Platform Leadership

How Intel, Microsoft, and Cisco Drive Industry Innovation

Annabelle Gawer

Michael A. Cusumano

HARVARD BUSINESS SCHOOL PRESS

Boston, Massachusetts

Requests for permission to use or reproduce material from this book should be directed
to permissions@hbsp.harvard.edu, or mailed to Permissions, Harvard Business School
Publishing, 60 Harvard Way, Boston, Massachusetts 02163.

Library of Congress Cataloging-in-Publication Data

Gawer, Annabelle, 1969-
  Platform leadership : how Intel, Microsoft, and Cisco drive industry innovation /
  Annabelle Gawer, Michael A. Cusumano.
     p. cm.
  Includes index.
  ISBN 1-57851-514-9 (alk. paper)
     1. Technological innovations–Management.   2. Leadership.   3. Computers.
  I. Cusumano, Michael A., 1954-   II. Title.

T173.5.G39 2002
658.5'14–dc21

                                                        2001059374

The paper used in this publication meets the requirements of the American National
Standard for Permanence of Paper for Publications and Documents in Libraries and
Archives Z39.48-1992.

The authors would like to dedicate this book to the loving memory of Nancy Staudenmayer.

Annabelle Gawer would also like to dedicate this book to Salomon and Myriam Gawer, and Reina Botbol.

Contents

Preface

The interaction between business and technological change impacts the world every day. The personal computer, the embedded microprocessor, the Internet, cellular telephones, mobile computing, and the wireless Web are just a few recent innovations that have affected millions, perhaps billions of people around the world. Some of us are creators of these technologies; many more are users and observers. Hundreds of firms have emerged over the past two decades to bring new products and services to market based on these new technologies. Some companies, like Intel and Microsoft, have become household names; other firms, including many of the dot-com variety, have appeared and vanished like flares in the night.

For investors, employees, managers, suppliers, and customers of these and other high-tech companies, the stakes are enormous. There are billions of dollars to gain and equal sums to lose. Products are "hot" one day and obsolete the next. The way these companies compete is also complex and often difficult to understand. Information is not the problem. Every day, the business press reports in great detail on what the giants of the high-tech world are doing—what new products are in the pipeline, what acquisitions they have consummated, what agreements they have reached. But often, these reports seem superficial. How are we to understand the motivations for the strategic moves and countermoves that technology companies make on a daily basis? We believe that, behind their actions and the myriad innovations that the press reports on so frequently, there is a larger game at stake: the game of technological platforms.

This book is the fruit of several years of collaboration between the authors. It started off in 1996 as doctoral thesis research at the MIT Sloan School of Management. Annabelle Gawer was interested in probing the dynamics between technology platforms and innovation networks, and began investigating several hardware and software companies. Michael

Cusumano, who had studied the software and PC industry for many years and recently visited the Intel Architecture Lab, suggested Intel as a case study. This company quickly became the focus of the Ph.D. research, which Gawer completed in January 2000 under Cusumano's supervision. After Gawer joined the INSEAD faculty in Fontainebleau, France, in February 2000, the authors extended the study to include other platform leaders and "wannabes" with somewhat different strategies—Microsoft, Cisco, Palm, NTT DoCoMo, and the open source movement.

These companies and initiatives provide a range of platform strategies and technologies. Understanding different cases is important because technology platforms come in many forms, ranging from consumer products such as color television sets and videocassette recorders to PC hardware and software and fax machines; that is, almost any product based on unique technical standards. Companies in many markets want their products to become part of a ubiquitous platform, like Microsoft Windows or the Intel microprocessor family. This book tries to bring together what established and emerging platform leaders have learned about how to make their strategies work: How companies can shape their business environment by creating a vision of technological and business innovation and by manipulating the processes of competition and collaboration. Platform leaders are unique in that they can drive a broad network of innovation within and around their industries. They can determine not only their own competitive futures but also the kinds of technologies and products that become dominant and commonplace in everyday life. For an increasing number of companies in a wide variety of markets, learning how to play the platform game is essential for their survival and long-term success.

Acknowledgments

Many of the insights generated in this book would not have been possible without the contribution of close to eighty managers at Intel whom we interviewed in depth, many of them several times. Here, we wish to thank several people in particular. First, Craig Kinnie, Dave Ryan, and Carmen Egido from the Intel Architecture Lab made this study possible. They provided the initial access and cooperation, and gave generously of their time and enthusiasm. Dave Ryan also read the thesis manuscript with great care and provided many valuable comments that we have incorporated into the book. Andy Grove supported the project from the beginning and granted an exciting and valuable interview. Other Intel executives and senior managers—especially Les Vadasz, Gerald Holzhammer, Dennis Carter, Ron Smith, Dave Schuler, Will Swope, Claude Leglise, Herman D'Hooge, Bill Miller, Jim Pappas, Abel Weinrib, Dave Johnson, Dan Russell, Dave Carson, Bala Cadambi, Sanjay Panditji, Michael Bruck, Jonathan Khazam, Sally Fundakowski, Tom Marchok, and Steve Tolopka—shared with us valuable insights from their many years of experience. David Yoffie, a professor at Harvard Business School and a member of the Intel board of directors, provided an introduction to several Intel executives in 1997.

The research on which this book is based is inscribed in a larger intellectual conversation about issues of innovation, modularity, strategy, and industry leadership. This work owes a large debt to the many researchers who have contributed to clarify and refine our understanding of the phenomena at play here. We cannot cite all the authors whose reflection inspired our work, but we wish to acknowledge our debt to Baldwin and Clark and their exemplary work on modularity.[1] The research by Langlois and Robertson helped us understand the relationship between modularity and innovation in the computer and stereo industries.[2] Fisher, McGowan, and Greenwood's work on the history of IBM enriched our understanding of how IBM influenced the evolution of the computer industry with the modular IBM/360.[3] Shapiro and Varian's book[4] summarized and clarified many years of work by themselves and other economists such as Farrell, Saloner, Monroe, and Katz[5] on the dynamics of standards wars, an essential element of platform leadership strategies. Bresnahan and Greenstein's work on technological competition and the structure of the computer industry provided rich insights.[6] Sanchez and Mahoney,[7] Schilling,[8] Gomes-Casseres,[9] Garud and Kumaraswamy,[10] and McGahan, Yoffie, and Vadasz[11] also contributed to our reflections on standards, modules, market leadership, and innovation with their discussion about openness versus proprietary standards, complementary products, and coordination between firms.

Both authors, and Gawer in particular, would like to thank Professor Scott Stern—who was at MIT during 1995–2000 before joining Northwestern University—and MIT Professor Rebecca Henderson. Both played a pivotal role in developing the ideas present in this book. They also served on the thesis committee. Over several years, many discussions with Stern and Henderson helped refine our understanding of the forces at play in high-tech markets. Their influence is present throughout this book.

Gawer also wishes to thank MIT Professors Frank Fisher, Michael Piore, Ed Roberts, Eric von Hippel, Jim Utterback, Bengt Holmstrom, and Lotte Bailyn for their constant encouragement and feedback. Beyond MIT, she would like to thank Northwestern Professor Shane Greenstein for his interest and support. At Wharton, Professor Daniel Raff provided an opportunity to present this work while still in progress, and Professor Sid Winter gave valuable comments and encouragement. Professors Allan Afuah from the University of Michigan, Will Mitchell from Duke University (formerly at Michigan), and Michael Tushman, Adam Brandenburger, Marco Iansiti, and Mary Tripsas from Harvard Business School provided important encouragement for this work. During 1999 and 2000, Gawer also presented parts of this work in seminars at the London Business School, HEC, ESSEC, the Ecole des Mines de Paris, and the Technion in Israel; she wishes to express her appreciation for the invitations and the useful feedback these opportunities provided. At INSEAD, Professor Yves Doz offered helpful comments on the draft, while Professors Philippe Haspeslagh, Jo Santos, Gareth Dyas, Landis

Gabel, Luk van Wassenhowe, Laurence Capron, and Ludo van der Heydn were available and inspiring. Gawer would also like to express her gratitude to the cohort of friends and MIT colleagues who provided good humor at much needed times. Long-time friends come to mind first: Sarah Juliette Sasson, Ania Marchwinska, and Demetra Lambros are pillars of friendship. At MIT, Kwanghui Lim, Jeff Furman, Neil Mayle, Pierre Azoulay, Sonali Shah, David Hsu, Lin Xu, Steve Freeman, and others provided feedback and support.

Cusumano would like to thank Professor Lee McKnight (now at Tufts University) and Professor David Clark at MIT for support through the MIT Internet and Telecom Consortium. MIT Professors Erik Brynjolfsson and Glen Urban provided support in later years through the MIT Sloan School Center for eBusiness. In addition, he thanks Paul Bosco of Cisco Systems for discussing the study and Donna Dubinsky of Handspring (formerly of Palm) for her comments during the research. Campbell Stras of Cybergnostic checked some of the technical discussions on routers and networking. David Yoffie and Mary Kwak of Harvard Business School generously provided a manuscript version of their book *Judo Strategy*, which contained a discussion of Palm. Joost Bonsen, a former MIT student, suggested the case study of Linux. MIT Professor Bengt Holmstrom provided comments on one of the chapters. The Technology and Operations Management Seminar at Harvard Business School offered an opportunity to present the research with Gawer in the fall of 2000, which helped move the ideas forward. The MIT Sloan School Center for eBusiness and the MIT Industrial Liaison Program provided other opportunities to present the research findings.

This work benefited from the financial support of several institutions. At MIT, the Sloan School Doctoral Program and the Internet and Telecom Consortium provided funding for Gawer during her Ph.D. research. The MIT Sloan School Center for eBusiness and the MIT Center for Innovation in Product Development provided funding for Cusumano. At the Internet and Telecom Consortium, Sharon Gillett, David Clark, and Bill Lehr provided much valuable feedback to Gawer in the early stages of the study. They also arranged many opportunities to present the work in progress and gain access to interesting companies, such as Hewlett-Packard and Nokia, to test out some of the ideas. The

Centre de Gestion Scientifique at the Ecole des Mines de Paris also provided early support for the project.

Both authors would like to thank two anonymous reviewers and reviewer David Reed (formerly of Lotus Development Corporation) for their detailed, constructive feedback on the first complete version of the book manuscript. David Reed also granted us an interview. In addition, the authors would like to thank Carol Franco and Hollis Heimbouch of Harvard Business School Press for their early and eager interest in the topic. Heimbouch and Genoveva Llosa were helpful in commenting on the manuscript, encouraging us to meet deadlines, and ensuring that the manuscript became a book.

Finally, both authors would like to acknowledge the memory of Professor Nancy Staudenmayer, who died in November 2000. Nancy was a former doctoral student at MIT who became a close and cherished friend. She taught at Duke University after graduating from MIT. She was a promising young scholar, working on the problem of organizational interdependencies, especially in software product development. Nancy inspired us and many other people with her drive for excellence, her enthusiasm for life, and her untiring dedication to scholarship as well as to friendship. We think of her often and miss her deeply.

Annabelle Gawer
Paris and Fontainebleau, France

Michael A. Cusumano
Groton and Cambridge, Massachusetts

November 2001

Platform Leadership

Chapter One

Introduction

[W]e are tied to innovations by others to make our innovation valuable. If we do an innovation in the processor, and Microsoft or independent software parties don't do a corresponding innovation, our innovation will be worthless. So, it really is a desperate situation for us.

—DAVID B. JOHNSON, DIRECTOR OF THE MEDIA AND INTERCONNECT TECHNOLOGY LAB, INTEL ARCHITECTURE LAB

In many industries, conventional wisdom has said, a position of leadership bestows authority, strength, even invulnerability. Powerful companies have always been able to get what they wanted—the components required to build their products—from suppliers. In some cases, suppliers also needed to provide not just the components of the product per se, but add-ons, or complementary products. These *complements* (another term for complementary products) were necessary additions to what the main producer provided; for example, tires for cars or film for cameras. Firms that made the main—or "core"—product (i.e., the car or the camera) had relationships with the suppliers of complements that reflected some interdependency—but by and large, the balance of power lay with the core product producer.

1

Given this balance of power, firms that commercialized successful products in the past did not have to worry much about innovation coming from the side roads. Focusing one's attention on the competition was the main thing to do. Managers, therefore, devoted less attention to external firms that were neither competitors nor buyers. "Core" firms expected suppliers to design and manufacture specified components. Suppliers could innovate, but fundamentally, their product or process improvement had little chance to shift the existing balance of power between the core firm and its suppliers.

In some modern industries, especially the high-tech sector, this centralized approach to business has changed. Matsushita, for example, could hardly design and build VHS recorders oblivious to the decisions being made by the producers of videotapes—without which their recorders would be worthless. Nevertheless, once it established the format (the VHS standard, developed by engineers at Japan Victor Corporation, a Matsushita subsidiary) and convinced major developers of videocassettes and distributors to adopt it, Matsushita's leadership was ensured; its position of strength would not be challenged.[1]

But unchallenged positions of industry leadership are becoming more and more rare. Today, in an increasing number of industries, the interdependence of various products and the widespread ability for many actors to innovate require that every company, no matter how big or how small, makes its fundamental decisions while taking into account what every other company active in the network of interlocking parts is doing. One would expect the kind of desperation mentioned in the quotation with which we began this chapter to come from a cash-strung fledgling dot-com company. In fact, the quote is from a manager at Intel, the most powerful chip maker in the world, who was discussing Intel's flagship product, the microprocessor.[2] Since microprocessors are an essential piece not only of all the personal computers (PCs) in the world but of the increasing number of programmable devices as well, Intel would seem to be sitting atop a high-tech gold mine. The idea that Intel may be vulnerable to the whim of external firms is, at first blush, inconceivable.

Yet managers at Intel and at many other high-tech companies claim that they are facing a problem that is pervasive and fundamental. What exactly is the problem? In a word, it is the character of the modern high-tech *platform*—an evolving system made of interdependent pieces that can each be innovated upon. This definition highlights two fundamental phenomena currently impacting the high-tech world: (1) the increasing *interdependency* of products and services and (2) the increasing ability to *innovate* by more actors in the high-tech world. The interaction of these two phenomena gives rise to three distinct but related issues that these companies face:

1. Maintenance of the integrity of the platform
2. Platform evolution
3. Market leadership in platform environments

First is maintenance of the integrity of the platform—of how the pieces fit together. Who will be in charge of it? Which mechanisms will ensure integrity as technological innovation constantly threatens the necessary internal coherence of the jigsaw puzzle? Second is the issue of platform evolution: Who will take charge of it, and by which mechanisms? Third is the related strategic question of how to achieve or preserve market leadership in platform environments. The balance of power among component providers is tenuous because continuous innovation on components can alter the drivers of demand. As a result, positions of leadership, whether technical or market-share leadership, are in a constant state of challenge—a challenge different in significant ways from those faced by dominant companies in the past.

Relevant Industries

For which industries are the lessons of this book relevant? The most obvious are the computer, telecommunications (telecom), electronic appliances, and automotive industries. However, we believe that our ideas are relevant for the increasing number of industries that make complex products of varying types. What are *complex products*? We are surrounded by them: bicycles, cars, refrigerators, radios, computers. All consist of different interrelated components that have to fit together.

Complex products made of interdependent pieces have existed for centuries. The idea that making complex products requires strong interrelationships between components is also not new. Building the Egyptian pyramids, for example, required the architects to specify the shape and size of the stones (the components) that made up these constructions. The design of the pyramids dictated the specifications of the components. These had to fit together, otherwise the internal coherence of the structures would be threatened and they might collapse.

Although complex products are not new, an increasing number of industries that make these products share the following characteristics:

- Independent producers make the different component pieces of the product.
- Many developers of components can innovate.
- The rate of technological progress is fast.
- Demand for future complements is uncertain but could be strong.

The two fundamental forces we have singled out—interdependency and innovation—are particularly powerful in these industries.

In many high-tech industries, developers of components have the power to innovate on their products—and their efforts can increase the attractiveness of the overall system of which they are a part. In some industries, new complementary products can act as a trigger to attract new customers to buy the core product. For example, new software applications can spur a customer to buy a new computer, and the availability of movies on videocassettes can encourage potential buyers to purchase a videocassette recorder (VCR). In these examples, the core product is the computer or VCR, and the software applications or video-cassettes are the complementary products.

Modularity and Industry Evolution

At the birth of many industries, a few firms develop all or almost all the components necessary to make the products. As industries evolve, what generally happens is that specialized firms emerge to develop certain components of the larger puzzle. An increasing number of industries today consist of *different* firms that each develop one component of a big jigsaw puzzle. Economists refer to these industries as "de-integrated." This evolution has happened in the computer industry, where companies like vertically integrated IBM and Digital Equipment Corporation (DEC) have left center stage for a specialist, hardware component maker, Intel, and a specialist, software component maker, Microsoft—and the plethora of complementary developers around them.

The reasons industries evolve this way are widely discussed, but a central tenet of many theories is the concept of modularity. A *module* is a unit whose structural elements are powerfully connected to each other and relatively weakly connected to elements in other units. Clearly there are degrees of connection, thus there are gradations of modularity.[3] Many industries of complex products have evolved toward a more modular architecture, including the computer, telecom, and automotive industries. Consequences of modular designs reach far beyond the purely technical characteristics of the products, for example, the physical shape of the product or its internal structure.[4] Design decisions affect the organization of production, and modular designs provide the means for people to divide up the work in tasks or groups of tasks that are relatively independent of each other. Modularity in product design has a powerful impact on innovation: Innovation can happen on modules of the product without having to impact (and thus threaten the integrity of) the overall system.

In addition to modular designs, the vast improvement in tools of communication is another factor accelerating the pace of innovation. The development of the Internet, for example, has reduced tremendously the difficulties of coordinating work on discrete modules or components across distant locations and fostered collaboration on new products.

Another aspect of modern industry is the ubiquity of software. Organizations and individuals have used software tools in a pervasive manner to achieve improvements on products and processes. Software expertise—fueled by developments in computer higher education and the ubiquity of cheap PCs—has also reached unprecedented levels and availability. The combination of these factors leads to the fact that technological innovation—once restricted to the labs of rich and powerful companies—has never been so prevalent and widely distributed. Barriers to innovation are at a historical low.

The ability for an increased number of actors to innovate separately on different modules of systems is radically altering the nature and stability of relationships between the firms that make core products and the developers of complementary products. This book analyzes the strategies that executives at Intel, Microsoft, Cisco, Palm, NTT DoCoMo, and supporters of the Linux operating system, have developed for facing these challenges. Their strategies differ in many respects, but they also share many similarities. Each group, in their own way, follows an approach that we have called platform leadership.

Platform Leadership

Platform leadership refers to the common objective sought by the companies we talked to: to drive innovation in their industry. The increased breadth of innovation described earlier creates the necessity for either one firm or a group of firms to ensure over time the integrity of an evolving platform. It also creates strategic opportunities to channel the direction of innovation on complementary modules or products. Ensuring the integrity of the platform and driving its evolution become strategic imperatives in industries where distributed innovation constantly challenges established relationships of power between suppliers of complementary products.

More and more firms want *their products* to become the foundation on which other companies build their products or offer their services; that is, they want to become platform leaders. A platform leader can benefit from—but is also highly dependent on—innovations developed at other firms. Platform leaders might rest easier if they had the resources to create the core components and all possible complementary products themselves for every market around the world. But this is impossible. No single company can replicate all the innovative capabilities of a market, especially at a time when tools and knowledge necessary to innovate are more widespread than ever. As a result, nearly all the platform leaders we observed have had to work closely with other firms to create initial applications and then new generations of complementary products. Platform leaders and complementary innovators have great incentives to cooperate, however, because their combined efforts can increase the potential size of the pie for everyone.

From the perspective of the platform leader, complements are both a curse and a blessing. They can be a curse when a firm that depends on complements developed externally fails to get them created in a timely manner or at a high enough level of quality or volume. On the other hand, complements can draw new customers in, inducing them to buy the core product. For Microsoft, whose core product is the Windows operating system, a large number and variety of complementary Windows-compatible software applications are a blessing because it encourages potential customers to buy Windows-based computers. Likewise, having a large number and variety of movies on VHS-compatible videocassettes available in video stores pushed the sales of VHS recorders. The availability of a large number of complementary products *adds value* to the core product. Innovation on complementary products, therefore, constitutes a great opportunity.

In short, in industries that center around platform products, the value of a platform increases when there are more complements. The more people who use these complements, the more incentives there are for complementary producers to introduce more complementary products, which then stimulate more people to buy or use the core product, stimulating more innovation, and so on. It is, therefore, in the interest of a platform leader to stimulate and channel innovation on complementary products.

The game is risky, though, because platform producers may fail to get other firms to cooperate and innovate, and this failure can lead to greatly reduced sales for everyone tied to the same platform. Since platforms are made of components that interact following standard interfaces, standard wars are necessarily part of platform strategies. Examples include Sony and the Betamax standard, which failed to dominate the VCR market, and the Apple Macintosh line of PCs, which has found some resurgence in recent years but has not unseated Windows machines as the mass-market standard. DEC's Alpha microprocessor failed to garner much of a following, mainly because of a lack of software applications. Informix has found a niche in the corporate database software market, but lost out to Oracle and Microsoft as the industry standard. QUAL-COMM is in the midst of a global struggle with companies such as Nokia, Ericsson, AT&T, and Motorola to establish its technology as the international standard for next-generation wireless cell phones.

The Navigator browser, which fit into a platform and once had a market share of around 90 percent, declined sharply in popularity as a result of Netscape's inability to keep it as the industry standard.[5] Microsoft's Pocket PC operating system may suffer a similar fate at the hands of

Palm or other competitors if Microsoft cannot persuade more companies to adopt their system for their handheld computers and personal
digital assistants (PDAs), cellular telephones, or cable TV set-top boxes.

In other words, it is quite possible to *fail* to become a platform leader
and to *mismanage* the process of stimulating and channeling complementary innovation. The result is an inability to exploit the dynamics of
markets driven by the economic forces we have described. Of course,
there are no guarantees of success in high-tech markets, where change
can be quick and brutal. The VHS platform for the VCR and what has
been called the "Windows-Intel" platform for the PC are now standards,
but their originators did not win their markets easily or by accident.[6]
Managers and engineers at Intel, Microsoft, Cisco, Palm, and other successful platform leaders, as well as platform-leader "wannabes," must
work hard to establish, maintain, and grow their dominant positions.

Framework: Four Levers of Platform Leadership

Based on the companies we studied, we developed a framework that
managers can use to design a strategy for platform leadership or make
their existing strategy more effective. This framework—which we call
the Four Levers of Platform Leadership—allows platform leaders or
wannabes to design and test the validity of their strategy, given the circumstances of their industry and the competences of their corporation.
Here is an outline of the four levers:

1. *Scope of the firm*: This lever deals with what the firm does inside
   and what it encourages others to do outside. Is it better for firms
   to develop an extensive in-house capability to create their own
   complements or to let the market produce complements? Is
   there a "happy medium" between these two extremes? If so,
   when is that the best approach?
2. *Product technology (architecture, interfaces, intellectual property)*:
   This lever deals with decisions that platform leaders and
   wannabes need to make with regard to the architecture of their
   product and the broader platform, if the two are not the same.
   In particular, they need to make decisions about the degree of
   modularity, the degree of openness of the interfaces to the

platform, and how much information about the platform and its interfaces to disclose to outside firms—potential complementors who may also become competitors.[7]

3. *Relationships with external complementors*: This lever centers on determining how collaborative versus competitive should the relationship be between the platform leader or wannabe and the complementors. Platform leaders and wannabes also need to worry about how to achieve consensus with their partners, and how to deal with potential conflicts of interest, such as when the platform leader decides to enter complementary markets directly and turns former partners into competitors.

4. *Internal organization*: This lever allows platform leaders and wannabes to use their internal organizational structure to manage external and internal conflicts of interest more effectively. Options include keeping groups with similar goals under one executive, or separating groups into distinct departments in order to address potentially conflicting goals with outside constituencies. The issue of culture and process comes in here: We found that since innovative, modular industries are often ambiguous environments, where a complementor today can become a competitor tomorrow, an internal atmosphere that encourages debate (or at least tolerates ambiguity) accelerates the strategy reformulations that are sometimes necessary. At the same time, efficient internal communication of corporate strategy, once a decision has been made at the top, facilitates the implementation of strategic reorientations.

We believe that each of these levers is critical for achieving or sustaining platform leadership. The Four Levers cover both strategy formulation and implementation issues, which are intertwined. The levers are distinct but closely related; therefore, platform leaders or wannabes need to make choices on these dimensions in a coherent fashion.

The decision of what complements to make inside and what to leave to external firms is probably the single most important issue that platform leaders and wannabes have to decide—and keep deciding. It is not a onetime event because firms innovate continuously on their products and add new functionalities that may well have been performed previously by external firms. This decision encompasses choosing appropriate levels of investment in venture capital activities or acquisitions aimed at evolving the platform or helping the complements business.

Decisions on the architecture or design of the product and on how to treat intellectual property (i.e., whether to keep product interface specifications "open" or closed"), tend to have a major impact on the incentives and ability of external firms to innovate on complements. And deciding how to treat external firms is, of course, related to the scope of the firm because it requires a decision on whether to compete or to collaborate.

We shall also see that platform leaders and wannabes need to be mindful of the consequences of encroaching on the territory of developers of complements. There is a strategic trade-off between systematically entering any complementary market that seems to hold the promise of profit and maintaining goodwill and collaborative relationships with developers of complements. While some companies invest a lot of effort in building a strong reputation for not encroaching on complementors' turf, others are less careful where they trample. We shall explain the external circumstances that can justify these different behaviors and clarify the risks involved with these two approaches.

We shall also see that platform leaders or wannabes need to establish an internal organization that supports their objectives. In particular, when the objective is to maintain collaborative relationships with complementors, certain organizational design decisions—such as whether to keep particular groups under one executive or to separate groups into distinct departments—impact the ability of a platform leader to convince third parties that it will not recklessly infringe on their turf. Distinct departments reduce the fears that third parties might have to invest in complementary products and new technologies.

The important point here is that platform leaders usually need to perform a delicate balancing act between competing and collaborating with complements producers, whose products are necessary to create demand for the platform. The firms we studied relied on various means to influence outside firms, ranging from specific technical choices and organizational decisions to initiatives to enhance their external relationships and reputations.

Plan of the Book

We decided to present the strategies adopted by Intel, Microsoft, Cisco, and relative newcomers Palm, Linux open source supporters, and NTT DoCoMo because they each met two criteria. First, they have been particularly successful or sophisticated in their approach to platform leadership. These five firms have driven innovation in their industries and steered the direction of complementary innovation in a manner that was useful to them, while also providing business opportunities for external companies. Second, these firms and Linux supporters have implemented different strategies to achieve platform leadership. These differences are rich in lessons.

A substantial portion of this book is devoted to Intel. Chapters 2, 3, and 4 discuss the company's platform strategy and what we can learn from it. The microprocessor is a key component in a broader system or platform—the PC. The value of Intel's microprocessor (and the PC itself) depends on products that other firms create: the software operating system, software applications, software development tools, and hardware components such as monitors, keyboards, storage devices, and memory chips that make up the PC system. Probably because of its situation as a component maker for a platform that customers buy for the applications it can perform (more than for the sheer power of the microprocessor), Intel exists in a "desperate situation" because its market success depends so heavily on the decisions of other firms to develop complementary innovations.

For example, Intel spent around $2 billion developing and preparing to manufacture a new 64-bit microprocessor (the Pentium 4), which it introduced in mid-2000. This new product doubled the information-processing capacity of the current generation of 32-bit microprocessors, which handled information in batches of only 32 bits, and brought mainframe-computer power to the desktop PC. Yet this innovation provided little benefit to users *unless* hundreds of companies, beginning with giants like Microsoft and Oracle, *redesigned* their software products to take advantage of the new 64-bit architecture.

Intel chose (and still chooses) to harness the power of complementary innovation and work with outside firms to make its new products successful. Intel also invested heavily in activities aimed at driving architectural changes of the overall platform and orchestrated many industry initiatives. The Intel Architecture Lab plays a major role in Intel's platform strategy. Chapter 3 describes in detail Intel's rich portfolio of platform activities, and the many projects we have gathered data on allow us to present an unprecedented study of all aspects of Intel's strategy for platform leadership.

Chapter 2 presents the story of Intel's first attempt to move the industry—the PCI bus initiative. This effort lay the groundwork and provided the template for Intel's subsequent actions as a platform leader. Chapter 3 describes what Intel did to strengthen its leadership on the PC platform after the success of PCI. It extracts Intel's strategic principles for platform leadership, including stimulation and coordination of complementary innovation, relying on our Four Levers framework.

Chapter 4 focuses on the trade-offs involved in Levers 3 and 4 by examining the difficulties Intel faced in implementing its platform leadership strategy. Of particular interest is how Intel handled internal and external tensions and conflicts of interest—issues that seem to us inescapable for any firm attempting to pursue platform leadership. We argue that the ability to manage internal as well as external tensions constitutes an organizational capability that is necessary to implement a platform leadership strategy. This chapter also examines the management processes involved in communicating commitment to third parties and suggests the importance of organizational design choices such as enforcing the separation of interests among groups that aim to achieve potentially conflicting goals.

Not all platform leaders need to act like Intel, though they may pursue similar goals. Aspiring platform leaders might follow other strategies to try to minimize conflicts of interest and maximize potential gains from their investments. These alternative approaches include making essential complementary products yourself (like Microsoft), or buying promising third-party complementors (like Cisco). In chapters 5 and 6, we examine some of these alternative approaches to platform leadership that have had varying degrees of success. In chapter 5, we present the strategies of established platform leaders Microsoft and Cisco. In chapter 6, we discuss the strategies of three "wannabes" struggling to become platform leaders: Palm, NTT DoCoMo, and supporters of Linux. In these chapters, we illustrate the Four Levers by looking at the choices these companies have made.

For example, analysis of Microsoft, Cisco, and Palm's platform strategies allows us to explore in more detail the trade-offs involved with Lever 1. Recall that this lever concerns the scope of the firm: Does the platform leader make its own key complements or rely on external firms (such as partners or suppliers) to do this? Here, Microsoft and Intel differ. For many years, Microsoft made its own key complements—software applications such as Word and Excel, and now Office—products that account for about half of Microsoft's revenues and profits. In contrast, Intel makes some complementary products (including chip sets, digital cameras, teleconferencing equipment, and a new MPEG audio player for home consumers, introduced in January 2001), but complements are not a major focus of its business.

We also discuss in depth the different approaches of these companies with regard to Lever 2. Recall that this lever is concerned with technological choices such as open or closed interfaces. Microsoft, for example, relies on proprietary product technology for its Windows platform, even though it released considerable information on the interfaces to help other firms build software applications and compatible computers and networking systems. The Windows interface technology, therefore, is "open but not open" in that Microsoft dominated the underlying technology (the Windows source code) and drove the evolution of the interfaces, but is relatively liberal about sharing interface specifications. Both Microsoft and Intel have kept the inner details of their products proprietary, but made their external interface specifications widely available because they wanted companies to build products around their products. The connection details are thus open but subject to the control of the firm that discloses the interface specifications (as opposed to a group of firms or a standardization body). Both companies sometimes give preferential access to interface information to companies who are partners, as opposed to competitors.[8]

The conclusion, chapter 7, summarizes the strategic choices facing firms that want to succeed as platform leaders and offers advice on how to organize for and implement a platform-leadership strategy. The strategic issues involve not only how open to make interfaces and how much of a complements business to build in-house, but also how best to influence innovation activities occurring outside the firm. It is possible, for example, for a platform leader to become actively engaged in standards organizations as well as in venture capital activities and acquisitions. As we discuss throughout the book, however, platform leaders walk a fine line between promoting what is good for them and their platforms versus what is good for complementors, customers, and the industry overall.

Chapter Two

Intel's Rise to Platform Leadership

The Story

The [industry] power structure hadn't worked itself out yet. IBM wasn't dead and Compaq wasn't king and there were lots of new small players coming into the market at all levels.

—GERALD HOLZHAMMER, CO-DIRECTOR, INTEL ARCHITECTURE LAB

[Andy] Grove concluded that . . . we needed to provide leadership to the industry to cause the platform to evolve more quickly, to get new applications and new uses for the platform . . . Andy essentially asked me—his specific words—to become the *architect for the open computer industry, to help the industry figure out how to evolve the platform.* A narrow view of that would be to pretend that I was in a large company like IBM and that all these other companies worked for me and for my boss, and that we could work together.

—CRAIG KINNIE, DIRECTOR, INTEL ARCHITECTURE LAB

Today, Intel and Microsoft are considered platform leaders in the PC industry. Intel contributes the core hardware product, the microprocessor, while Microsoft contributes the core software product, the operating

15

system, as well as some key applications.[1] Intel and Microsoft determine—or at least heavily influence—the evolution of the PC system. But things were not always this way.

This chapter presents not only the economic and technological context that surrounded Intel's rise to platform leadership but also the key actions that Intel took to transform itself from a simple component maker, supplying to a system architecture that it had not designed, into a major source of influence over the evolution of this system. Here and in the next two chapters we focus on Intel because we know of no company that has devoted more thought and resources to platform issues and the broader problem of how to increase "the pie" for (almost) everyone participating in its industry while preserving a leadership position within a thriving ecosystem of companies.[2]

A historical account of what happened at Intel seemed to us the best way to present our ideas in this chapter. Firms' strategies do not spring fully formed from the minds of visionary leaders who understand everything before everyone else. Context matters. Events and circumstances, as well as a keen understanding of what their firm can do, allow managers to develop a vision that they then try to make real by taking strategic actions. Implicit in this approach to the Intel story is an understanding of strategy development as an iterative, even messy, process. This understanding preserves a role for visionary leaders, but circumscribes the nature and the impact of their actions in an environment where strategy is emerging from the interaction between the firm's external and internal environments, mediated by managers' perceptions of opportunities and actions to influence their environment.[3] This is why in our writing we chose to remain close to the reality of events as they unfolded. We tried to capture the broad direction of these events without losing a sense of their complexity, and even sometimes the "messiness" of the organizational response to the strategic issues as they arose.

Intel's Problems

In growing its microprocessor business rapidly and profitably, Intel faces the problem that end users of computers don't buy microprocessors—

they buy PCs. Microprocessors constitute only one element of the PC, albeit an essential one. Users experience their computers through interacting most directly with software applications and peripherals such as the screen, keyboard, mouse, and printer. The microprocessor itself is "hidden" to the user in a complex, multilayered system of interdependent products. How users view the microprocessor is therefore greatly affected by other products that Intel does not make. The larger problem that Intel faces is ensuring continued demand for its ever-evolving microprocessor. In accordance with Moore's law, Intel has continued to push out new generations of its microprocessor every eighteen months or so. This "law" refers to the prediction by former Intel chairman Gordon Moore that the performance of the microprocessor would double every eighteen months due to improvements in design and manufacturing processes. A key strategic issue is that Intel must make multibillion-dollar investments in product designs and manufacturing facilities with each new microprocessor generation to make this law a reality—*without any guarantees that new customers will appear in volume for the new products.*

For example, PCs made since the mid-1990s are all enormously powerful. There are also thousands of software applications already available that are not only "good enough" but contain far more features than most people would ever use. But if there is no demand for the latest Intel microprocessors—or for more computing power—then computer manufacturers, peripherals manufacturers, and software producers will not make PCs or software applications that take advantage of the latest Intel technology. Intel and many of its partner companies will cease to grow.

An analogy from the automobile industry helps explain Intel's platform problem—and how Bala Cadambi, a manager at IAL, saw the solution:

> Intel is in the business of providing the engine for the PC, just like Honda is in the business of providing the engine for the automobile. That engine is doubling in capacity every 18 to 24 months—that's Moore's law. It increases the capacity in terms of efficiency, scalability, power, and the kind of things it can do with multimedia. *What we really want is to ensure that the rest of the platform goes*

with it. This means that if the engine gets better, the tires get better, the chassis gets better, the roads get better, and you get better gas mileage. You can have navigation systems that are scaleable—and everything that goes with having a better experience. The platform around the engine limits the engine. *So we want the platform— which is everything that's around the microprocessor—to be keeping pace and improving and scaling, so that the microprocessor can deliver its potential.*[4]

This quote is representative of the dozens of Intel managers we interviewed in that they all believed the company would be better off (and so would the end user) if all the firms that develop the complementary products would innovate in a way that would be optimized to function, all together, with the next version of the microprocessor.

But exactly *how* could this alignment in innovation happen? By which mechanisms would the coordination between developers of complementary products occur? We shall see in this chapter how Intel influenced its environment to achieve these objectives. But first, we turn to Intel's industrial and strategic environment at the time it began to envision itself as a platform leader. In the early 1990s, executives at Intel perceived that it was becoming increasingly difficult to grow demand for PCs. There were at least two root causes to this problem: an increasingly obsolete PC architecture and the lack of industry leadership to advance the PC "system"—hardware and software included.

Obsolescence of the PC Architecture

When Intel started to develop microprocessors for PCs in the mid-1980s, it was in no way an architect of the overall system it operated within. Intel's noted entrance in this market was as a mere supplier to IBM for its first PC. Intel was a supplier of an important component, but it was IBM that had designed the overall platform. IBM was the architect of the PC, and its architectural legacy remains to this day in the architecture of current PCs. By *architecture*, we mean the partitioning of the system into components of a given scope and related to each other functionally and physically through given interfaces. From a given architecture flows the design of components' functions and how they relate to each other. If a system's architecture is compared to a geographical map, the components of the system are the countries' territories and the interfaces between components are the countries' borders.

The architecture of the PC had evolved in stages, reaching a plateau in design during the mid-1980s. In 1979, IBM had brought together a team in Boca Raton, Florida, to develop a new PC that would compete with Apple. The team, not bound by the usual IBM rules of using proprietary technology, had picked the commercially available Intel 8088 microprocessor. IBM offered Microsoft's disk operating system (DOS) as the main operating system, along with several application programs, such as the VisiCalc spreadsheet program.

Soon after, the IBM PC-compatible business emerged because IBM had not made exclusive agreements to control the core hardware product (the Intel microprocessor) or the core software product (Microsoft's DOS). In other words, both Intel and Microsoft could sell their products to other firms that wanted to produce PCs compatible with the IBM model. Then, in 1984, IBM introduced the more advanced PC-AT, which was an instant success because it was easy to expand the capacity of the AT design. Demand exploded for IBM machines and IBM PC-AT clones. Intel executive Albert Yu, in his 1998 book on innovation at Intel, recalled how other firms were able to clone the new IBM machines as well as the older PC technology:

> This stable PC platform was a dream for many new companies
> eager to build compatible PCs to satisfy the huge demand. In
> addition to many hardware start-ups, many software companies
> were launched to offer new products for this fast-growing market.
> These were the formative years of the huge PC market. As the
> leader of this emerging market, IBM was the most powerful player
> and set the directions that others followed.[5]

IBM's architecture was now a common good and the standard for all PCs (Apple computers excluded). At first reluctant, IBM had come to accept that IBM clones would be produced by independent companies across the globe. IBM's decision to allow the PC system interfaces to remain open spurred the production, commercialization, and adoption of PCs all over the world. As the PC became ubiquitous, a fundamental transformation occurred in the computer industry: Previously vertically integrated companies (e.g., IBM, DEC, Univac, Wang) started to lose leadership to specialist providers of hardware and software components—among them Intel, Microsoft, and Motorola. Integrated PC makers like IBM and Apple still existed, but suppliers of components started to gain more and more power to dictate their conditions to their business environment.[6]

Intel owed its big entry in this market to IBM, but the PC-AT architecture soon became akin to a tight shirt for Intel's microprocessors. The fast evolution of Intel chips created the perception among Intel executives that the shirt was about to split apart at the seams. By the late 1980s, according to both Andy Grove and Craig Kinnie, the then-current PC architecture had become obsolete. The architecture affected the performance of the overall system—on which the business of all component makers depended, including Intel. The PC architecture had not changed from the PC-AT, introduced by IBM in 1984. Meanwhile, the microprocessor was getting faster and faster. Intel executives could not help but complain that the old PC architecture was, in effect, "hiding" or limiting the real potential performance of Intel's microprocessors from end users.[7]

PC-clone makers used the IBM architecture and purchased components directly from Intel and Microsoft. The ability to use standard components vastly increased the volume of PCs being made. But as Yu noted, this modular approach did not help evolve the platform:

> The downside of this cookie-cutter approach was that the PC architecture was frozen at the IBM PC-AT generation. One of the biggest problems with this design was the speed of the ISA [Industry Standard Architecture] bus was very slow. As a result, anything that was connected to the bus—hard disk, graphics, and so on—ran very slowly. As time went on, several attempts were made to improve this bus. In the mid-1980s, IBM proposed a bus called MCA [MicroChannel Architecture] to improve the performance of its PS/2 PC line. To counteract that, Compaq Computer proposed another one called EISA [Extended ISA]. A battle of the buses—EISA versus MCA—ensued between IBM and Compaq. There were stories each week in the trade press about which side appeared to be winning. Actually nobody much cared, as neither bus offered

discernible PC performance improvements. Because of the confusion, most manufacturers stayed with the cheaper ISA bus. As a result, the PC industry was stuck with a slow bus for years.[8]

A *bus* is an internal highway within the PC. Just as a real bus transports people in groups, a computer bus transmits data in bunches in the form of electrical signals or bits between components. Bus performance is measured by its "bandwidth" or "speed": the faster the bus, the faster the transmission of data. Speed is a common performance metric used to evaluate the PC and microprocessors. Buses are important in the PC architecture because the computer's overall performance depends not only on the performance of each individual component but also on the performance of the links between the components.

Lack of Industry Leadership

As the quote above illustrates, Intel executives were disturbed that no computer manufacturer had stepped up to advance the PC platform. It was clear the industry had evolved away from vertically integrated firms that made every component of a computer system in-house. Now, many firms contributed the components that made up a PC. The industry was also moving away from proprietary technologies controlled by individual firms. But where it was heading was not obvious. It was unclear which firm or which industrial organization (e.g., standards committee or consortia) could take the lead—to either impose new architectural standards or coordinate key activities and "system optimization" work among firms developing components of the PC. This lack of platform leadership in the industry restricted innovation at the system level. Kinnie, a director at Intel and the head of the IAL, recalled that Intel came to the conclusion that the PC platform itself was not moving as fast as the speed at which Intel was able to develop more processor power.

> When the PC industry was young, leaders like IBM or later Compaq would advance the platform and everything was wonderful. But it grew up as an "open" industry, which was a very different thing. . . . The leaders weren't there. What they had left behind was getting old, whether it was the PC platform itself, graphics, software—it was all aging. We were coming out with processors, and it was as if our processors were like V-8 engines and we had a chassis

like the Volkswagen Beetle. The end user doesn't get the benefit of the V-8 when you do that.[9]

The problem was serious for Intel because it had recognized that its primary business of developing microprocessors (then primarily for PCs) was a big growth industry. The problem was also difficult to resolve because of its systemic nature. Many companies (in particular, all the suppliers to this given architecture) had a stake in the PC design. No single supplier could evolve the overall system by itself, let alone overthrow it.

Intel executives were also thinking ahead, to the trajectory of innovation they envisioned themselves upon. With Moore's law in mind, they planned to develop and commercialize a stream of ever more powerful microprocessors in the subsequent years. A solution to the problem of the PC architecture was required to accommodate Intel's future vision.

Creation of the Intel Architecture Lab

In 1991, Intel executives came up with the idea of establishing a laboratory within the company to address these fundamental challenges. This group would be called the Intel Architecture Lab (IAL). Grove, then CEO, initiated the creation of IAL by asking Kinnie, who had been involved in previous system efforts within Intel, to tackle the PC platform obsolescence problem. Grove wanted Kinnie and his lab to become the "architect for the open computer industry."[10] IAL, therefore, was Intel's first organizational response to the architecture problem that was slowing demand for PCs.

Although the architectural issue was significant, it was only one of several issues that could be tackled to increase the appeal of the overall platform. Intel executives began to realize that compelling new uses could increase demand for PCs and consequently drive up demand for Intel's products. New uses for PCs could do wonders for demand for the powerful chip. But all sorts of technical roadblocks (not necessarily related to the PC architecture, such as the slow appearance of new software applications and computer peripherals) prevented innovators and end users from finding new ways to use the PC. As a result, Intel management gradually expanded the scope of IAL to more than simply trying to redefine the technical architecture of the PC. Kinnie recalls:

We looked at *what people would want to do with the PC if it was as good as it could be....* [W]e set a goal of about five years for interactive applications like conferencing. Our view was that if the PC was really delivering on its promise, why can't we do these things? Then we started looking at *what was preventing the industry from delivering on that goal.* Not what Intel was doing, but what the industry limitations were. They were technological as well [as] structural: channels and distribution.[11]

So, IAL was charged with the goal of moving the PC platform forward. The creation of IAL coincided with the moment that platform leadership became an explicit goal at Intel. Intel's vision of platform leadership required IAL to marshal human, capital, and technical resources. Although IAL did not work alone, it played a central role in Intel's platform leadership strategy. It continues this pivotal role today. In 2001, this research organization included some 550 engineers.[12] Most employees were software developers—and *none* worked directly on designing new versions of Intel's microprocessors.

Carmen Egido, one of the lab managers, explained: "Our primary job is to expand the market for high-end microprocessors. The role of [IAL] is precisely that: to provide enabling technologies and grow the market for microprocessors by finding new users and new uses for PCs."[13] In most cases, facilitating new uses required facilitating the development of new software applications. This is why IAL consists mostly of software engineers. Gerald Holzhammer described the decision to focus on software in an attempt to stimulate growth in demand for computers:

There was a master plan . . . that said *we need to encourage innovation on software applications.* It all came about fairly naturally. . . . If the end user doesn't see really immediate added value by buying the next-generation processor, then Intel will not grow. Intel will have a huge problem. We are spending billions of dollars building these new manufacturing plants. If people don't come, don't buy, we will fall off a cliff. So, fundamentally, [we need] to obsolete our old product. That's the premise. That's the reason why we have an Intel Architecture Lab, *whose fundamental mission is to grow the overall market.* We need to amortize our manufacturing capacity in a large number of units. That will happen only if there are new applications. How do you grow a market? Intel has 80, 85, 90 percent market segment share for CPUs [central processing units]. You don't grow by getting another 2 percent. *You grow by growing the entire pie.* How do you grow your pie? By getting new applications, find new users for the PC. This is pretty unique to IAL. IAL is charged to grow the overall market.[14]

Before the birth of IAL, in 1987, Intel had tried—without initial success—to "move the industry" in a direction favorable to one of its new products: the 80386 chip, with its capability for a 32-bit flat address space. Intel tried to convince a reluctant IBM to adopt its new chip for the IBM PCs. But IBM, which still had many orders to fill for PCs loaded with Intel's previous 80286 chips, was not interested. Microsoft also did not go along with Intel's desires and began to pursue a "split-platform" strategy with IBM OS/2 (the IBM operating system) for the 286 and 386 running as the 286, while building into its Windows 3.0 the capabilities for support of 32-bit code—thus playing Intel and IBM against each other. It was Compaq that first commercialized the 386 with its Compaq 386, and was extremely successful at selling it. Consumers came to believe that "386" was a Compaq brand. Intel later launched its "Intel Inside" marketing campaign to gain some recognition in the eyes of consumers and therefore increase its own bargaining power vis-à-vis the other actors in its ecosystem. Although the introduction of the 386 was not initially a great success for Intel, that relative failure apparently served as a lesson and a warning. Intel could not be insensitive to the dynamics of the industry and the motivations of possible adopters, original equipment manufacturers (OEMs), and complementors to the Intel chip.[15] With the creation of IAL and its first project, the PCI bus initiative, Intel started to do things a little differently.

Expansion of the Mission

During the mid-1990s, IAL's mission evolved; it became "a catalyst for innovation in the industry."[16] Specifically, IAL became proactive in helping Intel with what company people called "Job 1"—selling more microprocessors. What is referred to internally as "Job 2" concerns all activities aiming to enter, compete, and make a profit in businesses other than microprocessors. As of 2001, most of Intel's profits came from Job 1-related activities.

By driving or "orchestrating" innovation activities at other firms that complemented Intel microprocessors, IAL engineers tried to create new uses for PCs and thus generate demand for new computers—most of which would probably use Intel microprocessors.[17] According to an internal document, IAL's mission has become even broader: "to establish the technologies, standards, and products necessary to grow demand for the extended PC through the creation of new computing experiences."[18] As a result, IAL got involved in three areas: driving architectural progress on the PC system, stimulating and facilitating innovation on complementary products, and coordinating outside firms' innovations in an attempt to drive the development of new system capabilities.

Context of the PCI Bus Initiative

IAL's first project, in 1991, was the development and driving of industry adoption of the peripheral component interconnect (PCI) bus initiative. The PCI bus initiative was a remarkable effort to transform the internal architecture of the PC. The IAL developed a new connector or "bus" technology that linked the many pieces of the PC system. The initiative was a resounding success: Not only did the PCI bus become the standard for most firms in the industry, but, as IAL's first assignment, it paved the way for all the architectural initiatives that followed. Thanks to PCI, Intel grabbed the position of platform leader as it went from merely "supplying silicon to a well-defined architecture"[19] to become "the architect of the industry."[20]

Intel Chairman Andy Grove claimed in our 1998 interview that PCI was a pivotal event in Intel's transformation into a platform leader. Prior to the 1990s, Intel was a component maker that supplied its microprocessors to IBM's well-defined system architecture. By sponsoring a change in the bus structure, and providing a chip set that implemented these architectural changes in an actual product, Intel entered a territory that, until then, PC producers (the OEMs) had reserved for themselves. This strategic move marked a change in the dimensions of competition in the computer industry. Intel finally recognized that it could influence the environment and the direction of innovation—to its own benefit. Grove recalled:

> The change in our recognition was sometime between 1989 and 1991. This was coincident with IBM proving either lack of interest or inaptitude in moving the PC platform forward. The major thing we undertook was the definition of a new bus structure, PCI. It didn't seem that big a deal then, but PC bus structure for the previous decade had come from IBM. If it didn't come from IBM, it came from a reaction to what IBM was doing.[21]

To a large extent, the failure of PC manufacturers such as IBM and Compaq to take the lead in evolving the PC platform created the opportunity and incentive for Intel to get involved in architecture design, by specifying a new and better bus technology, for instance. The transformation of the computer industry of the 1980s from vertically integrated computer makers to arrays of specialist component makers and OEMs (the system integrators) revealed many specialized firms but no real leader. Hardware and software producers hoped that "open standards" as well as the activities and incentives of individual firms would result in integration of their different components. But to overcome technological roadblocks and optimize the performance of the PC platform required direction. Kinnie, IAL's director since its creation (except for a brief period in 1997 when Holzhammer served as acting director), related to us the reasoning behind Intel's decision to become a platform leader:

> [It wasn't clear] whom to deal with. If you know who the king is, you go talk to the king—right? If there isn't any king, who do you go talk to? [Designing a bus] was the right thing to do. To think that any person could do it was bold. But it puts you in the right mindset [to understand] the scale of the problem you want to take on. So we set the goal and asked what was preventing the industry from getting there. We identified the roadblocks, and we found plenty of technological roadblocks really close to home in our chip sets and in our memory controllers. We started to work on those first. The first thing we did, as an example, was to invent a bus

called Peripheral Component Interconnect [PCI]. We picked it because it solved a range of problems: It solved a graphics problem; it solved plug-and-play problems; it solved interrupt problems; it solved performance issues.[22]

As this quote illustrates, Intel managers were unwilling to continue tolerating a "bad" PC architecture that limited the performance impact of their core product, the microprocessor. The PC's internal interfaces were too constrained in bandwidth (i.e., the capacity to transfer data back and forth between the different components of the PC). "For us," Grove said, "the danger was a Pentium processor power would have been choked off by the ISA AT bus."[23]

While a faster microprocessor increased the speed at which the microprocessor processed data, it was still the input/output (I/O) bus that determined the speed at which data arrived at and exited the microprocessor. Hence, limits of the system architecture restricted how much Intel could affect performance of the overall platform, the PC.[24] Will Swope, an Intel VP and director of platform planning, explained the problem of the I/O bus "bottleneck":

> The common problem Intel has is that we cannot get enough data into our processor to operate on. . . . Say you're just trying to write a picture on the screen. If you don't have the data to operate on in the processor, you can't then feed the pixels to the screen. The processor . . . usually takes 64 bits of data at a time at the clock rate of the bus, which is 100 MHz. That's 100 million times a second. So it would be really good if you have 64 bits of data to grab. Otherwise you go click to grab the next data. It's like being able to run very fast to the door to open it, but there's no one there when you get there.[25]

Dave Schuler, a senior sales and marketing manager who would head the PCI project along with Dave Carson (who would become PCI's principal architect), was frustrated by the slow graphics system on the PC, and feared that users would not see any improvement, even with Intel's next-generation microprocessors. "[G]raphics was such a bottleneck in the system that you could make the processor go twice as fast but what you saw on the screen didn't speed up."[26]

Another problem for Intel was the growing expense that went into trying to fix this architectural problem. According to Carson, getting stuff in and out of the computer was becoming the bottleneck: "We were spending more and more money, and a bigger piece of the expense of building the box was going into the I/O rather than into the processor. Well, that's not Intel's interest. Intel built the processors. We didn't build this other stuff, so we didn't want three-quarters of the cost going into that stuff."[27]

At the same time, IBM was attempting to evolve the PC architecture in a proprietary manner with a new bus project: MCA. That strategy was in line with IBM trying to maintain (or more precisely, to revert to) a "vertical" industry; that is, a structure of industry competition where highly integrated firms made most of their own components and competed on the merits of distinctive, proprietary architecture. Intel also would not have benefited from proprietary approaches from OEMs that might have led to what some Intel managers called "fragmentation." Clearly, a battle of PC systems was not in the interest of Intel: For one thing, Intel wanted to be able to provide the same microprocessors to all the OEMs it did business with. Different PC architectures might not allow that. Intel managers firmly believed that this would be detrimental for industry growth. Eventually, IBM was unsuccessful with its proprietary MCA proposal because other industry players opposed such an overt attempt to introduce a proprietary technology. The prospect for a fast-growing PC business had become clear to many of the new companies that had emerged and started to sell PCs. Many economic actors wanted to have a share of this growing pie. The times called for a more consensual approach. Nevertheless, a few companies stepped in to drive the process of industry alignment, and Intel was prominent among them.

Intel Takes the Architectural Lead: The PCI Bus

For Intel to attempt to change the PC's interfaces was truly a bold, strategic move. It was also a risky one. Until this time, Intel engineers had only designed the microprocessor, a critical but small piece of hardware that relied on many other hardware components not to mention the operating system and other basic software. The changes Intel was contemplating could affect the entire PC system and the entire industry because it would change the architecture of the system and thus affect how new pieces of a computer that had a PCI bus would have to be designed.[28]

The willingness of firms to adopt this architectural change, moving from one bus (IBM's ISA) to another (Intel's PCI), and from following one firm (IBM) to another (Intel), would mark the beginning of a change in leadership in the computer industry. Until then, who designed or made different parts of the PC pretty much followed the template IBM had introduced with the original PC in 1981. But IBM failed to continue as the platform leader for all PCs being manufactured in the industry. IBM's weak and unsuccessful attempt in the mid-1980s to recapture the architectural lead by trying to get the industry to switch to yet another new proprietary bus technology, MicroChannel, may have contributed to the decline in its influence.

Intel, by contrast, did not try to benefit from proprietary architectural interfaces for the PC. Instead, the company made sure that the new PCI specification was free and open to everyone. The reason Intel did this reflected its particular approach to platform leadership, which contrasted with IBM's. Intel-proprietary interfaces could have resulted in further fragmentation among the PC manufacturers' choice of system interconnect. This outcome would not have been good for Intel, which supplied microprocessors to these companies. It was in Intel's best interest for all PC manufacturers and developers of complementary products to plug their products together in the same way to make the development of complements as easy and as cheap as possible.

The PCI bus was an internal interface whose definition potentially affected all the companies that designed and manufactured other parts of the computer attached to the bus. Therefore, altering the bus was a major architectural change involving significant risk. Not only did Intel have to succeed in designing a bus that worked faster, but it had to convince other firms to adopt this new standard and invest in new products that used it. Not surprisingly, winning over other firms was perhaps the most difficult part of the PCI effort, and Intel's success here was in no way guaranteed. Intel had to rally firms around the new standard. As Kinnie described, "When you invent something like PCI it's not just a matter of Intel deciding it's a good thing. People have to be prepared to invest their own innovation and their own companies. Lots of little graphics companies bet their livelihood that this was it."[29] Large companies like IBM, Compaq, and DEC also had to bet that PCI would be the next standard and design their new products using the new technology.

Solving Industry Architectural Problems While Thinking Ahead

Once the PCI project was underway, Intel found out that other industry players had also started to work on a specification for an improved bus. But where these other groups seemed intent on designing interfaces tied to particular microprocessors, Intel was wary of the potential for competing chip sets that were "wired into a specific generation of the processor." Carson explained:

> Here we are, thinking about *providing a specification for the whole industry to use*, which may in some people's estimation have been rather presumptuous on Intel's part. It was a new thing, but it turned out—unbeknownst to us at the beginning—that we were also doing it in the face of an industry standards organization, which had the same task. Once we found out, we decided to continue anyway—because we didn't at all approve of the approach they had taken. Technology-wise, they were just doing something that was more wired into a specific generation of processor. When we would go to the next generation of processor, they would have had to make a bunch of changes to keep following it. We wanted to be transparent. We wanted the processor to be able to move transparently to all the rest of the stuff in the box. *You shouldn't have to redesign the entire box every time you change processors*, otherwise the processor-change treadmill is way too slow. There's too much baggage.[30]

Contrary to their counterparts, Intel engineers designed PCI so that future versions of the microprocessor would *not* require a redesign of anything else in the PC architecture. Seemingly an arcane technical detail, this design decision was strategically brilliant. The design left enough room for Intel's chips to evolve and find their place in the PC architecture without requiring further approval or extra coordination between other actors in the industry—thus reducing an important hurdle for the adoption of Intel's future chips.

The technical approach Intel chose to avoid rewriting the interfaces every time there's a new microprocessor was to create a "buffer layer" of programmable instructions (or "logic") within a special chip set that sat between the microprocessor and the connections to different devices or software programs.[31] The chip set also manages the memory for the whole system and provides the connection to the processor. This chip set spawned the PCI bus and a lot of other connected devices. Most important, Intel could change the chip set layer as needed with new microprocessor generations, without the complementors having to do anything.

> So, we c[ould] turn the chip set and just change the processor connection, put a new processor down—a new version of the chip set *where all of the design for the rest of the system stays constant*. Then you've got 500 vendors out there in the industry that are providing add-in boards for various functions that plug into PCI. They don't have to know that any of that changed.[32]

What had happened in this episode is worth a pause for reflection. The industry as a whole had a shared, specific problem—the insufficient capacity of the bus—but only the solution proposed by Intel was capable of solving that common problem while also creating a technical and industrial environment in which Intel's future innovations could find the PC system as a convenient cradle. The PCI and chip set designs introduced a local modular architecture into this part of the PC that decoupled Intel's zone of innovation from the rest of the computer.[33] The advantage for Intel? If Intel were to develop new microprocessors—which Intel knew it intended to do frequently and regularly—there wouldn't be a need for other industry players to redesign their products in order to be compatible with the new Intel chip. Such redesign and coordination of work among companies making interdependent products is a costly hurdle; one that usually prevents the adoption of innovations that affect the design of multiple products. Therefore, Intel's brilliant design move proactively reduced a major barrier to adoption for Intel's future chips. This approach—solving a common problem in a manner that will facilitate the realization of one's future plans—is, in our view, a key part to platform leadership. But let us get back to the story.

Indecision within Intel, Tensions with PC Manufacturers

Even among Intel executives, commitment to PCI wavered. They could not agree on how aggressively to push the PCI bus. Some managers feared that strong support would create too many tensions with PC manufacturers. Grove recalled, for example, how PC manufacturers thought that Intel should not try to change the PC architecture because this was none of Intel's business. What was a component maker doing dabbling in architecture? There was a real risk that PC manufacturers would *not* follow Intel's lead. Architectural innovations and decisions had been the exclusive province of firms that produced and sold entire PC systems.[34] Grove reflected on the risk that Intel faced by stepping onto the turf of its own clients, the OEMs:

> The notion that a silicon producer could define a computer bus architecture was a very strange thing. But nobody was doing it or nobody was capable of doing it. So, around 1990, we started a pretty major effort to develop our own chip sets as well as the bus architecture. . . . Around that time, all the larger manufacturers made their own chip sets. . . . It was a pretty controversial move.[35]

Compaq and other large PC makers worried that Intel's move into PC architecture would threaten their ability to design unique products that differed from the competition. If PCI succeeded, they feared they would see stiffer competition from a myriad of smaller firms that had been at a disadvantage because of the expertise and resources needed for chip set design. If Intel provided chip sets, then what would distinguish the products between large and small PC manufacturers? Grove remembered the debate:

> [Large OEMs would] lose their ability to differentiate. Compaq would have been, or was, a viable threat for IBM. [They] had to redo chip set development, but those masses of PC producers can't afford to do that. And we have excellent engineers and excellent computer architects. So we got to do a particularly good bus definition—a chip set definition—and our computers are going to be much better at using microprocessors. If they relinquish that, they lose a possible technical differentiation, a performance differentiation. The whole industry was already the same in one way: They are all using the same microprocessor. Now it would be the same in another way: using the same bus architecture with the same chip set implementation. This was, for the larger OEMs, a controversial

issue. For the smaller OEMs, this was wonderful because it gave them an opportunity to compete for a larger audience on the same footing. So, the industry's reaction was complex.[36]

Carson noted that Intel executives made the situation worse by continually changing their minds about PCI.

> Intel never could really decide whether we wanted to do PCI or not. It [posed] the whole issue of Intel: This is a processor company, a company that builds chips. Compaq takes those chips and builds whole computers out of them, and for the first time we're going out and saying, "Here is an industry standard that will impact everybody, that doesn't have anything to do with our processor but has to do with the way you build the box. We're writing it, and here it is." That was the first time we'd done that. So there we were, suggesting, "Hey, you guys who build computers aren't building the right bus, and we're going to help you do it right." Actually, it was further complicated because we were not aware at the time we started, but, by the time we got along the path to defining this thing, we found out there was a standards organization doing a parallel job called VESA bus, for Video Electronic Standards Association. They were writing a standard there. We looked at what they were doing and said it's not the right thing technically and it won't migrate across our processor families. That wasn't very good for us because they had marshalled several companies already to create and endorse a standard. It turns out there was only room in the industry for one of these two standards. Nobody builds a VESA local bus anymore.[37]

Indecision among Intel executives was not a good signal to other firms in the industry, especially the smaller suppliers of complementary products. Why should they invest in a new standard if the champion of that standard wasn't aggressively backing it? Carson empathized with his customers' hesitation to follow Intel's sometimes confusing signals:

> Say you're a little company that builds graphic chips, and there are a half-dozen big ones at the time and a dozen more little ones that sell a few parts. The half-dozen big ones are all competing wherever Intel is shipping platforms via Compaq or Dell or IBM. These six

guys are competing to get their part on all of those systems. That's not a very high-margin business. . . . So these guys don't have a lot of money to do speculative investment. . . . Bear in mind now . . . that there's a standards organization producing an alternative. So now they're looking at both of these and saying, "Which one do I do?" Now here comes Intel into that environment, having produced this alternate standard, and Intel is saying: "Maybe they won't follow us. Maybe we should quit. Let's not get too serious about this. We might not be successful. Let's stop." Somebody comes along and says to Andy Grove: "Intel, you're doing it wrong." He doesn't know for sure whether we're doing it wrong or not, but he says: "We don't want to be embarrassed. We're more a processor company. We can get off here." . . . For three years during the development and diffusion of PCI, there was a major pullback in March of every year.[38]

Despite their hesitance, Intel executives did end up pushing PCI. Grove insisted, however, that Intel had to find at least one "big-name OEM" (preferably IBM) to get on the PCI bandwagon. Although the reality was that Intel's top management had not fully committed to PCI, the grassroots work of Intel's field engineers created a perception in the industry that Intel *was* firmly behind PCI. This perception discouraged competing proposals from other firms. Eventually, Intel convinced IBM to adopt the PCI design, even though this decision probably weakened IBM's own PC business.

Intel Decides to Make the PCI Chip Set

To convince IBM and other firms to adopt PCI, Intel executives realized they had to demonstrate Intel's commitment to the new standard and put their own "skin in the game."[39] Intel did this by starting the mass production of PCI chip sets at its Folsom, California, division (later renamed the PCI Component Division, and then the Computing Enhancement Group). The chip set played a technically crucial function. It was the "most strategic interface" in the PC because it provided a direct link to the microprocessor and had to change with every new generation or at least every other new generation of the microprocessor. Grove recalls that PC manufacturers such as IBM and Compaq ultimately went along with Intel because they wanted to ship PCs that took advantage of the latest Intel chips as quickly as possible. Designing complete PC systems on their own at the pace Intel introduced new microprocessors was turning out to be too expensive as well as technically complicated. Grove argued that Intel had to make a complete solution available to PC manufacturers:

> It turns out that the development of these chip sets or computer platforms was getting much more complex. So, it was getting increasingly difficult for the larger OEMs to keep up. Economically, the notion was that everyone was going to do their own different chips but, in the face of the rising chip complexity and cost, that was an impossibility. It was a big burden for them, and it became evident that we were going to succeed. That was several years later, when we came out with a complete solution in 1993—chip, bus, chip sets, and motherboards that implemented it. So, you could buy from us, or get a specification from us and do your own development, or get a chip set from us with which you could do your own motherboard, or you could buy the whole motherboard that implemented the same thing.[40]

Usually, chip sets were made by chip set manufacturers such as Chips and Technologies. At the time Intel was trying to push PCI, however, the market for the PCI bus was not yet established. Hence, chip set vendors were reluctant to invest enough resources to make a functioning PCI chip set "right" and in a timely manner.[41] Waiting would mean further delay in PCI implementation, and therefore delay in the establishment of PC systems that could take advantage of the capabilities in Intel's newest microprocessor—the Pentium. The result would probably be a lack of demand for Intel's latest products. Claude Leglise, former head of Intel's Content Group, described Intel's predicament:

> At one point, we became limited in our ability to sell because the chip set manufacturers were not ready with products that matched our processor. We ended up with two strategies. One was to tell them ahead of time what we're going to do, technically and volume-wise, so they could design products that match and be prepared to produce them in significant quantities. And we had a second strategy, which was to build the chip set ourselves such that it wouldn't be a limiter to our core business. We told the chip set

manufacturers, Chips and Technologies, for example, our vision of how big the market was going to be and where it was going to be. We'd tell them the kind of products we were building. We have 6 MHz, 20 MHz, 30 MHz, and you guys need to have the stuff that matches. . . . Typically, we would tell them a little after beginning our investment—once the bet was pretty clear, but before going to market: a year or two before, depending on what was needed. . . . It ended up that today we're the leaders in chip sets. I don't know if we ever intended to be. *We got into it because the other guys didn't move fast enough or didn't produce enough or didn't have the right quality.*[42]

At that time, Intel did not have a good record in rallying other firms around its initiatives. Kinnie recalled that Intel's entry into chip sets was necessary to break the "logjam" in putting together all elements of the new platform:

One of the ways we broke the logjam was doing our chip set. PCI would not have happened if Intel hadn't decided to do the chip set. It was the catalyst that showed we were really serious. Once we did the chip, we did what's called a cell library, we designed a graphics controller interface, and we made that cell library available to the graphics vendors so it would be easy for them to do a PCI. So, we gave them design assistance. That's how we lowered their investment burden to get them to hop on our bandwagon.[43]

Intel also had a technical motivation to enter the chip business. According to Bill Miller, Intel's director of worldwide media relations, the company's engineers were concerned that other chip set manufacturers did not fully understand the PCI standard and would not provide the proper chip set designs.[44] Without the right chip sets, Intel would not have sufficient demand for the Pentium or newer microprocessors to "ramp" up demand:

It took us five years to establish PCI. One of the things that were most troublesome was that it was really hard to get the other chip set vendors to do PCI "right." Because it was so close to the processor, we wanted them to do it right. Our product ramp, and therefore our revenue ramp, our distance from the competitors, our margin, our earnings per share, and therefore our market cap, were all driven by how fast we could ramp Pentium. And ramping Pentium was gated by the fact that you needed a PCI bus to do it. The ISA bus, or whichever equivalents at the time, were too stinkingly slow to show the benefit. PCI was a specification that told everybody to design this way and then all the various pieces from you guys will connect. We got impatient and we said, "That's not fast enough." So [we] entered the chip set business. We ended up building our own implementation of a chip set that has PCI so it is compatible with the specification, but we are not the only suppliers by a long shot.[45]

Even with the official go-ahead, convincing Intel's internal chip set group to bet on PCI itself was no minor task. Despite the number of valuable patents involved in the PCI chip set, the group, already facing an uncertain future, was reluctant to invest in the new PCI technology because there was not yet a market for it.[46] Kinnie recalled:

We had to convince our own chip set group, which was about to go out of business. They had tried to bet with IBM on their bus, and they had tried to bet with Compaq on their bus, and the market went with the old bus. The group said they didn't know what to do, and they weren't going to change but instead stay with the old bus. And we asked the chip set group: "Why not do a PCI chip set?" But it wasn't a slam dunk. It was very difficult for Intel to decide to invest in the PCI chip set. There was no market yet for PCI chip sets. The OEMs were not asking for it. We were inventing this thing. There was no business case for it. It was a lot of money to invest, although not in the grand scale of things. Still, it was a couple of million dollars, but it was the life or death of the chip set business. That's what made it more difficult. If they bet on PCI that would mean they didn't do the other thing. But we argued that they were about to die anyway.[47]

In addition to chip sets, Intel soon expanded its motherboard business, a major component of the PC that combined the microprocessor with essential chip sets for peripherals as well as memory chips. The motivation was the same: Suppliers were slow to move, and Intel wanted its customers to be able to take advantage of its latest microprocessor technology.

> We did something similar with motherboards. We had become very dependent on our customers' ability to design motherboards. Every one of our 300 or 400 customers had to hire engineers to design motherboards and that meant it took longer to make a profit. So we started designing, producing, and selling motherboards to accelerate the ramp.[48]

We will discuss in chapter 4 the strategic implications of Intel's move into chip sets and motherboards, and the tensions this expansion created with external chip set vendors. Despite some resistance, this move was an effective mechanism to get chip vendors to move faster in the direction that Intel wanted.

PCI: Template for Further Evolution

On the surface, Intel's seminal initiative on PCI appears to be focused on the technical development of a PC data pathway (the PCI bus), but its strategic significance lies in the shift of balance of power among the actors involved in the process of evolution of the overall PC platform. The creation and development of IAL was an essential factor in this radical shift.

PCI was just the beginning. IAL later initiated the design of several such interfaces and, with the collaboration of other Intel groups, encouraged the adoption of these interfaces as PC architectural standards by the vast majority of other companies in the PC industry. From the PCI project, Intel managers had learned that there was a process they could follow when working with other firms that made their efforts more likely to succeed. The approach Intel had followed with PCI provided a template when Intel wanted to rally industry players around other new standards such as the Intel-sponsored universal serial bus (USB) and the accelerated graphics port (AGP) technologies.[49] With more credibility and a process to follow, it became much easier for Intel to "move the industry" after PCI. Several Intel managers commented that thanks to the PCI experience, Intel had learned the ropes of what would become in the next few years a systematic set of activities set out to influence industry innovation and drive platform evolution.

Chapter Three

Intel's Strategic Principles for Platform Leadership

The Four Levers

To a large extent, PCI set the tone for the other initiatives. . . . Intel realized through this experience that, when we set out to do so, we can move the industry in some useful direction.

—DAVE CARSON, MANAGER, INTERCONNECT ARCHITECTURE, MEDIA ARCHITECTURE LAB, INTEL ARCHITECTURE LAB

This chapter takes up the question of how Intel strengthened its platform leadership after the success of the PCI bus project. Intel's platform leadership strategy, detailed in this chapter, included three main roles: (1) sponsor of systemic architectural innovation, (2) stimulator of external innovation on complements, and (3) coordinator of industrial innovation that spanned across many firms' boundaries. We link the key activities Intel engaged in to the more general framework of the Four Levers (introduced in chapter 1) to facilitate the reader's understanding of platform leadership strategy.

Four Levers for Platform Leadership

From our study of Intel, Microsoft, Cisco,[1] Palm, NTT DoCoMo, and Linux,[2] we have found that the main levers of strategic action in the hands of managers who aim for platform leadership are the following:

1. *Scope of the firm*: What to do inside the firm, and what to let external firms do.
2. *Product technology*: Make decisions regarding system architecture (the degree of modularity), interfaces (the degree of openness of the interfaces to the platform), and intellectual property (how much information about the platform and its interfaces to disclose to outside firms).
3. *Relationships with external complementors*: How collaborative versus competitive should relationship with complementors be? How will consensus be created? How will conflicts of interest be handled?
4. *Internal organization*: How to organize the firm to support the above three levers.

Platform leaders need to think about and implement these four levers in a coordinated fashion. Some external constraints or strategic choices on some of the levers create specific options (and sometimes constrain the possible remaining choices) for the other levers. It is the internal consistency of the Four Levers taken together that can ensure a successful platform leadership strategy. In the following section we analyze Intel's platform leadership strategy using the Four Levers Framework.

Driving Systemic Architectural Innovation

The PCI bus had been a significant step toward a better PC system architecture—and it was enough for a few years. However, with the ever-increasing performance of its chips, in the mid- to late 1990s Intel faced again the problem that relatively slow internal buses or interfaces in the PC did not allow customers to see any measurable performance improvement, even when they ran on powerful chips. The PCI bus initiative was only the first in a series of architectural changes that Intel championed.

In the late 1990s, Intel sponsored several new initiatives. Whereas PCI was an I/O bus that conveyed data to and from PC subsystems surrounding the processor, the AGP was a fast interface that transferred data between the microprocessor and graphics cards. AGP was geared especially toward boosting the performance of computers running graphics software applications. Intel also got involved from the early stages of design in FireWire, a serial bus interface standard offering high-speed communications from the PC to peripherals.[3] Carson observed:

> To a large extent, PCI set the tone for the other initiatives. We had to do a lot of pioneering in that one. We were pretty much turning over new leaves legally—in terms of intellectual property ownership, licensing agreements, and technical control of specifications—at the same time we were building the actual content. . . . I think two things happened. One, Intel realized through this experience that, when we set out to do so, we can move the industry in some useful direction. We don't have to be timid; we know we can do it. Two, the rest of the industry learned it. So, when we approached USB—which we approached a bit differently—we knew from the outset we're going to do this. Let's go pick the right five companies—Compaq, Microsoft, etc.—and form a consortium and just go do it.[4]

The various initiatives that Intel sponsored illustrate its use of the different strategic levers. For example, Intel decided to allocate resources to the development of an innovation, USB. However, Intel needed the involvement of external companies to work on complementary innovation as well as further specification of the interface itself. The choice of exactly what needs to be performed outside versus what needs to be developed inside is the prototypical Lever 1 choice. Right from the start, technological choices such as intellectual property treatment are singled out as important: This is Lever 2. Last, the mention of creating consortium is a way to organize relationships between Intel and external firms: This is Lever 3.

Universal Serial Bus

The USB initiative began in the mid-1990s when it became apparent to Intel executives that there were other platform bottlenecks to overcome. Limited bandwidth between the PC and peripheral devices—such as printers, scanners, joysticks, and digital cameras—was slowing down the overall PC performance.

The USB was a new interface linking a PC to external devices such as the keyboard, scanner, and printer. It was a "universal" plug into the PC: A user could connect several peripherals into one USB plug, which was not possible with legacy serial connectors such as those using the small computer system interface (SCSI).[5] The problem here, again, was the architecture: IBM and other PC manufacturers had designed the PC so that each peripheral device needed its own individual plug in the back of the PC. The USB removed this limitation. Miller recalled the origins of USB: "The concept of a serial bus that was essentially plug-and-play and could simplify the user experience was formulated in IAL. It was part of an overall media architecture that was being worked on at the time."[6]

Jim Pappas, the director of platform initiatives in the desktop products group, explained to us that USB "breaks the old one-to-one correspondence between the number of connectors in the back of a computer and the number of devices that could be plugged into it."[7] It lets users "daisy-chain" (i.e., connect to each other in a sequence or in hubs) up to 127 peripheral devices. USB works at 12 megabits per second (Mbps) and allows "hot plug-and-play," meaning that users can connect new peripheral devices without switching off the equipment before plugging in a new peripheral.

As with the PCI bus, Intel had a vision not only of what USB could do, but also of what the rest of the industry could do with USB: Create new peripherals that would augment the usefulness of any PC with a USB interface. Intel's architectural innovation on USB reinforced the modular design of the PC (Lever 2) while adding to its value by stimulating external innovation (Lever 3). As a universal connector, USB had a different goal than PCI in that Intel expected it to accommodate many peripherals and stimulate further innovation on existing products such as joysticks or other hardware products yet to be invented. USB allowed greater flexibility in connecting existing or future devices to the computer and therefore augmented the versatility of use of a PC—in effect, growing the PC platform. IAL executive David Johnson believed that USB, as a new standard, would stimulate innovation in peripheral devices:

> [The USB is] a connector: We hope that all kinds of peripherals will plug into it and it will generate a whole new class of peripherals for

the PC because it's easy to do and you can do it temporarily. Most things you plug into the PC get left there. It's like a mixer where you may have a bread dough hook and you may have something for a different kind of batter. Or like a food processor with lots of different blades. What we have with USB is great; there are all these games, and you just unplug your keyboard and you plug in the joystick or steering wheel or whatever, and when you're done you unplug it and you plug the keyboard back in. *The whole reason we did that was because we wanted to stimulate lots of other things getting plugged in.* That's our only motivation. So, to me, it was only useful if a lot of various external innovations happened.[8]

By defining a functional connector to many pieces of the PC, most of them yet to be invented, Intel pursued a modular approach to the evolution of the PC system (Lever 2). By attempting to stimulate innovation on products that could connect to this interface, Intel also acted on Lever 3 (relationships with external firms) by creating business possibilities for many third-party companies. Many became complementors of the PC platform by adopting the USB interface. Creating collaborative opportunities was a win-win situation for Intel: The demand for USB-compatible peripherals could create attractive business opportunities for many companies (and good will toward Intel). At the same time, the creation of such peripherals reinforced the diffusion of the USB interface, which was in line with Intel's vision of selling more revenue-generating microprocessors.

Before March 1996 Intel started to integrate the necessary logic into PC chip sets and encourage other manufacturers to do likewise. Widespread availability and support for USB began in the second half of 1997. Today, almost all PCs shipped in the world have a USB interface.

Intel's System Mindset

We describe in this section Intel's approach to Lever 2 (technological choices) in the context of its attempts to encourage innovation through industrywide collaboration. We were struck by how many IAL employees shared this philosophy for how to improve system performance and growth prospects for PCs: They wanted to help the industry to innovate. Intel translated this desire to facilitate industry innovation into major efforts to sponsor interface standards. These interfaces became the technological mechanism for channeling external innovation, ensuring platform integrity through compatibility of complementary products, and creating an industrial consensus on platform technological evolution. We describe further in this section Intel's efforts at sponsoring interface technologies to make them into standards. This endeavor requires a "system mindset"—focusing on the overall PC platform, of which the microprocessor is only one piece. It also requires a belief that Intel's success, and the success of the entire PC industry, depended on cooperation among key industry players and a common understanding that the industry needed to create new uses and thus new users for the PC.

IAL's work involved new standards. Egido commented: "IAL doesn't stand on its own. It has to reach out into the industry as a whole because the way we do our work is frequently through standards efforts. We participate in standards efforts and drive standards into the industry that then move the entire industry."[9] Early on in IAL history, its director Kinnie became convinced that, if IAL could establish better technical interfaces for components of the PC platform, the costs of product development would dramatically fall for all companies in the industry:

> What we decide is where in the stack we need to have interfaces such that innovation can occur in these segments independently. If the interfaces aren't there, innovation has to happen on a vertical stack all the way through. That takes a long time to happen, and there are usually big losses. We're breaking down the cost to innovate. A company can innovate in this layer and not worry about what's going on in these other layers because we have interfaces on either side of them. If they weren't there, we'd have to make the entire investment—and not very many people can afford to do that. Our work in the industry enables smaller companies, innovative companies, to make smaller investments and yet potentially win large market share in a segment they can own. And there are more of them that participate, so we get broader innovation. That's why this industry moves so fast: because you know there is still a chance for small innovators to plug in and succeed. You can't do that in the consumer electronics industry. You can't compete with

Mitsubishi; it's really hard. In our industry, little companies can thrive. It doesn't matter whether it's software, hardware, or chip sets.[10]

This quote presents a classic argument for the benefits of modular architectures for computers and similar types of systems. Tightly coupled with this philosophy of modularity was a stance on the importance of so-called open standards. Craig Kinnie, Andy Grove, and other Intel managers believed that many more innovations could emerge from a computer industry organized in layers of specialized firms that created products able to interact through "open" interfaces. Modular architectures with open interfaces between components make it possible for many firms to participate in the innovation process.[11] Intel executives believed that if their company played a key role in designing those interfaces, Intel could help this "ecosystem" flourish as well as position itself more firmly—and perhaps permanently—at its center. Intel executives proposed a strategy to capitalize on this belief. This strategy involved two key dimensions: (1) stimulate complementary innovations that enhanced the PC and (2) define the parameters of compatibility (embodied in interfaces) among the complementary products made at other firms. This second dimension involved playing a coordinating role to stimulate innovation at other firms.

Coordination at the interface layers facilitates innovation in complementary products as well as competition in markets for these new products. Because properly designed interfaces and a common standard for connections can "lower the cost of innovation," Kinnie saw IAL's role as trying to minimize "confusion" regarding how to connect to the PC:

> We want to define how these companies will hook their pipe to the PC and how application writers can take advantage of that pipe that we control and that we can have an effect on. I don't know which company is going to win, but they all will connect to the PC in exactly the same way. That's not the way it would have happened if we hadn't been around. Every company was figuring out a different way of doing it. Some companies were going to use add-in cards; some were going to use Ethernet cards; some were going to hook to the parallel port—and the software was even worse. We

said, "Wait a minute. We're Intel. We care about the PC. If you all want to save some money, the best way to hook to a PC is this way. Here's the hardware way; here's the software way." *Coordination here now creates a common connector. Now they all have to compete.* If they were all allowed to have a different connector and one of them won, there wouldn't even be competition. It would be one guy or two. Because we said there's one way to hook to a PC and we're going to make it happen, they all now have to compete to deliver to that socket. There's a time aspect: This causes the indecision to be resolved faster. When you have multiple competing standards, there are market forces and it takes time. If we come out and make it clear and say there's only one way to hook a pipe to a PC and it's this way, we resolve all of that confusion. And everybody invests in a common direction more quickly.[12]

Intel managers believe that IAL's efforts to help define interfaces for the PC made a significant contribution to the success of their company. IAL helped Intel establish and maintain a leadership position in the computer industry as well as generate great momentum behind their microprocessor product line. Providing the interface specifications, ensuring coordination with groups inside and outside Intel, and building consensus around key interfaces also spurred competition in complementary product markets and thereby increased demand for Intel products.

In addition, IAL helped Intel raise the barriers to entry for any firm that might want to compete directly with the Intel-sponsored, industry-backed architecture; for example, by trying to introduce a new microprocessor standard that used different technical interfaces. Kinnie acknowledged these barriers to entry, but emphasized that defining the "right" interfaces was mostly about enabling industry innovation rather than inhibiting competition. Defining the interfaces required vision about the evolution of the PC platform as well as a sense of the business opportunities for potential complementors. The task also involved difficult technical choices:

The location of the interfaces has to . . . be well defined. . . . [T]hose interface points have to be in the right place. You could pick the wrong place. The trouble with the VESA bus [replaced by Intel's PCI bus] was that they picked the wrong place. It could do graphics but nothing else. It has to be well designed, well architected from a technical point of view. It has to be robust enough for the rigor of all the applications that are going to be put on it, all the technologies that will be thrown at it. It will have to last for a fair amount of time.[13]

Building Momentum around Interfaces

Intel developed a sophisticated approach to Lever 3 (managing relationships with external firms). Its strategy involved establishing strategic interest groups and gradually building momentum.

Getting outside firms to support new standards such as PCI or USB required time and patience, as well as planning. IAL had learned this with PCI, and thus decided to proceed gradually rather than with a burst of publicity and investment. During the early phases, IAL generally initiated relationships with a small group of outside firms and brought them together in strategic interest groups (SIGs). Then, in collaboration with SIG members, IAL engineers designed the first features of the new standard. Even influential firms like Microsoft and Compaq tended to back Intel's proposals because they had a chance to participate early on in the design process and to influence the evolution of the standard.

Intel's SIGs usually had between three and seven members. For PCI, there were five companies: Intel, DEC (now part of Compaq), Compaq, IBM, and NCR. For USB, there were seven: Intel, DEC, Compaq, Microsoft, IBM, Northern Telecom, and NEC Technologies. For any standard involving software, rallying Microsoft was essential. For hardware designs, IBM, Hewlett-Packard, and Compaq were commonly involved. Pappas believed that keeping the number of early participants small was important because a small group made faster decisions:

> A thing I think is pretty key at this point is to keep the number of companies working on it small, just from an efficiency standpoint. Otherwise, if you have too many companies with too many diverging points of views, you could spend years trying to find [agreement]. And you want companies that have something to offer, and

are motivated to offer something, and that share that vision with you. Hopefully, they can offer something you need in the process. Having more people who don't offer anything you need doesn't really help.[14]

Intel's selection process for partners went beyond trying to keep the numbers small. The basic strategy, according to Bala Cadambi, the IAL manager responsible for peripherals issues, was to bring in a few firms that would have long-term commitments to the new technology, lend credibility to it, and attract other firms to the new standard:

> *Typically, we start with a small group of companies that are able to invest for a long period of time*—experts that are related to the kind of thing we're trying to accomplish. They have to be the leaders and the experts in that area, and have industry credibility—meaning if they come together and say, "here's what we agreed on," everybody else will say, "well, those companies talked about it, and it must be good for all of us, because they must have talked about it quite a bit."[15]

As we have already seen, decisions on Lever 3 go hand in hand with decisions on other levers. With USB, Intel had to make decisions about Lever 1 (what to do inside versus what to leave external firms to do), and also about Lever 4 (how to organize internally to support the above mentioned decisions).

USB was more complex technically than PCI because it involved so many parts of the PC system and industry—hardware and software makers of many different types. But the standardization process that IAL directed was markedly similar in both cases. After IAL generated the USB concept, Intel invested internally in some necessary development work. Then Intel recruited partners outside and inside the company, forming a new SIG to promote the new standard. Miller reflected on how the process unfolded:

> USB was near but not fully within Intel's traditional core competency. We had to enlist an entire industry because we had to get peripherals out there that took advantage of it. We had to get an operating system to support it and we had to get the device drivers

written. We actually pulled together a working group or a SIG—or a consortium, to use a more generic term—of industry players.

Intel had to put the necessary support into the chip set, which took some internal convincing. IAL has a budget, so the initial exploration was paid for. For the other money—that's where the convincing comes in. . . . Every quarter, we review budgets with Andy [Grove], Craig [Kinnie], Gordon [Moore], and the CFO. And we say: "Okay, that's a corporate-sponsored program, so we'll give you slight relief in your budget because you're working on the right stuff." . . . The outside world never sees this. They assume that we're one monolithic company that just marches in step. But when you look at our culture, there's plenty of internal debate.[16]

The first part of Miller's statement refers to actions on Lever 1, and the second part refers to the internal processes needed to implement the above choices: This is Lever 4 (internal organization and processes).

Because USB touched so many components from many different companies, Intel had to hone its persuasion skills to succeed. By contrast, it had been relatively easy for Intel to push PCI forward because it involved fewer partners. Intel had been able to implement the PCI standard mainly by introducing a chip set and getting Microsoft to make some basic changes in the operating system software.[17]

Another contrast is the world of Apple, which controlled the Macintosh hardware and software platform, including the design of peripheral devices. One company could make most of the interface decisions by itself. Intel, as Miller noted, had no such luxury. It would take two years to get everyone in the industry on board for USB. Intel managers had to have a long-term goal as well as a deliberate plan of action:

> *USB is more complicated [than PCI] because it involves more pieces of the industry, and so more pieces of the stack have to change.* USB is a peripheral specification that many other pieces of equipment can connect to. So, you have to convince everybody: vendors of equipment that connect, like printers, joysticks, mice, scanners, monitors, keyboards—everything. And it's not as if Intel has a 99 percent share of the keyboard market segment. Then we could just write a

memo: "Change your device output." We used to joke about how easy it must be to change standards at Apple. You just send a memo that says: "You will now do USB." And the response is easy: "Yes, sir. I'll now do USB." In our case, it's a two-year process to convince the keyboard manufacturers this is good for them.[18]

To advance the new USB standard further required more detailed as well as broader planning: This was the next step. Intel managers and engineers drew up a five-year implementation plan for getting internal groups and outside partners lined up. Miller continued his explanation:

We sort of size it and say: "Okay, we're going to do some industry initiative work. We're going to have to do some peripheral component work. And we're going to have to do some of our own chip set work. Oh, and then—by the way—we probably have to do some work with Microsoft and the BIOS [basic input/output software] companies." And we put that all together. That becomes a master five-year plan. It's really driven primarily out of IAL in this case. The implementation is then basically disseminated to people that will run the working group and will put it in the chip set and work with Microsoft, et cetera, et cetera. . . . *You have to be the master planner for the industry*. You have got to keep a scorecard in your head or on paper—we keep it on paper—of *which dominos have to fall for this capability to be established*. In the case of USB, it continues to take massive evangelism with the peripheral guys to get them to make a small-leap investment in the development effort to come out with a different skew. It takes some convincing. For example, HP does not just want to double its inventory because that is a significant cost for them. So you have to cajole them. It really helps when Intel puts [a USB-ready design], say, in the chip sets. It shows we're committed. It makes it pretty likely it's going to happen. It really helps when Microsoft puts the support in the OS. Those are two things that sort of sanction it and make it a no-brainer. That's it. USB will take four years.[19]

This long, complicated process has costs, but also benefits. The trade-off between Apple's approach and Intel and Microsoft's is that even though it might be easier for Apple to coordinate all new components of its platform, Apple cannot count on all the innovations developed by the thousands of complementors to the PC platform that Intel and Microsoft contribute to.

Relinquishing Royalties on Intellectual Property

Intel's treatment of intellectual property (IP)—part of Lever 2—was a key piece of its strategy. Intel did not require potential adopters of the PCI, AGP, or USB interface specifications to pay any fees for use of the technology. This approach to interface IP differed from that of standardization bodies that sponsored an interface standard. Industry standardization bodies such as the Institute of Electrical and Electronic Engineers (IEEE)[20] or the International Telecommunications Union (ITU)[21] usually encouraged firms to charge a "reasonable" price for licensing their standards technologies. In the realm of interfaces, however, Intel made the decision to create a space for "free and open IP." Pappas recalled that this approach has remained a stable feature of Intel's interface standardization efforts:

> We made a decision pretty early on that what we wanted was something *open* and *royalty-free* that the industry could adopt without huge concerns about infringing IP or having to pay high royalties. Actually, we wanted no royalties, and I think we've achieved that. When I say "open," I mean that our policy is different than standards-setting bodies like IEEE or ITU. Generally, their policy is that any interface IP that is introduced into a specification has to be licensed under "reasonable and non-discriminatory terms." But, "reasonable" is a very subjective term. What some people think of as reasonable, others think is completely unreasonable. And "non-discriminatory" means that you can't exclude people from the licensing agreement. So, if people want to come, you have to offer them a license, and you have to do it under reasonable terms. This is different from giving things away for free. I believe PCI was the thing that pioneered this, and we extended it and did an even better job on USB with what we call "open and royalty-free." We would license any interface IP we had to anybody else in the industry. So it's open, and anybody can have it. And royalty-free means at zero cost to license.[22]

Although Intel did not charge royalties, it did not give away its interface technology without some tit for tat. It usually required companies to agree to "reciprocal" licensing, which created a zone of free IP that covered technological areas in which several companies were involved. Intel also insisted on access to other firms' patents that covered the same areas. Pappas explained:

> [We treated IP] under reciprocal terms: Anyone who would have access to [our] IP—if they had any [of their own IP] in that area— would have to make their IP open and available to the industry as well. That's a condition when they license the technology. This applied to any IP related to the implementation of the interfaces to the specification. For example, the USB bus has electrical characteristics: how the pins work, the voltage level. We would make this available to anybody in the industry who wants it. They just have to sign an agreement with us. Maybe they have a patent on something else, like the "plug-and-play" aspects of it, or how you would recognize a new device that was plugged into the bus. There're a million things you could have patents on. Nobody will sue anybody on these things, because they know it's an open space. *The open IP policy was really critical because it created a sense of openness around USB in a period when the industry was on the verge of accepting something that they were concerned that they'd have to pay a lot of money for.* . . . Royalties slow the adoption of standards. I think our process with PCI and USB . . . *drove rapid adoption on the PC, and that is what drove lots of other companies to invest in the technology.* Whether it's cameras, telephones, scanners, printers, mice, or joysticks, all these things that are now becoming available for USB were driven by the fact that there were lots of PCs being shipped with USB, which in turn was driven by the fact that it was relatively low-cost, both from an implementation standpoint and from a royalty standpoint.[23]

The Intel approach to IP rights on system interfaces also contrasts with that of other firms in the industry. A case in point is Apple's sponsoring of an interconnect technology called GeoPort.[24] Apple wanted to charge royalties for GeoPort, while Intel and other firms such as Compaq thought royalties would deter many people from adopting the standard and reduce the number of complementary products that third parties might produce. Pappas recalled:

> Apple had a head start with the telephony industry. They had AT&T and Siemens, and part of an IBM networking division. They had formed an organization called Versit, whose purpose was to promote the connection of computers and telephony equipment. They were promoting several different technologies, one of which was an interconnect technology called GeoPort. Apple's primary interest, I think, was to promote GeoPort. They wanted to make this a PC standard, but the issue we had was that GeoPort was very slow.... We decided it wasn't a good solution from a technical standpoint. Also, all of us were particularly worried about the royalties—not just Compaq. Apple, which definitely had patents, was very difficult to deal with about licensing terms. They were not forthcoming, and it was pretty clear that they were interested in using this thing as revenue-generation for Apple. A lot of our PC company customers were concerned about that.[25]

There was another rationale for having standards technologies that are free and open for anyone to license: to prevent any one firm from exploiting a standards technology for its own commercial advantage. Ben Manny, the Intel manager responsible for the "Home RF" initiative, started in 1997, which aimed to establish a radio frequency (RF) standard for computers to communicate wirelessly between different places in the home, contrasted Intel's approach with the IEEE approach of encouraging firms to license for a reasonable fee:

> One important thing for us is to ensure that the specification itself is unencumbered, so that any company can license that specification—which really defines an interface, how these devices talk together—without having to pay a royalty to use that specification. This has become a common practice for us. In contrast, when IEEE does a specification, they have the clause about licensing at fair and non-discriminatory rates. So, it's not free. But it must be fair and non-discriminatory. *We believe free is better.* It prevents companies from trying to push a particular technology because of the business advantage it would give them if that technology were accepted.[26]

It was not always easy, however, for Intel to convince other firms to give up the right to charge royalties on technologies they developed. Manny recalled some objection to this "open IP" among third parties involved with the Home RF initiative:

> We had an agreement that the five promoters signed. We came up with a participant agreement, which is what we wanted the companies that had [RF] technology to sign, and then we had an adopter's agreement. Basically, a participant agreement allows the company to contribute ideas, and an adopter agreement is a license to use the specification to build products. The participant agreement had a couple of terms and conditions dealing with [IP] that were very objectionable to these other RF companies *because they're not used to giving away IP*. It also had some nondisclosure provisions. So it was a little tricky to navigate through these companies. There was pretty strong push back. They really wanted to kind of drive this. But we held pretty firm and said that, if they wanted to tell us what they have, they need to sign this agreement—and that covers the IP and so on.[27]

THE PARADOX OF INVESTING IN INNOVATIONS AND RELINQUISHING ROYALTIES   The paradoxical strategy of relinquishing royalties on innovations that are costly to develop yields an insight about the economics of interface design. There is a fundamental difference between the economics of innovating in products for which there is a market (i.e., that can be sold by themselves) and the economics of innovating in the design of a system's architecture (such as defining new links between PC components).

We can think of products as goods or services that companies can put a price on and sell in markets where multiple firms compete with one another. When a firm invests in developing an innovation, it is—usually—in the hope not only to create value for consumers, but mainly to capture value as well. Firms usually capture value by making it difficult for others to imitate the product innovation (through secrecy or patents), by having a stronghold on key suppliers in the market, or by having a strong brand that says to end users that competing products are no substitute. These barriers to entry help innovators profit from their investments.

Things are different when a firm invests in developing a new platform interface.[28] To understand Intel's rationale in pouring money into developing innovations that they relinquish royalties on, we have to understand that buses (the internal highways within the PC) are fundamentally different from real products. These are *enabling technologies*. They contain valuable content or information that probably could have value (i.e., a price) in the marketplace. But protecting that content, such as by hiding the detailed specifications of the hardware or software interfaces, would defeat their entire raison d'être: Interfaces exist to entice other firms to use them to build products that conform to the defined standards and therefore work efficiently with the platform.

Enabling technologies channel and facilitate complementary innovation, thereby reinforcing the architectural leadership of the firm that sponsored them. We do not see large numbers of companies competing to sell these enabling technologies to consumers (in this case, developers of complementary products). Instead, enabling technologies are "hooks" into real products and work better when they are openly available and free. The goal is to encourage other firms to innovate around these enabling technologies over long periods of time, rather than generating quick revenues by treating these technologies as products and trying to sell them.

By designing the interfaces and successfully rallying other firms around these interfaces to make them a standard, Intel ensured that it would benefit from the innovative activities at other firms (the complementors). Relinquishing royalty rights on PC architectural interfaces (a Lever 2 decision) was therefore a judicious decision for Intel.

Using Public Forums to Generate Momentum and Refine Standards

The next stage that Intel went through in its efforts to establish a new architectural interface for the PC platform was to open up the discussions to larger public gatherings, including what Intel called Developers Forums and Implementors Forums. These forums are organized by members of the Desktop Products Group (DPG), in particular its Platform Marketing department. DPG is separate from IAL but works in conjunction with it. Through these forums, Intel brought together thousands of independent software vendors (ISVs) and independent hardware vendors (IHVs). Dan Russell, a director of platform marketing in the DPG, was the manager responsible for organizing these events. Their main objective, said Russell, was to "create momentum in the industry" for whatever standard Intel was trying to promote:

> Momentum is when all the developers in the industry, when all the venture capitalists who are looking at investing in small companies, when all the managers who have budget decisions that have to be made . . . are thinking about this as one of the key areas they have to go work on this year. All of them. So, you start having all the different companies working in the same direction. We also bring the press and analysts together so that they can hear about all the stuff—because ultimately the press and analysts have a tremendous impact on momentum.[29]

The larger public forums were useful not only to build support for a standard, they also allowed a broader set of companies to provide feedback and help refine the specifications, which always contained some ambiguities. Different engineers interpret the same information differently, so it was important to find out—sooner rather than later—where potential misinterpretations existed. Cadambi pointed this out:

> You want to have the specification at least before you actually go into a Developers Forum to *disseminate the information*. The kind of information that we disseminate consists of specs, but it goes beyond the specs. A spec is a document, a piece of paper. When I write a specification, I'm limited by my mental block, my bias, my assumptions—and so that specification is limited by my style and my background. When others read the specification, they're limited by their style, their background. . . . What we try to do at the developers conference is disseminate, from the perspective of the authors of the specification, why we did certain things a certain way. We provide some examples and walk people through all the do's and don'ts, so they know the barriers, the trip points, and can make sure they avoid all these problems.[30]

To ensure its proposals had adequate time for broad debate, IAL organized forums for new standards proposals approximately twice a year. The meetings usually lasted three days and were "the premier technical event for debating and discussing the direction of the PC."[31] These forums also served an education function—they disseminated a lot of information on the latest status of the specification. But, as Holzhammer observed, "the loop doesn't end there. People send mail, respond to it, and the senior architects and OEMs are always engaged." To communicate with thousands of third parties, Intel also set up Web sites that allowed for the exchange of questions and answers. Russell explained:

> If you are going to do broad enabling, you have to have constant communication. With smaller groups . . . it was easier to do that. One of our architects would work with five or six people in the industry. All of a sudden, we're talking about working with 3,000 or 4,000 different developers. We had to have a way of constantly communicating what is going on with these technology initiatives. So the other thing we did was put together a technology-oriented newsletter Web site called the Platform Solution Newsletter Web site. You can subscribe and get the newsletter sent electronically once a month. We also use the Internet to communicate with a large number of people on an ongoing basis.[32]

Intel let this process of openly critiquing a new specification proposal go on for a few months or longer. But it had to end the period of receiving suggestions to give itself and other firms the time to develop products that used the new standard before it became obsolete. "After a point," said Pappas, "any changes are only to correct mistakes that have been made in the specs."[33]

Compliance Workshops: The "PlugFests"

Another type of forum that Intel relied on to refine a new standard and help companies develop prototypes was *compliance workshops*—referred to internally as "PlugFests." Intel held these workshops every three months or so. Between 100 and 200 companies usually attended, sending two or three of their best engineers, often from design and quality assurance, to make sure the prototypes worked.[34] These events provided an invaluable opportunity for hardware vendors to come together, literally with prototypes in hand, to test the interoperability of their equipment and their compatibility with a newly evolving standard.

At the same time, successful compliance workshops helped create legitimacy and popularity for a new standard because they demonstrated that companies were already committed to designing compatible products. They were a key part of the process through which a new technology supported by one or a small group of firms gradually becomes a standard. Many of the people we interviewed highlighted the importance of the compliance workshops. Russell, whose group ran all of the technical forums, emphasized that the PlugFests were the "lifeblood in trying to create these specs."[35] Since the specifications were usually evolving as different companies offered suggestions, the compliance workshops also made it possible for firms—including competing firms—to test and retest their prototypes to make sure they still worked properly. Holzhammer made this observation:

> After participating in the Developers or Implementors Forums, you need to go to this compliance workshop, where everybody brings their products and tests them against the specification and against each other. A specification is never an ironclad thing. People can read it differently and people can make mistakes in implementation. So, in the early phases of the first implementations, you avoid problems by having everybody come together in these "PlugFests." That's not always an immediate thing because these are *competitors* who will show up with their products. Sometimes we have to go to hotels and go to different rooms, and one company tests theirs, and then an hour later another company with a competing product tests theirs on our platforms. But these compliance workshops are very important.[36]

The August 1998 PlugFest in Milpitas, California, illustrates the atmosphere of these compliance workshops.[37] Intel reserved nearly all the rooms in a large hotel for the event; each company had a room. Taped to each door was a schedule listing appointments every half-hour or hour for other firms that wanted to sign up to test the compatibility of their equipment. The coordination among these companies—which developed both complements and rival products—was striking. The event was simple and lacked the flashiness that one finds at events such as Comdex or Interop, where keynote speakers, multimedia presentations, and demos appear in large exhibit halls with thousands of industry vendors and visitors.

As Miller put it, the PlugFest was "like watching the layers of the industry come together."[38] Engineers walked from room to room with oscilloscopes, other testing devices, and their own prototype peripheral products to conduct tests (behind closed doors) of interoperability with workstations, computers, and other equipment. Firms had to trust each other, as well as Intel, to reveal early versions of their products to competitors. But, as Cadambi pointed out, there were mutual advantages for everyone to share information:

> The compliance workshop is basically a forum to get people together at every stage of prototyping, all the way until they go to production. Even after they go into production, we want them to come back and continue testing as they improve their model— every six months, every year, when they have a new capability coming out or a new feature. We want them to come back and help test their peripheral device against the next one that is coming— which might be a competitor's—to make sure that when one ships it doesn't cause another to stop working. We do this in a fairly open environment, where there is a lot of trust. *Basically, we get a good-will agreement that even though you have some information about another person's prototype hardware or software, you'll not use the fact that it's working well or not working well to market against them.* Surprisingly, this has not been very hard to enforce. This has been a refreshing surprise for us in the last three or four years in USB. As the market has grown, there is more incentive for these companies to come back and continue testing. There's been almost no instance of somebody using information about other products, about early failures, as marketing collateral against them. The main issue is bringing them to the event. Once they see it succeeding and they see all the other people who are participating, it reinforces itself.[39]

The Milpitas PlugFest was also striking in that it combined an *open and public* space (the hotel, with the identity of participants listed, and where everyone could see everyone else carrying their products) with a *sense of privacy* (evident in the allocation of time to one-on-one interaction in private rooms). As Cadambi emphasized, companies agreed not to use "information about non-compatibility" against each other. To protect the confidentiality of sensitive information being exchanged, Intel also generally did not allow outsiders such as journalists to observe the PlugFests.[40] As a result, competitors usually felt comfortable coming together and helping each other build complementary—and compatible—products:

> The PlugFests are something fairly unique in that every one of the companies that is making USB products is a competitor of the other companies. Typically, you would think that these companies wouldn't want their unannounced product prototype, hardware or software, to be seen in a public forum. On the other hand, they realize if they have a product that goes out there and doesn't operate or can't operate with other products, it's bad for them because the end user will be unhappy and return the product—and then there's no market. The common good basically says that the market segment is going to grow and that the growth of the market segment is more important than the share of the market we have. So, if we have 50 percent of a very small market segment, that is less interesting than having 25 percent of a much bigger market segment. That's what gets the discussion going.[41]

Creating and Distributing Enabling Tools

Another step for IAL, with the cooperation of other Intel groups, was to create and disseminate technical tools that enabled companies to use the new technology in product development. The tools consisted mostly of software programs and components that helped engineers build other software programs, for example, to analyze program logic, operate peripherals (programs called "device drivers"), or process Internet telephone calls or streaming audio and video over the Internet. Intel generally used its Implementors Forums and Developers Forums to distribute tools in the form of software development kits (SDKs) and device development kits (DDKs) and to train people in how to use them. Cadambi explained why these kits included software libraries.

> By using the library, it's almost as if you have a prefabricated set of building blocks. These are standard building blocks being used repeatedly, and nobody has to go down to the lowest level. It's like you're building a house where the bricks are already made: you

don't have to go and find clay to make the bricks. And because the bricks are all the same size, you're using standard building blocks.[42]

This modular logic for building software made Intel's tools essential building blocks for innovation. SDKs and DDKs are increasingly common practice in the computer industry. To be effective, they need to be widely disseminated and used by complementary developers. The development and diffusion of these tools is costly. However, the economic logic of tool development and dissemination is similar to the logic of innovation on interfaces: By facilitating and channeling complementary innovation, these enabling tools reinforce the architectural leadership of the sponsoring firm.[43] Intel started to aggressively disseminate such tools along with specifications information contained in informal working documents such as white papers. These actions helped Intel create a cadre of designers who could use a new technology and build momentum behind it. Russell explained that in order to create momentum and "broad enabling," Intel had to train multiple designers in the industry. Tools, and the collateral white papers, are developed and disseminated through various venues (e.g., the Developers Forums) to train the designers and help them develop appropriate complements.[44]

> These tools are created all over the place inside Intel. IAL creates tools; our motherboard group creates tools; our graphics group creates tools; our chip set group creates tools; our performance analysis group creates tools. There are all these different things that happen and [our engineers] have been doing it primarily for their own benefit. I realized that if [these tools were] beneficial to Intel engineers, [they] would also benefit the engineers in the industry. It would be a great way for us to get them going on their own without us having to support them. We collect them from different parts of Intel and channel these tools out to third parties.[45]

Over the years, Intel developed expertise in developing these tools and disseminating them to an ever-larger number of possible complementors, both through forums and the World Wide Web. All the interface initiatives that Intel got involved in have a Web presence that typically offers forums for discussion of the specifications, prototypes, a list of members, announcements about products that are compatible with the interface standard, and a list of training events for learning how to develop products compatible with that standard.

For an interface to become a standard, firms need to start building products that are compatible with this standard. As Intel managers got more and more involved in challenging and innovating upon existing PC interfaces, Intel realized that they were just starting to "peel the onion."[46] A key strategic issue was how to encourage and direct the vast array of interrelated innovations that would make the PC system work better.

Stimulating Innovation on Complementary Products

Intel's efforts to stimulate innovation on the PC was a logical extension of its goal of increasing demand for PCs and for their own microprocessors. With the PCI project, Intel began to engage in multifaceted activities aimed at facilitating and stimulating the development of complementary innovation. Its strategy has consisted of three main activities. First, to facilitate complementors' innovations, Intel typically discloses private information about the design of its products (road maps) as well as computers containing prototypes of Intel's upcoming chip. Second, Intel sends skilled engineers and savvy marketers to transfer technical expertise and share knowledge about the market. And third, Intel makes equity investment in third parties. Examples of external innovation spurred by this strategy include three-dimensional (3-D) graphics, video games, multimedia, and Internet applications.

Because the PC is a system, an innovation in one part has repercussions in other parts. Innovation on one component often requires that other components change to ensure smooth operations or improved performance of the whole product. It took Intel managers several years to grasp the nature of this "system problem" fully. David Ryan, the director of technology marketing in IAL, explained:

> For computer users to have a greater benefit, advancing the processor is necessary but not sufficient. The rest of this computing solution needs to advance as well, in appropriate ways and in coordinated fashions. We didn't have this perspective at the beginning. We were very oriented toward the processor. We thought that the issues were all in the hardware platform. As we worked with

that larger focus, we peeled the onion. We realized that there were software issues. It's not just hardware. It's hardware and software. As we got involved in the software, we realized it's not just the software platform. It's the add-in cards, and it's drivers. And then we discovered that there are communication issues. Over time, we learned.[47]

Marketing Campaigns

All the while, Intel was continuing to churn out ever more powerful chips. In fact, managers at Intel had first begun to care about stimulating demand when cheaper clones of its microprocessors started gaining market share in the late 1980s and early 1990s. The company fought off challengers by stepping up its investments in new product development and manufacturing. No other maker of Intel-compatible chips has been able to keep up with Intel's level of investment.

In 1990, around the time of PCI, Intel managers also decided to build Intel's brand name. They launched in November 1991 the ambitious multimillion dollar "Intel Inside" marketing campaign. This advertised to the world whose microprocessor technology was inside those Compaq, Dell, and IBM boxes, and encouraged consumers to go with the Intel brand rather than buy PCs with microprocessors from other companies. The campaign was a great success in creating brand awareness among consumers. Thanks to it, "Intel" connoted quality and innovation.[48] The campaign also allowed Intel to gain bargaining power vis-à-vis suppliers, and increased Intel's competitive position vis-à-vis other chip makers by increasing end users' willingness to pay for Intel's products.[49]

Roles of Other Intel Groups

Intel would not have been able to exert much influence over suppliers, complementors, or end users if not for its ability both to churn out increasingly faster chips and establish relationships with other players in the PC industry. Because other authors have discussed Intel's internal innovation capabilities, we focus here on some of the work Intel did with external firms to stimulate external innovation.[50]

Intel management wanted to appeal to as many outside firms as possible to increase the potential sources of innovation. IAL was the key internal organization in this effort but, to be effective, it required the support of other Intel constituencies. Management created new groups within Intel to provide this support: the Computing Enhancement Group (CEG) to develop chip sets, the Content Group to establish good working relationships with external software developers, and the Corporate Business Development Group (later renamed Intel Capital) to invest in third parties. The choices Intel executives made with regard to how to allocate internal resources to back up the platform leadership strategy belong to our framework's Lever 4. As always, these decisions are interdependent with other levers. For example, the work of the Content Group and of Intel Capital also relate to Lever 1 (what to do inside versus what to let other firms do) and Lever 3 (management of relationships with external firms).

INTEL ARCHITECTURE LAB   The IAL had primary responsibility for fostering external innovation requiring a relatively long-term horizon (i.e., three to five years). IAL's activities include identifying lead firms (or "rabbits") to get certain innovations going in the marketplace, conducting "ethnography" studies of end users to find out how customers actually use PCs and other computing and communications devices, and holding events that allow IAL engineers to display their ideas for complementary products to a broader audience.

IAL also develops software tools and basic technologies that Intel might license or distribute as SDKs or application programming interfaces (APIs) in areas where there is underinvestment in complementary products (e.g., videoconferencing). Johnson explained that IAL's job is to "sell up" computers equipped with new chips.[51]

> Our goal is be a catalyst, to be whatever it takes so that new applications happen or new uses of applications happen that take all of the CPU power we can produce. Then that's an incentive for someone to say: "That new Pentium II 400 MHz can do something better that's important to me, so I ought to go buy it." That's our goal. We want people to say: "That use or application is important to me. And to do that well, I need to buy a new processor."[52]

CONTENT GROUP   The Content Group, formally established in 1994, grew to 220 employees by the late 1990s. The Developer Relations Group (DRG) within the Content Group was created in 1994 by Leglise. The DRG has one team devoted to consumers and another to businesses (the latter team was added in 1996). Together, these two teams strive to establish good working relationships with external software developers. The overall goal of DRG, according to Sally Fundakowski, director of the seventy-person business subgroup, is to "facilitate the development of leading edge, most compelling business or consumer content applications and services available for Intel-based PCs, and in particular, to use the advantages of new versions of the PC platforms as they come out, and to make sure that those are taken advantage of by the best business content that comes out."[53]

The Content Group originated in 1993 as Intel was getting ready to launch the Pentium chip. For the launch, Intel needed applications that would promote the use of the Pentium chip as a multimedia tool. Therefore, Intel needed to encourage developers to create multimedia applications for PCs. In 1993 to 1994, ten people from the Marketing and Sales Group were working on these relationships. After the big success of the Pentium in 1994, Ron Whittier, who had comanaged IAL along with Kinnie, hired Leglise and the DRG staff and started to marshal the internal resources to help external developers create content that would enhance demand for Intel's chips. The Content Group was linked from the start to the IAL, with the goal of "trying to get that technology out there and really create compelling value for PCs through content."[54]

DRG's objective is to facilitate the creation of software products within one to two years or so and to make sure they are available by the time Intel is ready to mass-produce and sell a new line of microprocessors. To achieve this time-sensitive objective, members of the DRG begin discussions, information exchange, or negotiations with outside software companies as many as eighteen months before the launch of a new microprocessor. Specifically, these activities might include subsidizing external software development efforts, loaning computers loaded with prototypes of the forthcoming microprocessor (still being refined by Intel), and sending Intel engineers to exchange advance technical and market information.[55]

DRG provides software companies with prototypes of the new chips and then makes Intel technical experts, who have intimate knowledge of the new microprocessor specifications and of what the chips can do, available to software complementors. Leglise, the director of the consumer side of the DRG, outlined his role in our 1997 interview:

> We do three things for [software companies]. First, of course, is what I would call strategy setting. We tell them—under the appropriate legal nondisclosure—what it is that we're going to do.... Now, that software company has the ability to plan because we're sharing our plan, our best view of the market segment, and they have the opportunity to plan.... [Second, we] give them early access to the technology. I will give them access to the latest generation of microprocessors six to twelve months before the market, which means six to twelve months before their competitors.... Clearly, we have our self-interest at heart. We want to sell more chips. And I'm very direct and above-board about that. But we believe that if we tell them what we're doing, they will sell more software.... My number-one job is to make sure that the day we announce a new set of computers we have applications on them that justify the purchase of a new machine.... People are more likely to buy software when they just bought their machine. They have a brand new toy, and they buy a whole bunch of stuff. In fact, I know it's $605 for Year 1 in software; it's $225 in Year 2; and it's less than $100 after that.[56]

Leglise divides software companies into two camps. One follows what he calls the "traditional strategy," preferring to wait until there is an installed base of users and then develop products for that existing base. The second group tries to be "first to market with a new generation of hardware."[57] Leglise and his staff prefer to work with the latter—companies willing to risk being an early or first mover—though he recognized that this strategy could be high risk if Intel changes its plans or demand for a new product line does not materialize:

> It's a pretty big bet for them. So some [software companies] tell us to go away—not a lot, but a few. And there's some who say this is absolutely perfect, it's exactly what they want to do because if

they're first they'll end up being a leader. A good example on the MMX generation is a company called UB Soft, in Paris. They were practically unknown outside of France. They said: "Bingo. We like this." They designed a great driving game for the MMX technology generation, and now everybody knows who they are. That's the trick. For them, it was a great strategic thing. But companies either like the idea of being first or they don't.[58]

Paying software companies to develop new applications is not how Leglise and other Intel managers prefer to operate. They want software companies to invest in their own new products and make a legitimate profit from these investments.

The one thing I have consistently refused to do is to pay people to do a job. Maybe we've done it once or twice, but it wasn't a good idea. I tell them I want this kind of software and I'd like them to build it. We don't know software; they do. . . . I will help mitigate the risk by paying half [the cost]. They should pay the other half. I want them to have some skin in it, so they are interested in making it successful. Look at the history of IBM and OS/2. Rumor has it that IBM spent a billion dollars on applications for OS/2, but they bought people. They'd say: "Here, do this for me." When the companies said it was done, IBM asked: "Aren't you going to sell it? Market it?" The companies said: "No, our deal was to develop it. You've got it now. Good luck." The same happened with Phillips, which had CDI. They sprinkled money over the entire industry. CDI was a home, interactive CD-ROM thing, and it did terribly. They had all these developers developing stuff, but there was no business model—except "I'll pay you." *We have to trust that the people who make their living doing that will have a better idea of what kind of things will sell. The only business model I can see [working] is theirs, not mine.* We have to be very conscious of that. So, it comes right back to the ecosystem. I want them to be successful on their own with their business model.[59]

MICROPROCESSOR PRODUCT GROUP   The Content Group cooperates with the Microprocessor Product Group (MPG), which makes microprocessors and is Intel's largest group. For example, the job of

Jonathan Khazam from MPG is to make sure that all collaterals support-ing the new microprocessor—for hardware designers, for software designers, for tools and libraries—are coming along at the right time. Most of his work is "focused on what Intel needs to do to get the devel-oper community ready to accept new technology."

> There's a whole lot of work on building the foundation and the things that the [DRG] needs to rely on in order to be successful with the ISVs. DRG can't be successful unless operating system support, if it's required, is in place. It can't be successful unless it has the compilers, assemblers, and debuggers to take out as the tools for ISVs. It can't be successful unless the key providers of software components and libraries and APIs to the software devel-opers are ready.[60]

MPG's function is to "understand what are all the pieces that Intel needs to provide and then ensure that they are being developed, so that they can be ready when the Desktop Products Group needs them in order to enable the application developers."[61] MPG not only defines what the microprocessors are (such as the technical goals for the next generation of the product) but also defines the market needs that Intel must address and coordinates the collaterals for each new microproces-sor launch. What Intel executives call the "planning time horizon" at MPG is typically much longer than in the Desktop or Consumer Prod-ucts Groups. Those groups focus on the launch of microprocessors and are thus involved with managing the product and the marketing around that product approximately eighteen months before it gets to market. But, meanwhile, to make new technologies happen, a significant amount of work needs to happen well before eighteen months.[62]

> For the launch of our MMX processor, the [DRG] was responsible for working with ISVs to get them ready for product launch.[63] With MMX technology, they started to ramp up mid-1995, and by 1996 they were fully up to speed. But the software-enabling work for MMX technology started in 1994. Our focus would be on things like understanding where and how the instructions get used, understanding the types of tools that we need to get to developers,

understanding the chain of dependencies in the software development process, and understanding what the complete portfolio of tools and collaterals are that need to go along with that product launch. And then making sure that at least until other parts of Intel are ready to manage them, that those things are in place and happening.[64]

The companies that Intel "enables" to get ready for its new chips include many small firms as well as such major players as Microsoft, the PC manufacturers (Dell, Compaq, and IBM), and other OEMs.

> OEMs have to update their designs when Intel changes the specs of its products. Compaq, for example, builds motherboards and integrates the PC systems. When Compaq buys the components from Intel, it needs to design the boards that will accept those components, and needs to work together with Intel, which works to enable Compaq to be able to accept Intel's component.[65]

ORGANIZATIONAL EVOLUTION   Intel management makes modifications to its internal organization structure almost yearly. For example, a mid-2000 reorganization made several changes to promote broader thinking about platforms. Intel expanded the mission of its Content Group to emphasize working with outside companies to provide broader solutions, depending on what customers wanted. Some of these solutions involved different computing platforms, such as Internet systems built around UNIX servers from Sun Microsystems or computers running the Linux operating system.[66] Management also created a new group charged with developing what it called "platform-based solutions" for different markets: enterprise (servers and workstations), desktop (PCs), and mobile (wireless, handheld computers). Intel formed other new groups to focus on comprehensive Internet-based solutions for the business and home markets, with a special emphasis on alliances for creating e-business solutions.[67] Intel management also placed its laboratories, including IAL and MPG, under the direction of one executive in order to encourage the labs and associated business units to collaborate more closely on providing customer solutions that cut across the expertise of particular labs or business units. In addition, Intel formed another new group to work on solutions-oriented tools, such as Extensible Markup Language (XML) accelerators.[68]

INTEL CAPITAL   Intel's venture arm, originally called the Corporate Business Development Group, was renamed Intel Capital in 1999. It provides funds to start-ups that aim to develop technologies or products that will consume a lot of processing power. By supplementing their funding, Intel facilitates the development of these firms' technologies.

Tight links exist between Intel Capital and the [DRG]. It is not unusual to find people in DRG that report to two managers, one within DRG and the other the head of Intel Capital, Les Vadasz. One such employee, P. S. Kohli, not only handles equity investments—within the scope of Intel Capital—but also nonequity investments, and manages them from a business perspective for DRG. DRG makes nonequity investments to develop content or to help coproduce content in situations not suited to equity investment. For example, DRG has sent Intel engineers, usually from IAL, to work with external content developers.[69]

Picking "Rabbits" to Provide a Competitive Stimulus

As part of its strategy of stimulating innovation, IAL managers encourage outside complementors to compete by picking one firm (called a "rabbit") to be a leading proponent of a new technology or standard. The goal, according to Johnson, is to provide "a competitive stimulus . . . a driver that then can get other people interested in pursuing a competitive product that will build on the PC platform."[70] Miller commented on identification of the "rabbit" and the strategy in general:

> We want people to do unnatural things. You have to look at the industry and analyze who is in the best position to take that risk with you. . . . The best way to break a logjam is to find somebody you can hold up as a shining example. We call them the "rabbit." . . . It's a hunting analogy, where the rabbit runs ahead and the dogs chase it. . . . You say: "Okay. This technology company picked this initiative direction and—wow—look at the good publicity they're getting. Look at the fact that their stock price is going up. Look at the fact that their products are successful." You make a big deal

about it. . . . Again, it's all about the momentum you create. We have to do that a lot to break the logjam. The logjam would come from people not wanting to take a risk.[71]

Intel often tried to find more than one rabbit to stimulate a particular market:

> We do not necessarily want just one rabbit. In the end game, you want to get the people with the most volume in that particular layer of the stack. Say you wanted to compete and change the modem standards. You would [target] the top three. But you may not get the top three because they actually have the most to lose from change. So you may want a rabbit who has the most to gain or has an innovative technology. You may want to work hard with them and make them successful. You start a rabbit off, and the other ones say: "Well, it's just a little rabbit. Don't worry about it." Then the rabbit gets bigger and bigger, and soon it starts eating market share. Pretty soon, the others are going: "Wow! That's pretty important." And they'll move. . . . So, you pick rabbits for one of many reasons, and then you promote the hell out of them. The Platform Marketing Group and the marketing function within IAL play a major role in picking them and bringing them along. As for PR, we come in at the end and help with the tactics and the placement.[72]

Intel invests in marketing and public relations support to focus industry attention on the rabbit as well as on the market in which this firm is trying to establish itself as a leader. Intel's attention often draws capital to these complementary products. Intel people had several examples of how the rabbit concept had spurred complementary innovation. Miller cited the case of the USB connector technology for hardware devices like printers, scanners, and the mouse:

> Take a capability like USB. You've got to pick a peripheral rabbit. At any time, the rabbit varied. . . . Actually, we had a rabbit in each subcategory of peripherals. Storm Technologies was our scanner rabbit, and Logitech was our digital rabbit. They had to have the little Photoman digital camera, which was before digital became really hot. Microsoft was our mouse rabbit. But we picked one

person in each category who would be believed. The smaller ones had nothing to lose and everything to gain; the big names saw this as a way to consolidate their position.[73]

Intel also needs to ensure the standards and technologies it promotes evolve along with the industry. Rick Yeomans, head of IAL's Technical Marketing Engineering group, remarked that with the arrival of broadband and new generations of multimedia devices, the original USB standard had become somewhat obsolete. In response, Intel promoted a second-generation standard: USB 2, and had to find themselves a new rabbit.

In addition, IAL worked to evolve the AGP standard, and data compression technology that enables Internet users to view objects in three dimensions. The Web 3-D work was a continuation of several earlier unsuccessful efforts, including the "Chrome project," in which Microsoft was the rabbit. Chrome was aimed at building a high-end 3-D Web browser. These efforts were ahead of the market and never received broad support from software developers, although with the arrival of broadband and faster computers, 3-D on the Internet still had potential in the mass market.[74] IAL regrouped after Microsoft cancelled Chrome and worked with Macromedia on an eighteen-month joint development program, which resulted in the launch of a new version of the popular Director/Shockwave Web media platform that included 3-D as a new native data type.

Coordinating Role

To establish new system capabilities, working one on one with a single external company would not be enough. As part of its platform strategy, Intel began to coordinate multifirm innovative activities to develop new systemic capabilities, such as DVD (digital video disk) and TAPI (telephony application programming interface). Table 3–1 shows IAL's seven broad initiatives for 2000.

To deliver some PC capabilities to the end user required coordination among different actors in the industry. Most Intel managers we interviewed said coordination among firms was necessary for their innovations to be valuable to consumers. Intel managers thought a lot about

Table 3-1 IAL's Seven Initiatives for 2000

INITIATIVE	OBJECTIVE	FOCUS
Connected Home	Working to establish affordable, easy-to-use, and widely available connectivity to and within the home	*Devices (appliances) that "think," high-speed Internet access, home networks*
Digital Entertainment	Working to create new ways to play in the family room through the emergence of digital entertainment devices and formats	*Music and other digital media, content protection, interactive Web with digital TV, new media appliances, virtual entertainment, interactive sports*
Information Management	Working to organize and access personal information automatically	*Information organization and personalization, sense-making and understanding, knowledge capture and publication*
Internet Building Blocks	Working to open the Internet to proactive services and products	*Trusted managed networks, open networking, Internet services technology, Internet telephony*
Internet Media	Working to make rich multimedia experiences pervasive on the Internet	*Internet media technologies such as 3-D and quality video, multimedia authoring tools, Internet media applications, open specifications for rich media development*
Manageability	Working to make it easy and cost-effective to manage Intel Architecture systems any time, anywhere	*Tools and specifications to lower the cost of ownership for desktop, mobile, and server computer systems, such as the Intel Wired for Management initiative*
Scalability	Working to scale platforms and application capabilities	*Design guidelines and specifications to enhance platform performance, to handle demand for more functionality and bandwidth, and to simplify system setup, installation, and configuration*

Source: Data compiled from Intel Web site <http://developer.intel.com/ial/ourinit.htm> (accessed April 2001).

how to direct this coordination toward improving the PC platform as a system. Ryan commented:

> This picture of a stack [see figure 3–1] represents the industry layers with which we need to interact in order to deliver a complete capability to computer users. We frequently find that, for a technology advance to be delivered to the computer user, or for the computer user to have a new capability that may be unrelated to a particular hardware advance, changes in many of these layers need to occur accordingly. For the user actually to see that new capability, some companies need to make new hardware. Some companies need to make changes in the operating system. There need to be new types of networking or new products developed, or new applications developed and Internet changes that may be needed to take advantage of this new opportunity to deliver content. So, to get a new use or new capability to occur, we have to work simultaneously across all these layers. The players in the layers are different. They are really different industries and very different companies, with different marketing requirements in each of those areas.[75]

As with the sponsoring of the PCI and USB architectural interfaces, Intel needed a critical mass of industry players to specify new products that corresponded to the new initiatives' capability objectives or specifications. For example, Intel invested significant resources into developing the basic technology for DVD and TAPI—and then created or participated actively in a consortium that promoted the use of these technologies. Intel's approach to intellectual property was the same as for PCI and USB: It shared the technology with the consortium members without asking for royalty payments and expected members to reciprocate on this policy.

In playing the role of coordinator, effective communication is crucial. To communicate with other Intel departments as well as with third parties about new initiatives, IAL people typically used what they called "capability stacks" (see figure 3–1). These diagrams identify all the activities and actors necessary for some new or improved capability to happen. The systemwide nature of these innovations required the coopera-

Figure 3-1 **Industry Capability Stack**

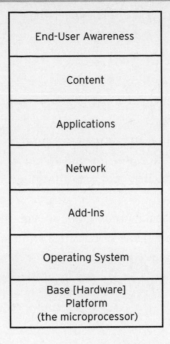

End-User Awareness
Content
Applications
Network
Add-Ins
Operating System
Base [Hardware] Platform (the microprocessor)

Source: Intel in-house materials.

tion of many companies in the PC industry. This required IAL to take on the key role of coordinator and mediator—or "broker"—between external firms. In some sense, as one of our MIT colleagues suggested, IAL needed to act like the "host of a dinner party," although the party usually lasted years rather than hours.[76] According to Kinnie, it typically required between three and five years for Intel to fully establish a capability in the marketplace.[77]

Conclusion: Organizational Capabilities of Platform Leaders

In the process of learning to become a platform leader, Intel developed organizational capabilities that we believe can be helpful for any firm striving to achieve platform leadership. First is the *ability to cultivate internally a "system mindset."* This requires managerial attention, technical expertise, and resources at the level of the overall system or platform rather than limiting the focus to the inner details of the core product or piece of the system that is the firm's speciality.

Second is the *ability to create external momentum*. For Intel, the mechanics of this important capability involved the following:

- Communicating Intel's vision of the PC platform evolution
- Gradual garnering of consensus starting with small groups of influential firms
- Developing and distributing tools for development of complements that fit into Intel's overall vision
- Highlighting business opportunities for potential complementors
- Facilitating external innovation, be it modular and complementary or spanning firms' boundaries and requiring massive industry coordination

Now that we have exposed the mechanics of platform leadership à la Intel, chapter 4 looks at the challenges Intel faced in implementing this strategy.

Chapter Four

Platform Leaders and Complementors

How Intel Manages Conflicts of Interest

We think one of our core competencies is that we are a trusted partner for almost everybody in the industry. We can talk to the graphics group's competitors openly about their products and about our specification, and they trust that we honor that. But you can't just mandate trust. You have to earn it.

—CRAIG KINNIE, DIRECTOR, INTEL ARCHITECTURE LAB

Chapter 3 detailed the mechanics of how Intel became a platform leader. We saw how Intel managers systematically engaged in a set of activities they had learned through trial and error. This is not to say that it was easy. In fact, just how difficult it was to successfully implement these activities was a theme in most of our interviews with Intel managers. We chose to devote an entire chapter to these difficulties because we realized, after completing our comparative study with other firms, that the difficulties Intel had faced were obstacles on the path of any firm attempting to pursue platform leadership.

Trust and Tensions

First, we present in this chapter how much effort Intel put into building trust between itself and third parties that it encouraged toward a particular direction of complementary innovation. We explain why these efforts were crucial to Intel's rise to the status of platform leader. Developing trusting relationships between Intel and, in particular, small third parties, was akin to convincing these smaller players to dance with the elephant. That turned out to be an arduous endeavor.

The ability to convey a long-term commitment to cooperative relationships is essential for Intel to act effectively as a platform leader. In our Four Levers Framework, this corresponds to Lever 3. In the PC industry, IAL has acquired a reputation as a trustworthy and relatively impartial broker of information between Intel and third parties. Companies have come to believe that IAL people are not overly biased toward Intel's short-term interests but are looking out for the good of the industry overall—which is good for Intel in the long-term as well. IAL's special position allows Intel to rally consensus among industry players while having a voice regarding how specific PC technologies and standards evolve. IAL maintains significant influence over the design of interfaces that other companies use to interconnect their components to Intel's chips. Because IAL has successfully obtained this reputation for impartiality and has been able to influence industry standards, Intel can practically guarantee that there will always be a supply of innovative complements around its new microprocessors—unless a completely new platform and set of complementors to that platform were to emerge without Intel's influence or input.

We have seen that Intel's platform leadership strategy involved not only promoting new interface standards and architectural concepts to advance the PC platform but also orchestrating complementary innovation at the industry level. Following this strategy has led to conflicts of interest and resulting tensions, within the company and with outside firms. We classified the problems we observed into two types: *external tensions*, which occur between the platform leader and outside firms, and *internal tensions*, which occur between groups inside the platform leader. For both types, conflicts of interest and tensions that increase too much can become full-fledged battles among groups that are supposed to be working together.

External tensions can emerge when a platform leader encourages innovation outside the company. For example, Intel managers want other firms to innovate; but they also want to preserve their ability to diversify and potentially compete in complementary markets themselves. If Intel starts to compete with current or former partners, suppliers, or customers, this strains these external relationships.

Internal tensions arise when one department pursues objectives at the seeming expense of another department in the same firm. For example, all Intel employees probably agree that the primary corporate goal is to sell more microprocessors, Intel's largest product line. IAL's chief function is to achieve more microprocessor sales, mainly by facilitating innovation outside the company in ways that expand the use of computing devices. To do so, IAL encourages many external firms to deliver complements (e.g., digital cameras, applications software, or Internet content) that exploit the latest generation of Intel's chips. Intel product groups, on the other hand, follow a different strategy. They often decide to build complements themselves to profit in these markets.

Intel's lingo for different internal goals provides a useful way to differentiate among these objectives. Inside Intel, Job 1 refers to activities aimed at strengthening Intel's position as the leading chip maker (i.e., activities with the main goal of selling more Intel microprocessors). This includes all activities that have a demand-enhancing effect on Intel's chip. Job 2 refers to activities aimed at "building successful businesses in [microprocessor-]related technologies"[1] (i.e., activities with the main goal of achieving profits in complementary markets).[2] Intel's product groups often do Job 2 or explore new businesses, unrelated to microprocessors, that might evolve to become new core businesses for Intel in the future (this has come to be called Job 3 inside Intel).

Over the past decade, Intel has sold products ranging from motherboards and chip sets to complete computer systems, videoconferencing systems, and even some software development tools and application programs. The departments that have marketed these various products have often found themselves competing with companies that IAL views as partners, not competitors. None of these other products was likely to replace microprocessors in importance to Intel. Nonetheless, internal and external conflicts of interest emerged. These conflicts can be especially difficult for an organization such as IAL because it requires the cooperation of other Intel groups as well as the trust of outside parties to work effectively as the "architect of the industry." If managers at outside companies become too concerned about Intel moving into their markets, they might hesitate to invest in complementary innovations that Intel executives want them to pursue. Outside managers might very well fear that Intel could not only steal their markets but also exploit specific investments the complementor firms could not fully protect with patents or specialized know-how. This type of pirating happens often in high-tech industries because patents in computer technology can be difficult to enforce.

Intel managers are well aware of these tensions. Their strategy for platform leadership incorporates how to make sure internal and external relationships work more effectively. Let us pause a moment to review the types of problems that can arise between a platform leader and third-party complementors, and describe the steps Intel took to manage these external conflicts of interest (Lever 3). Next, we review the types of problems that can arise within the platform leader's organization (Lever 4). We examine the various Intel groups with which IAL worked and the steps Intel took to manage tensions with these groups. Finally, we address the more general issue of how managers in any company can best resolve external or internal conflicts of interest that inevitably come with a platform leadership strategy.

External Conflicts: Why and When They Occur

External tensions often arise when the platform leader and outside parties have different objectives—either perceived or real. The problems can become more intense when both sides have expectations that neither side fully meets. In our interviews at Intel, we noted three types of situations that gave rise to external conflicts of interest: (1) when complementor firms have to take large investment risks in uncertain markets, and have short time horizons for return on investment (ROI), (2) when the platform leader fails to follow through on particular commitments ("leading on" the complementors), and (3) when the platform leader decides to compete with its complementors. These types of situations seem most likely to occur when it is unclear whether an external firm is a complementor or a competitor relative to the platform leader. This type of ambiguity probably occurs most often in rapidly evolving markets, such as those in which Intel competes.

When Risk Is Too Big or Time Horizons Clash

Third-party complementors sometimes hesitate to support the latest version of a core product that is key to the platform in question, such as the latest version of yet another Intel microprocessor. The reason seems to be the investment risks involved. The most immediate risk for third parties is that they have limited resources (e.g., people, time, and money). They prefer to make investments that will pay off relatively soon. In most cases, the platform leader has already made its investment in the next generation of its technology. But the platform leader wants third-party firms to make complementary investments *before* the market has demonstrated actual demand. This results in agendas that conflict, even if only temporarily.

For example, Intel generally approaches potential complementors about twelve to eighteen months before it launches its next-generation microprocessor and asks them to invest in new products tailored to that product line. Usually, Intel wants complements that consume a lot of processor power or require the new microprocessor for other technical reasons, such as the way it handles graphics or streaming video. Of course, Intel wants to persuade consumers to upgrade to products that use its new microprocessors. Understandably, some companies hesitate to bear the technical and market risks of developing complements for a microprocessor that Intel has not yet finished developing or launched. Such development often requires these companies to divert substantial resources from their existing business, which might be barely profitable. David Johnson points out that the risk is especially high because demand for Intel's new generations of processors was often limited to a small part of the market, at least initially:

> One of the problems we have is that both the [Intel Architecture] Lab and the Content Group are focused on doing something that's good for the next generation of processors. What we've consistently

run into is that *this may not necessarily be in the best interest of the third parties. It may be difficult for them to buy into what we're doing because perhaps the new generations of processors are used in a tiny fraction of the market.* If I'm a producer of a software title or some content, and I use this Intel technology or these Intel dollars and target them for the very high end, I may not have near the success with my product because it doesn't work for the mass market. Yet, that's what we want people to do because the opposite is what we see going on by and large—third parties target the mass market, and therefore nobody sees the benefit of our new processor because a content creator doesn't take advantage of the new features and capabilities.[3]

In the long run, market demand moves toward the next-generation product. The platform leader, if it has been successful, usually has the resources to wait for mass-market demand to emerge. Intel certainly does. So does Microsoft when it tries to persuade customers to upgrade to the latest version of Windows. Complementors, especially smaller ones, may not have the resources to wait. They need each of their product lines to generate money sooner rather than later. Their time horizons for ROI may be very different from those of the platform leader. Bill Miller discussed this problem:

> The biggest force you have going against you is that you're asking people to change their business model. . . . The real issue, though, is that *not every change we want to have happen in the industry is going to be perceived as immediately beneficial in others' business models,* especially in the horizon that they care about that business model. Intel can take a couple-of-years view of some of these industry things. An OEM that is number seventeen in market segment share cannot do that. They have to take a six-month view. And if our initiative or our direction doesn't benefit them in the next six months, we have an awful hard time convincing them. They may not be there or *they may feel they can't afford the perspective.*[4]

Miller cited the Wired for Management initiative as an example. This program offered a technology to allow incompatible (i.e., proprietary) computer systems to talk to each other more easily. But it involved different time horizons for Intel and complementors as well as potentially different strategic objectives:

> The biggest challenge is pushing something before its time—like with "Wired for Management" back in 1993. . . . Nobody in the industry wanted to lift a finger to do that six or seven years ago. They liked their own little proprietary world. Companies were more likely to be old-line companies like HP or IBM, with their own vertical, proprietary mindset. Basically, we were coming in and saying: "Let's make this heterogeneous." Intel just stuck with it and stuck with it, even when there was no return on investment [ROI] in the near future. . . . We were trying to convince the industry that putting this management infrastructure in the computers was an important thing. It was a three-year ROI. PC servers hadn't captured the enterprise yet. So, they didn't see the need to invest there. For the next eighteen months, they needed to get to redundant disk drives, and they knew that that was the next thing. And for the next eighteen months, they were right. Looking out over three years, the Information Technology director would say: "I've got all these servers. I can't integrate them. I'm throwing up my hands." From talking to IT directors, we knew this. We tried to tell them. We were out there saying: "You must make this all interoperable." And they would say: "I can't. It doesn't fit in my budget. I don't have enough engineers to put on it right now." And we would say: "But in this time frame, you're going to need to care." They'd say: "I can't care about that now. I can only care about where we'll have to be in eighteen months."[5]

When Platform Leaders "Lead On" Complementors

Another source of external tension is when a platform leader fails to follow through on a commitment. In effect, it may "lead on" some third-party complementors. They make investments that go nowhere because the platform leader has changed its strategy, which it has the right to do. Reneging on a promise can happen for many reasons. In Intel's case, this sometimes occurred when a market did not pick up (even Intel managers have limited patience) or when a complementor failed to meet expectations. Intel's interest in pushing a certain complementary technology might also diminish over time, such as when the *relative* portion of CPU power it would need got smaller (because total CPU power was steadily rising). Complementary producers have to keep up with Moore's law and Intel's fast pace of new product development, or they might find that their complements are no longer so important.

This problem occurred with MPEG, a standard for compressing and exchanging video data.[6] As Johnson observes, Intel's interest dropped before the complementary market took off and third-party firms recouped their investments:

> In theory, there can be a lot of synergy in relationships with developers that are trying to develop complementary products. But there are downsides. *The downside is that we're both very focused on this high end, but we sometimes abandon the technology or the market segment before it is mature.* Let me give an example in media technologies. [W]e were very interested in MPEG encoding and decoding, which right now takes a lot of the CPU horsepower. It's something you can barely do [on existing PCs], and it takes lots of tuning. A year or eighteen months from now, maybe MPEG will take only 10 percent of a CPU, since the CPU power will have increased enormously by then, so by then we will not care so much about MPEG anymore: Who cares about 10 percent? We will be looking at some new media technology that takes 80 percent of whatever that CPU will be then. But it may be that in eighteen months the market is just starting to use MPEG for DVD players, archiving, or camcorders. We might be gone then, because we won't care.
>
> Our job at IAL is to help be a catalyst *so that new applications or new uses of applications happen that take all of the CPU power we can produce.* Then that's an incentive for someone to say: "That use or application is important to me. And to do that well, I need to buy a new processor." That's our goal. We call it "sell up." We want people to say: "That new Pentium II 400 MHz can do something better that's important to me, so I ought to go buy it." So, eighteen months from now, a Pentium II 400 MHz is going to be a slow machine because we are pushing ahead. As for the application that

was all-consuming in 1998, when we get to 2000, those of us in the labs and in the Content Group won't care about it.[7]

Johnson recalls another example of a complementary product in which Intel was likely to lose interest over time, the DVD—an exciting new technology that was replacing conventional CD-ROM drives. The reasons for this eventual disinterest were similar to the MPEG case:

> *One problem is that we sometimes exit—that is, drastically reduce the energy we put into it—before the market segment is mature.* That could either hurt the market segment or make third parties too dependent on Intel. Things like that may have, in fact, messed things up. For example, back in 1997 and 1998, DVD was very important to us in the Content Group and IAL. There were not many DVD players being sold, or applications to use DVD, or content available. But it was very interesting to us because it used a lot of the available CPU power. By the year 2000, we at IAL and in the Content Group probably will not care because DVD will be one of those apps that doesn't use much of the microprocessor power, and so it won't be very important to the market segment.[8]

When a platform leader fails to follow through on public commitments it has made to a new technology, the costs can be high. Not only might its reputation suffer, the platform leader can also harm the complementary market it once hoped to promote. One type of damage occurs when complementors refrain from continuing their investments or even entering the market because they fear direct competition with the platform leader. Another is when complementors become too dependent on the platform leader and fail to invest in complementary assets necessary to make their own investments successful. Johnson explains:

> The market segment gets hurt if third parties think: "Intel, the big guys, are there, so I don't want to be there. They're going to crush me." That's not good, and it's not what we want, because we're trying to encourage people to do these complementary things. Alternatively, if we make the people so dependent on us that they

don't set up an economic model that can be successful—that is, if they are very dependent on our subsidy or on free technology or something like that—then all of the things that then happen in the market segment may cause this to sputter and fail.[9]

The platform leader may run out of patience or time with a supplier that doesn't deliver on its promises. This occurred with Rambus, which introduced a memory chip in 1999 that had much faster access speeds than competing chips. The new technology promised to reduce the bottleneck between fast microprocessors and memory chips that could not send or receive data at comparable speeds. Without a reduction in this bottleneck, consumers had less incentive to buy new computers with faster microprocessors. But, as Intel CEO Craig Barrett admitted in a published interview, "We made a big bet on Rambus, and it did not work out."[10] Rambus delivered the special chips, but at a price twice or more than that of standard memory chips that performed almost as well for most PC tasks. Advanced Micro Devices also started selling its latest generation of very fast processors that worked well without the expensive Rambus chips. Although Intel might still rely heavily on Rambus in the future, these events helped persuade Intel to redesign its new processors so that they could work with either the Rambus chips or conventional chips.

When Platform Leaders Compete with Complementors

Intel's attempts to maintain goodwill in the industry to back up IAL efforts at coordination were hurt more than once by Intel's own moves to enter new, complementary markets. For anyone wishing to understand what it takes to be a platform leader, it is imperative to fully grasp the difficulties involved here. Entries into new markets (concerning Lever 1, the scope of the firm) present the most difficult challenge to platform leadership because they strike at the core of the trust-building efforts that platform leaders must make to rally around their projects the many actors of their industry.

Another way to restate this challenge is with the question: What are the effects of the Job 1 versus Job 2 dilemma on external complementors? As discussed earlier, most of Intel's activities are Job 1 (sell more microprocessors) or Job 2 (make a profit in complementary businesses outside microprocessors). Several groups within Intel work on Job 1: The MPG develops new versions of the microprocessor. Sales and Marketing help sell these microprocessors. IAL facilitates industry innovations on complements that enhance demand for Intel's microprocessors. To play that coordinating role, IAL tries to be a neutral industry broker. But other groups within Intel have a different agenda (Job 2). Product groups whose main objective is to enter and compete in complementary markets may clash with complementors, which creates external tensions between Intel and its complementors (and makes IAL's job more difficult to do, especially where trust building is concerned).

It is not surprising that tensions can mount when a platform leader steps into the territories of its complementors with its own competing products or technologies. This did not occur often in Intel's case—in contrast to Microsoft, for example, which deftly moved into many markets complementary to the DOS and Windows operating systems. Microsoft frequently challenged applications and networking software companies (e.g., WordPerfect [now owned by Corel], Lotus, Novell, Netscape, and Oracle). But even Intel occasionally stepped on some toes. In the mid-1990s, for example, Intel developed a new software technology called native signal processing (NSP) that it did not tie to the Windows platform. NSP allowed software developers to bypass Windows and give instructions, such as for handling graphics, directly to the underlying microprocessor. Microsoft interpreted NSP as a hostile move on Intel's part because it reduced Microsoft's control over software programming standards. Intel "caved" and abandoned the effort.[11]

In chapter 2, we described another case of competition with complementors when Intel pushed the new PCI bus standard, entering the chip set and motherboard businesses. Not surprisingly, Intel's moves provoked complaints from former partners, especially companies based in Taiwan that relied heavily on chip sets and motherboards for revenues.[12] Miller explains Intel's side of the PCI story:

> Why did we enter the chip set business? We got into the chip set business in a major way *to accelerate platform transitions*.[13] To unleash the power of the Pentium, we had to introduce the new PCI bus. We did start by giving specifications [to the chip set manufacturers]. We started with traditional enabling, which is you

give specs out, you evangelize that the processor is going to need it, you make the technical case, you make a marketing case, and you say that you're going to advertise it to make it important to the industry. But we realized that wasn't good enough because they weren't fast enough. One of the most troublesome things was that it was really hard getting the other chip set vendors to do PCI right. . . .

Our foray into the motherboard business used to be a manufacturing foray, and now is more of a licensing foray. We manufacture some, but mostly we have licensed our designs. This allows us to have influence over other areas of the platform as well. If you are defining how a certain percentage of the motherboards are designed, you then can make a good technical argument and have a good volume argument. Standards follow volume. The simplest way to get a standard [like PCI] established is to put in a product that sells at a high volume.[14]

Intel's entry in the motherboard business was extremely controversial and widely relayed in the business press. Interestingly, a posteriori, Intel managers explain Intel's entry into motherboards—and why Intel risked alienating its complementors—with a platform leadership argument: The "acceleration of platform transitions" (to use Miller's words) is no less than trying to put in place all the complements needed to accompany the launch of Intel's new microprocessors. It was only after the external market (the complementor motherboard makers) failed to launch motherboards corresponding to the new specifications that Intel decided to bring inside the activity of developing and commercializing these complements. Here we see an interesting example of the thought process of Intel's managers regarding Lever 1 (scope of the firm: What to do inside versus what to let external complementors do). Note that a decision on Lever 1 (here, bringing the chip set and motherboard businesses in-house) is bound to affect other levers: here, Lever 3.

INTEL'S FIRST CONTROVERSIAL (AND FAILED) ENTRY IN VIDEOCONFERENCING   Intel's initial attempt to market its own videoconferencing products is perhaps the best illustration of how damaging external conflicts of interest can become when a platform leader enters a market dominated by a complementor. What happened in this case is that Intel did not fully understand the dynamics of the market it tried to enter. It failed to understand the process of standardization in this market led by telecommunications firms. It also failed to anticipate the impact of the incumbent firm's reaction. Intel managers thought that their entry would stimulate more competition and innovation and ultimately grow demand for the PC. What happened instead was a panic and a freeze by that market's main player, PictureTel, made worse by a media outcry about how Intel was damaging this market. David Ryan recalls the beginning of Intel's entry in videoconferencing:

> We first tried a proprietary approach to videoconferencing. We tried to build Intel products and create a conferencing standard and say, "This is it. We're going to do it. Everybody sign up. It's not open, and there's no participation." We actually got a lot of people to put their name to it.[15]

Intel wanted to jump-start the market for inexpensive videoconferencing products by introducing its own videoconferencing offering called ProShare. The company spent some $100 million on development and marketing. Priced at about $1,000, ProShare competed with better-performing but much more expensive products from companies such as PictureTel, Vtel, and Compression Labs, which ran from $20,000 to $100,000. The confrontation with these other firms began over technical standards. Intel engineers concluded that they could not incorporate the same videoconferencing standard (called H.320) used in the more expensive systems because this would have brought the ProShare price to at least $4,000. Instead, Intel decided to establish a new standard to enable low-cost videoconferencing as well as sharing of documents on the PC. Michael Bruck recalls that PictureTel, the market leader, felt threatened by Intel's proposal and refused to go along:

> Our first foray in videoconferencing was a miserable failure.... We said, "Let's establish a conferencing-specific standard that would allow this low-cost video data conferencing to take place, based on PCs." And it's clearly superior to H.320. We had all sorts of advantages, including developing it ourselves.... What we didn't realize was that, first, we were dealing with the telecommunications industry, which does not follow the computer industry standards that are

set by groups of companies getting together. The telecommunications industry is very much driven by standards bodies, in particular the [ITU] in Geneva. [The telecommunications standards process] takes ten years, and we were not going to wait ten years. We needed to get this product out now, but we realized we needed interoperability standards.... Two of the large room-based video-conferencing companies were very open to establishing new standards.... We went to PictureTel, who was the leader at the time, and they said: "You guys are nuts. We think it's a dumb idea. We don't support it. What's in it for us?" ... They had a vested interest in maintaining the status quo. They probably looked at low-cost videoconferencing and said: "This is going to [change] our business." And it did change their business significantly. Not only were they not supportive, but they were extremely vocal and publicly unsupportive. They mounted a major public relations campaign against Intel for going out and establishing what we called a personal communications specification with the Personal Communications Working Group.[16]

Intel proceeded without PictureTel's support and created a new standard. Ultimately, though, as microprocessors and PCs became more powerful, Intel was able to use the H.3xx standards (H.320, H.321, H.322, and H.323), which ensured compatibility across the larger and smaller (i.e., PC-based) systems. Not surprisingly, PictureTel's business did suffer. After the initial confrontation, Intel took a $30.5 million equity position in PictureTel during 1999 to try to bolster the company's finances. PictureTel then took over the marketing of Intel's ProShare product line, which Intel had been operating at a loss.[17] PictureTel later experienced even more deterioration in its revenues and profits as demand for high-priced videoconferencing systems failed to grow amidst competition from cheaper Internet-based systems. The product lines acquired from Intel became a significant business for PictureTel.

Intel managers have a reputation for learning from their mistakes.[18] Videoconferencing proved to be an invaluable learning experience. One lesson, according to Bruck, was the realization that the platform leader had to deal with the incumbent leader in the complementary product market as well as with the relevant standards bodies and industry analysts. It had to "line up all the ducks" to get an industry to adopt a different technology:

> We really learned that we had to go not to the de facto but more the
> de jure standards committee. We thought we would be able to bring
> the product to market sooner by going our own way, but it didn't
> work. *The key lesson here is that we underestimated the strength of
> the incumbents.* It took just one company to derail the entire thing
> in an industry that was not quite open to it because it was not
> necessarily perceived to be in their best interest. Also, the telecom-
> munications press never bought our story. They never stated it was
> technically better and might have had merit. PictureTel was the
> market-share leader at the time. They were selling a competing
> desktop product, which was H.320 compliant, and they saw no
> benefit in what we were doing. In hindsight, *we should not have
> tried to do something when there already was a standard. . . .* We
> generally underestimated the fact that there was somebody in the
> lead market position who was influential, and that there were
> influential analysts in that business—one in particular. I don't
> think we had lined up our ducks well enough.[19]

Ryan admits that Intel erred by trying to introduce a proprietary technology that ignored the requirements of incumbent firms. The result, he claims, was an "unmitigated failure," until Intel got the support of Microsoft (in NetMeeting, a feature bundled in Windows that incorporated Intel's H.323 stack software) and other firms for the H.3xx standards for handling both videoconferencing and Internet telephony:

> Videoconferencing is a bad memory for people, so a lot of people
> have blanked it out. But we do remember the lesson from it: The
> model that works is industry collaboration and working together
> productively, where everybody is participating in what's going on
> and able to innovate their products. *That proprietary approach, sort
> of dictating a standard with a product, was pretty much an unmiti-
> gated failure.* So we cycled back around and worked on this H.3xx
> space, which was more the model of open industry participation,
> and that worked. . . . Now you have conferencing applications from
> all the vendors.[20]

Finally, Intel managers learned that their efforts to grow a complementary market could fail and have the opposite of the desired effect. Johnson recalls:

> We wanted to deliver an affordable product that would make videoconferencing a desktop PC add-on. We were so intent on videoconferencing as a method for selling CPUs that our own products drove the prices down to where the channel wasn't making money, we weren't making money, competitors couldn't make money—and, therefore, we didn't help the overall marketplace. Major players are still there, but they are weak. A number of the more peripheral players have left. Being a catalyst is very hard because, if you don't do enough, you don't really change the balance. You don't accelerate things. Likewise, you need to be careful not to come in so hard that you don't undermine the conditions in the market you enter. In some ways, what we did with ProShare was enter the market segment with a product and expect the market to respond. But then you have to be careful because you can undermine the whole market segment and not end up fostering innovation. Some people claim we did just that.[21]

The Source of External Conflicts: Are Platform Leaders and Complementors "Friends" or "Foes?"

Conflicts are an inevitable part of the relationships between platform leaders and complementors. This is the fundamental difficulty of managing Lever 3 (external relationships) of our framework for platform leadership. But why is that?

Fast-moving, high-tech markets often have product boundaries that are vague and continually changing. New generations of software and hardware products can take on capabilities that threaten the core products they once complemented. Internet browsers and networking software products, for example, blur traditional distinctions among operating systems, networking systems, and applications programs. Netscape's Navigator browser was once a wonderful new complement to Windows; later, Microsoft perceived it as a threat and built its own browser, Internet Explorer, to add to Windows. Industry specialists and judges then debated for years whether we should view the browser as a separate product or as a new feature of the operating system. Customers can launch software applications from Web servers that interact with Internet browsers, rather than with Windows, making the browser a competing platform. This is why Microsoft fought Netscape so hard to win the browser market.[22]

Personal digital assistants (PDAs) such as Palm Pilots and Pocket PCs are another example. Conceived as mobile complements to more functional laptops or desktop PCs, they began to evolve into handheld computers. Synchronization software, usually included with these devices, ensured that PDAs functioned along with PCs. At the same time, however, PDAs (and other small computing devices, as well as Web-enabled cell phones) began to cannibalize at least some PC sales. In addition, makers of these smaller devices had more choices for microprocessors and operating systems than PC manufacturers did. Were PDA makers complementors, customers, or potential rivals to companies like Intel? They were all three, simultaneously.

A platform leader must cooperate with many companies that it wants to develop complements. At the very least, the companies must agree on some interface standards to make their products compatible. At the same time, though, the platform leader must compete with its rivals for the attention and investments of potential complementors. Complementors can choose to develop products that work with one platform *or* another platform. In some cases, a platform leader might even find itself competing with third parties that are usually its complementors. This scenario occurred with chip set manufacturers when Intel introduced microprocessors with expanded functionality and decided to make chip sets itself.

It is especially confusing when the same firm—whether it is the platform leader or a complementor—plays multiple roles. Ron Smith, director of Intel's Computing Enhancement Group, said: "People may be complementors, customers, or competitors. Often, the same company is all three. And often we are all three to another company. [T]hat's the first-order effect you have to take into account."[23] Compaq is one example. The largest maker of PCs was a big customer of Intel as well as a complementor because it designed PC systems that worked with Intel microprocessors. But Compaq also sold computer systems that did not use Intel microprocessors. Did this make it a rival as well as a customer and a complementor? Yes. The problem is not that such confusion of roles exists, but what to do about it.

External Conflicts: What to Do about Them

Intel managers figured out, through trial and error, how to overcome conflicts of interest with outside firms and persuade them to adopt new standards or innovate in ways that support the Intel microprocessor line and the PC platform. Chapter 3 discussed the processes that Intel used to successfully rally other firms around systemic architectural innovations to push the industry along a particular trajectory. How did they overcome the conflicts inherent in these relationships?

First and foremost, Intel managers established trusting relationships with complementors (Lever 3). A gradual, low-key approach helped garner industry consensus around innovations impacting many firms. Second, Intel assured partners that critical technical information would remain open and that it would treat intellectual property fairly (Lever 2). All these play a decisive role to help a platform leader gain the trust of external parties. We believe that such trust building requires that the platform leader make a credible commitment to playing an active role in promoting industry innovation as well as establishing long-term, collaborative relationships with complementors.

Build a Reputation for Trustworthiness

Trust is an essential ingredient in platform leadership success. Intel managers, such as Jim Pappas, know this: "[Some complementors] certainly are concerned that you might also be talking to their competitors. Even though it's all done under nondisclosure and professional ethics, *you have to build trust before you're able to talk* across that boundary of product and business strategies."[24] Kinnie describes how difficult it was for Intel to gain the trust of industry players in adopting the PCI bus standard:

> We had to go out and earn the industry's trust. It took us probably three years, and *we had to demonstrate, time after time, that specs that were open didn't have hooks in them, and that we weren't going to get people some other way*. We didn't surprise people. We were just

persistent, deliberate, consistent—and we earned the trust of the industry. Now we have that.[25]

Intel in general and IAL in particular have earned a reputation for trustworthiness within the industry—and outside it. The fact that companies in other industries came to IAL in the late 1990s to help them promote new technologies—for example, the v.90 modem and DSL standard for high-speed Internet access over conventional phone lines—speaks to this reputation. But it was not built overnight. Kinnie said that it took IAL several years to achieve this stature, which it did by keeping the lab's agenda separate from Intel's product groups and insisting that specifications remain as open as possible.

For trust to develop, the platform leader must be careful not to "lead on" complementors. If the platform leader says it will support a new technology and not favor any one integral product group in order to encourage external companies to innovate, and these firms base their R&D and marketing investment plans on this commitment, the platform leader cannot change its mind midway without severely undermining its reputation. Will Swope, an Intel VP and director of platform planning, discusses the potential negative impact on trust of such events:

> The main challenge is that, if we commit to something and it doesn't happen, we have an impact on a lot of small companies. We've asked them to bet their company on this technology but, if it doesn't materialize, it's not just a case of us feeling bad about it. *It is a very damaging reputation to have. Maintaining trust is the real challenge.* That means having enough confidence that this is really going to happen; making sure we are betting our own money; making sure that we have the products; dealing with these road maps; and making sure that what we say will happen, does happen. There are inevitable changes and slip-ups. Then we have to make sure that the industry knows about them in a unified way, so at least we're not playing [favorites] or giving Compaq or Dell an advantage over someone else by telling them too early or not telling other people. It only works if you are a trusted source. Everybody is betting big-time that this next technology is going to happen in an organized way, in a way that adds a level enough playing field so that more than one person can participate and more than one

person can get some economic advantage. That is a big, big deal, and we put a lot of time into making that work.[26]

Another aspect of trust is concern for the long-term financial health of complementors. Intel managers echoed this concern, especially for smaller firms that could fail if an R&D project did not succeed. Kinnie reflects on Intel's widely shared sense of responsibility:

> Most often, first movers are young, innovative companies that don't yet have a market position. Someone who has established market position has more to lose. The young companies could win big if they bet their whole company but, if they lose, it's a very big deal. *That puts responsibility on us.* We're not interested in putting companies out of business. So, if we don't think the company has a real chance to succeed, we won't finish the deal. We sometimes won't know that until we engage them and find out who their people are, what their real skills are, and until they really do what we're asking them to do. If they can't, or it's a big risk, we'll say, "It's been nice talking to you" and go to somebody else. It doesn't do us any good if they fail, or if we squash a company and people's dreams and we still don't meet our goal. We're real sensitive to that. We could inadvertently run over little companies and hurt them, and we don't want to do that.[27]

Concern for and understanding of complementors' business is integral to trust-building efforts. Intel managers need a detailed understanding of the sales and profit potential of projects they promote to third parties and Intel product groups. If the platform leader demonstrates an understanding of the business model for the market segment—which industrial actor makes how much money, and from what activities—this instills in partner organizations confidence that they should be able to profit from their investments. Ryan, who is particularly fond of value-chain analysis, insists that Intel has to ensure that all companies in the chain can make money:

> There needs to be profit at every stage of the value chain. . . . [We] try to understand who the players are, who the actors are at every point in the network of value chains that work together to get a solution ultimately into people's hands. . . . We end up discovering business model barriers or completely different approaches to

doing the enabling. We shift the balance of our approach and try to find the way that the industry would in fact deliver new capabilities where everyone makes money. If every stage of the value chain is not making profit or finding differentiation or doing something positive with your business in a significant way, [the business] is not going to happen. The weak link will break the chain.[28]

We shall see later in the chapter that in order to establish trust, some internal organizational processes and aspects of Intel's internal culture revealed themselves useful, and others had to be put in place (Lever 4).

Exert Some Restraint over Scope of Activities

To maintain trust, the platform leader needs to act strategically (and with caution) regarding setting or changing the scope of its own activities and investments (Lever 1), especially when deciding to enter complementary markets directly. Intel sometimes reassured complementors that it would not crush them carelessly by invading their businesses. For example, Carol Barrett, an IAL marketing manager, sees her job as selling more microprocessors, not competing with complementors:

> My basic mechanism for diffusion is all about *partnering to provide solutions to the market*. We build media components. We don't build products that are full solutions, but components that really need to be incorporated into full 3-D editing and creation products. There are market segment leaders out there that are doing that; they are well established and have excellent products. [Firms] like Discreet, Light Wave, Interactive, SoftImage are the top-tier players making 3-D model authoring products. . . . We produce a component that could be included in their product. I definitely don't want to compete with 3-D editing companies. *My job is demand-creation. So, I'm trying to go ahead and help sell our next-generation microprocessors*. I'm not trying to sell 3-D engines.[29]

Claude Leglise, too, insists that the Content Group is not looking to compete with software companies that develop complementary products:

> I have no intention whatsoever of getting into the software business. Intel has no corporate competence in entertainment software. We don't know how to do video games, so forget it. We're not

trying to go into their space. We're trying to get them on the same strategic road map so that the *overall ecosystem* will benefit.[30]

Likewise, Ryan makes it clear that IAL, unlike Intel product groups, is not about to develop its own products. Its business is solely to make "components" and "enable" the industry:

> We don't make products at IAL. We make product components. The core—the conferencing standards, the engines for processing the standards-based data streams, and the engines to encode and decode video and audio—all those basic components were developed by IAL. They're pieces, component parts of a product.[31]

Although several managers at Intel spoke of this restraint regarding complementors' territory, this policy is not followed 100 percent of the time by all groups at Intel. As we shall see, this creates some of the conflicts that we discuss later in this chapter.

Take a Gradual, Low-Key Approach

When a platform leader pushes an innovation that affects many firms, it is best to take a gradual, low-key approach. As mentioned in chapter 3, Intel decided early on that it would try, when feasible, to establish cooperative relationships with complementors. This cooperative stance on external relationships shapes Intel's Lever 3 strategy. Several other aspects of this strategy followed from this stance.

First, Intel adopted a low-key approach that not only allowed other firms to participate in the definition of the standard or technology in question and make it as technically sound as possible, but also granted them an opportunity to shape it in a direction that was in harmony with these firms' vision for their product evolution. This approach increased the likelihood of getting "political" support from these external players—some, market leaders in their own segment—by giving them a chance to influence the technology in ways that were favorable to them.[32]

Setting new standards in high-tech industries is a delicate process, fraught with difficulties. There are often many ways of doing the same thing, and different companies can take different positions. The platform leader does not want to offend potential partners or turn them away. At the same time (as discussed in chapter 3), it is often best to keep the number of companies involved in formulating a new standard as small as possible to facilitate communication and consensus. Pappas elaborates on how to minimize conflicts and maximize results in the standardization process:

> One of the key things is keeping to a very small number of companies that work on the specifications, particularly in the early formative stages. It's like Jell-O: As things gel, it's okay to let other people in because you've got the basic shape of it set out. And then you want to modify it a little bit to make it more extendible. Just getting good, solid technical review is actually very beneficial. . . . The key thing here is you're looking for companies that are going to give you solid technical engineering. They actually have something to deliver. You really want somebody that's influential in a particular industry, that is going to be committed to this thing and develop products for it, and will help you put the resources on it. That's the best of all worlds. . . . But you never really have the best of all worlds. There's always some company that doesn't want to do it, or wants to do it some other way. It's a little bit like playing poker at the beginning. You work with them. . . . But sometimes there's company pride involved—they've already invested in one area, and you're asking them to switch. It's really delicate at the beginning, but we tend to work through those things. At some point, you can sit back and see the industry coalesce around a certain idea. Most people want to jump on at that point.[33]

Getting companies to talk openly about their ideas for a common standard is difficult to manage. A low-key, neutral approach from a platform leader can help make these delicate conversations happen.

Intel certainly found this to be the case with USB. To establish the USB standard, Intel needed to stimulate the external development of peripherals (e.g., scanners, modems, cameras, and joysticks) because this is not part of Intel's competence (a Lever 1 choice). So, in the process of writing the technical specifications for USB, Intel managers (mostly from IAL) sought out the industry leaders in each of these segments to help them define the corresponding parts of the USB standard. Bala Cadambi, the IAL manager for peripherals and interconnect technology, recalls how being low-key was a crucial factor of success in that delicate endeavor, especially in the beginning:

> The [USB] proposal was based on visiting more than fifty companies over about a year. . . . We do a lot of things in a very low-key manner because that's what it takes to succeed as an enabler. . . . Low-key is important as a leadership style. You must have credibility. You have to establish that you are here for the person's good, as opposed to for your own good, and that you're looking out for the industry's welfare. It's also important to keep things low-key because, when people come in saying they're "from Intel," everybody assumes they already have the magic answer—but they don't yet. The concern is that, in the absence of a standard, everybody has some idea about how they want to do it. And what you *don't want to do is to appear threatening to their business* in proposing a standard. That's the harder part of managing the transition because, in the absence of standards, everybody has some proprietary idea of how they want to go. . . . You also want to make sure that it's done so that *everybody feels that they have a say* in the marketing of the program, in providing the engineering building blocks behind it. . . . It can't be one-way.[34]

Several Intel managers said this low-key style was crucial at the beginning of technical initiatives that required bringing on board many actors of the industry, each with potentially complementary or even conflicting visions for where they wanted to take their product in the future.

Keep Implementation Specifications "Open" though Not "Free"

In the standardization process, outside companies are likely to worry that critical details of any new interface specification might not remain "open" or publicly available. The platform leader has a special responsibility to make sure this does not occur and to act as a neutral "enabler" of innovation for the entire industry. Dave Schuler, one of Intel's worldwide sales managers, recalls some of the intellectual property (IP) issues involved in the PCI bus initiative, where Intel people debated among themselves how much of the technology to open up:

> I'm really proud of what we did with PCI. And it's really changed the industry. Interestingly enough, there are people you can talk to

inside of Intel who say it's a failure. People in the legal department may say we gave away too much intellectual property, that we didn't charge enough or we licensed too freely. You can always make those kinds of claims with hindsight. At the time, it felt as if the prevailing mood in the industry was "Don't trust Intel. Big bad Intel. Obviously, they're hiding something here. They're going to get everybody excited about this bus, and then they're going to come back and say: 'And, by the way, we own some patents and you have to pay us royalties on it.'" We were starting to run into that. We really had no choice but to take a proactive stance. We said: "You know the IP around this socket? Well, we will provide reciprocity for the industry." In other words, we'll license it, and anybody who wants to use it just has to sign a license that says that they won't use it against us. . . . We're not going to create a tollgate. . . . I think we did what was necessary to get the industry to rally around the new standard.[35]

IAL managers developed a solution to this problem of how to handle IP. They made a distinction between what Kinnie called "specification IP" (proprietary information that described the functional details of a new technology) and "implementation IP" (proprietary information necessary to apply the technology in an actual product). Intel was likely to license or give away specification IP, but was more careful with implementation IP, especially if one of its product groups intended to compete in this area. Kinnie believes that IAL and the product groups usually could make these distinctions and settle any arguments on their own, without involving top management:

Specification IP and implementation IP are different, and what we got taught around PCI [was] we had to get real careful about that. If Intel wanted to participate as a business in an area around an open spec, Intel would be very deliberate about how it used its implementation IP—technology where there are multiple ways to implement that product. We would not necessarily go out and license everybody for that piece, but anything that was required to implement the product, then we would license freely. So we got more sophisticated in our ability to distinguish between the two. And so a lot of these debates internally were settled around the notion that IAL would sometimes assist an internal group with implementation IP because we understood this. Any acquired IP would always be open within what we called "open space." But sometimes we could settle these issues between us and the internal groups ourselves. . . . The groups would recognize that the open spec would broaden the market. But what they didn't want is for IAL to go out and help their best competitor to get in the market before they did. And so sometimes managing the implementation IP was a way to do that. . . . It also helped resolve the issue between us and internal partners because we weren't out just blasting away everything we had. We were reserving some for Intel's plays into these markets.[36]

Industry members must have confidence in the openness of a new specification to invest resources in the new technology. Key personnel within Intel, too, must have confidence—in their understanding of the businesses they affect and in their decisions. Andy Grove comments on this:

We have to be very careful [when we define interfaces] that we do it in such a way that people will have *confidence in the openness of the specifications*, or else they will not support it. We have to be meticulously fair. . . . It is very important for us not only to be fair, but also to have the confidence that we are fair about this. . . . Wired for Management is [an] example. The reason we were able to do useful work in defining the Wired for Management standard is because we were, and are, in the network management business. So again, you have the problem that we are in that business and yet we are defining an industrywide standard that our competitors should play with. So it was very important for us to play this fairly—and largely we have, so there has been very little pushback.[37]

Intel managers learned another lesson about technology: "Open specs" should not be "free specs." They discovered that one way to ensure no one made any money from a new technology was to give it away. Kinnie explains this painful realization:

Early on, we thought that, to get people to do things, we would give them technology and they would integrate. What we found was that that devalues the technology, and in the end nobody can make money—because we made the value zero—and no other company would invest in better or alternative things. That's when we started to trade technology for equity or to license. We wanted to give people an incentive to compete with us, to make a better version. That's okay because we wanted to foster innovation. It took us awhile to learn that free is not a good price. We discovered that, and we don't give technology away free anymore.[38]

Internal Conflicts: Why and When They Occur

A platform leader may encounter internal conflicts of interest for a variety of reasons, usually related to differing strategies or time horizons among the various groups within the firm. As already noted, nearly all activities at Intel are either part of Job 1 (sell more microprocessors) or Job 2 (make a profit in complementary businesses outside microprocessors). IAL usually tries to be a neutral industry broker, but Intel's product groups often have a different agenda.[39] Kinnie explains IAL's dilemma:

> Our mission is primarily to serve Job 1. But, as we're going through this process and trying to find partners, we may find that an Intel business is pursuing products in the space we're interested in. We would go to them and say: "Hey, we're all Intel. Do you want to be an early adopter of this technology and an early market segment mover?" Surprisingly, most of the time the answer is "no." They're businessmen, too. Their job is to make profit—Job 2—and they have to go out and compete and use their resources like all the other guys in the market segment. So, they're really no different.[40]

Two situations lead to frequent conflicts within Intel: (1) when IAL provides assistance to outside firms that Intel product groups see as competitors and (2) when some internal groups want to make investments in new businesses that other managers see as conflicting with the company's core microprocessor business (i.e., the Job 1 versus Job 2 dilemma).

When Assisting Complementors Conflicts with Internal Product Groups

Part of being a platform leader involves helping outside firms develop products that complement the platform. IAL plays this role, though it runs into disagreements with Intel product groups when they see themselves as competing with these complementors. IAL often clashes with Intel's chip set group over the kinds of assistance or technology IAL provides to firms the product group considers competitors. As an industry enabler, IAL prefers to license technology broadly and to help as many firms as possible create complementary products, even if Intel product groups are making similar products. Profit centers such as Intel's chip set group, on the other hand, prefer to sell products (such as PC extension cards) to firms outside Intel and make a profit.

Another issue is that Intel's product groups—like independent companies—might have timetables for new product introductions that differ from what IAL wants. They might even be slower or inferior compared to their competitors—creating another internal dilemma for IAL. The lab wants to make sure that the best technology can be diffused in the market as quickly as possible, whether the vendor is Intel or not. Dan Russell, one of Intel's senior marketing managers, relates Intel's efforts to strike a balance between "moving the platform forward" and accommodating the strategies of individual product groups:

> We have to balance two activities at any given time. On the one hand, what we're trying to do is move the platform forward—add new technology that provides new capabilities for the platform. But we have to balance that with any given product group's strategy. I'll give you a very clear example: Last year, we created an initiative we called visual computing. . . . We set out this visual computing road map. . . . And we laid out all the features that the graphics suppliers would need to put into their graphics chips, and that the driver writers would need to be able to build, and had some tools for them so they could verify what we've done. We had to go show the industry how to do that. . . . We had to go tell the independent hardware vendors that they needed to start putting these new capabilities into their chip sets, and then we wanted to go and get the whole industry to actually start building that. *Well, Intel also has a graphics business.* So, there are two issues. Number one, we are enabling competitors to one of our internal divisions. Enabling means working with the industry to get them to build this stuff. Number two, our internal divisions aren't moving as fast as some of their

competitors, and so we're actually helping the internal divisions get better. We have to balance the fact that we want to go sell graphics with advancing the platform along these visual computing lines. We have to make sure that we haven't gone and set expectations or created a demand that our own graphics product group can't meet.[41]

Smith admitted there were multiple sources of tensions with IAL, but thought the main source was disagreement over what information should be open versus proprietary when his department was trying to sell the same product. He understood that IAL had a more general mission than a product group, but he still felt there was a conflict of interest:

We may have a slightly different definition than the Lab about what is open intellectual property and what is proprietary because we are not interested in giving away details of what it takes to implement our product. All that does is help the competition. But we are interested in giving away information that helps people build other products in complementary areas where we are not invested. We make that distinction between the two probably much more clearly than [IAL] does. If you're running the microprocessor business, you might be predisposed to say: "Well, this isn't the only business I worry about. I'd like to see as many competitors out there in chip sets and graphics and everything else that goes around it as possible." So, I'd like to give them enough information that they can compete. Right? Because my focus is microprocessing. From the Computing Enhancement Group's perspective, I am not quite as interested as they are in having the other chip set guys succeed or the other graphic guys succeed—so there is tension. There is some tension with the Lab because their mission is to go out and drive general technologies and standards—"general goodness" for PCs. Sometimes it's a fine line between what is an open industry capability and what is proprietary. So, there is some tension there.[42]

Another internal conflict occurred with the DVD technology. One Intel group worked with suppliers to develop a new software technology for doing copyright encryption using the DVD format. Another Intel group worked with other companies to create an MPEG-2 player that ran on a PC with no additional hardware. Intel managers vacillated over what to do with the new technology they had helped to create. One debate concerned which format would dominate in the future, but the main problem was indecision over whether to treat the technology as helping Job 1 (give it away, almost for free) or Job 2 (try to make some real money from it). Mike Aymar, the executive responsible for this product area, recalls his frustration:

> Now, what do we do with that technology? If it's Job 1, we probably broadly diffuse it. We make it available to as many participants as we can so that as many PCs in the world from any supplier, any hardware supplier, any software supplier, all have this capability. . . . If it's not Job 1, if it's its own business unit, they don't want to diffuse it broadly. They want to take that cool software we developed and go sell it one-on-one to Compaq, Hewlett-Packard, and NEC in Japan. And they want to do that in competition with the other people who might be selling similar software. They don't want to enable the other people. They want to go win the business on their own. They want to charge money for it. They want to make a profit. So, you have two very different ways of acting. . . . *We've learned that we have to be more explicit up front about which one it is and which one it is going to be.* Some things, like that DVD example, have gone back and forth and back and forth. For three months it's here, for three months it's there—because it gets changed back and forth. So, we have got to have the discipline to be clear.[43]

Tensions also heightened when IAL or the Platform Marketing Group (which is closely linked to IAL organizationally) distributed enabling technology such as development tools, a common practice during the Implementors and Developers Forums. Again, the disagreements tended to be between IAL and Intel's chip set group. Pappas, speaking as a product group manager, cited the case of VHDL (VLSI Hardware Development Language—VLSI stands for "very large scale integration," which refers to the presence of millions of transistors integrated on each microprocessor). When companies joined Intel's USB initiative to design peripherals according to this new interface standard, Intel generally provided their hardware engineers with a working reference implementation of the USB interface written in the VHDL programming language. This implementation described a hardware design that would meet the USB specifications and could be compiled by standard tools into logic gates that could be incorporated into systems and chips.[44]

> We had a VHDL implementation of the USB interface logic. You would take the data inside of your peripheral or your computer, would feed it into this thing, and it would serialize it—the protocol. There are things that happen on the bus—byte stuffing and serialization and error correction—and it would do that function. . . . We made that available free to any of the companies. That's the kind of service the Forums provide. VHDL was designed by IAL, specifically by Bala [Cadambi]'s team. . . . Bala and I were "two-in-a-box" [Intel's expression for a two-person team, consisting of a technical manager and a marketing manager who shared responsibility for a project or the management of a unit]. We developed this code and gave it to our internal groups. In fact, our group in Chandler used it to do their chip. And we made it available to anybody in the industry. This is another example of knowing your primary objective. *I can guarantee there were times when the group in Chandler was livid that I had freely distributed this. They have competitors out there that are building products.* There came a point when they're out there trying to sell their chips, and they would go into an account and explain why they should buy the Intel chips. And the people would say: "Well, I'm trying to decide between you and this other guy, and this other guy uses the same VHDL as you do because they got it from the same [source at Intel]." As the other group sees it, *I took this stuff and essentially enabled their competitors.* They would say: "Jim, you have to stop distributing this thing. I want to sell my product, and you're adding credibility to these other people because they're using Intel circuits on theirs. And so we want you to stop that." I told them we weren't going to stop.[45]

Carol Barrett makes another point. Specific component technologies can lead to conflicts between IAL and product groups, as in the case of Internet video. Her solution is to place clear limits (field of use) on how

IAL lets partners use an Intel technology—if they were competing directly with Intel in a complementary product market:

> Sometimes we face [internal tensions] because there might be some components that other product groups care about. So, in the case of Internet on the video, I use a series of different co/decs [coders/decoders], and those co/decs are used by our TeamStation [another Intel videoconferencing product] group [and by] the ProShare group. So there can be tension about whom I want to partner with to bring my capability to the market, because the TeamStation group and the ProShare group *are not going to like the idea that I'm helping to create competition for them. You have to have a lot of real strong limits* around the use of the technology by the partner, so that they cannot go ahead and use it in a way that allows them to create a new product outside of the current business just because they've gotten our technology innovations and compete directly with our product groups. It's a business deal, so we just limit them in the license. We spend a lot of time on those.[46]

When New Investments Detract from the Platform Business

Another type of conflict within platform leaders relates less to the strategy of platform leadership and more to the kinds of problems managers responsible for corporate strategy face every day. The issue is how much emphasis to place on the core business—in Intel's case, the microprocessor product line (Job 1)—versus new opportunities, whether they be investments in potential sources of new complements (Job 2), or potential sources of new revenues and profits (Job 3).

This debate is an old one within Intel. Its first memory chips for mainframes and minicomputers in the late 1960s and early 1970s proved to have a limited market. Intel then moved into memory chips for PCs in the mid-1970s while making small numbers of microprocessors. When memory chips became a commodity market dominated by Japanese firms during the early 1980s, Intel exited the memory chips business. After 1990, as PCs became more of a commodity product, Intel began pushing the PC as a broader information device and expanded its range of businesses.[47] Intel evolved to supply microprocessors and some complete products for all sorts of non-PC applications, including communications and networking equipment, wireless devices, various embedded systems, and information appliances.

In the late 1990s, Intel also introduced a line of inexpensive Celeron microprocessors that ran the Linux operating system in screen phones, e-mail devices, and television set-top boxes—directly challenging Intel groups that designed the more expensive chip lines and supported Microsoft Windows.[48] Investments in products such as Intel-branded digital cameras and videoconferencing systems were examples of Intel's efforts to get closer to the end user. It expanded into Internet services, too, with server farms and Web-site hosting services. Through these investments, most of which aimed to take advantage of the Internet, Intel executives hoped to grow the company at a 15 to 20 percent annual rate, about twice as fast as the basic microprocessor business grew during the middle and late 1990s.[49]

This expansion of Intel's businesses beyond microprocessors involved extensive organizational changes and internal debates over focus and priorities. As for the organization structure, in 1998, Craig Barrett split Intel into five groups and began more aggressive investments in acquisitions, start-ups, potential complementors, and new areas for growth. In 1999 alone, Intel spent $6 billion on twelve acquisitions and used another $50 million to fund start-ups.[50] Barrett also established a New Business Investments (NBI) group, an internal venture fund, and placed this group as well as IAL under a single executive. In a speech at the IAL in April 2000, Kinnie discussed Intel's efforts to expand its core business and the role of IAL:

> One [for expansion] is get closer to the end user—developing heads for certain kinds of branded end-user products where Intel directly deals with the end user. Now, we haven't done that in the computing sector because that's where our customers are and we've played with that for a long time and decided that's not a really wise idea. But there are other sectors where we can participate in branded end-user products and perhaps some of those would be kingpins to the overall strategy of increasing our value there.[51]

Identifying opportunities in these new areas required expertise that not all Intel departments possessed. IAL was slated to play a key role in developing these new areas. It added its own new business development group and worked closely with Intel's venture group. Shane Wall, IAL's director of new business development, comments on the new venture activities:

> The model is very much like a venture capital model. The public numbers are $65 million that we use to invest per year on an internal basis. We invest it just like we would a venture capital firm. So the idea is we take technologies in the labs that we think fall in those cracks . . . and we will create new business opportunities around it and then fund them through New Business Investments for periods of six months to a year, anywhere from 3 to 8 million dollars. Then they are managed just like a venture capitalist. They have their own board. They manage by cash flow. They're not tied back to Intel's microprocessor business. In fact, they very much stay out of making a decision based on whether it would grow Intel's microprocessor's business or not.[52]

How did this shift in focus impact IAL? Kinnie said: "The more convenient and the closer you can get to the end user, there's more gold that goes into Intel's pocket. And so we want to continue to put our eyes there as a lab and to try to understand again full end-use capabilities or what it takes and then potentially Intel's role in this opportunity."[53] IAL in 2000 to 2001 thus took on a new role—to help develop new businesses for Intel, which could become new core businesses.

THE CHALLENGE OF DIVERSIFICATION   Diversification is difficult for most companies, especially if new business areas take the firm farther and farther from its traditional core of expertise. One potential problem with Intel's diversification strategy as of 2001 is that Barrett, Grove, and other company executives grew up mainly in the microprocessor business, and that is their expertise. Intel is also slow (compared to firms such as Cisco) to promote executives from acquired companies into its senior management ranks. Helping Intel cope with this limited expertise creates additional pressures on IAL managers to help Intel diversify and invest in venture opportunities. Kinnie notes that IAL holds a meeting every Friday morning to review venture deals, rather than talk about new research areas or initiatives.[54] Ryan sees these new responsibilities not as a distraction but rather as a healthy broadening of IAL's original mission:

> It's an important change for us in terms of the space that we are applying our mission or, if we're talking about IAL, now it's broader. The mission is the same. . . . The mission in this organization is to grow the opportunity, grow the innovation which is occurring in the ecosystem that's creating opportunity for all of the actors in the ecosystems in which Intel can participate. Intel's corporate focus has shifted, moving and expanding from the computing mission statement to the Internet economy mission statement. The implications on the IAL are that the ecosystems that we're looking at are broader. We still do what we do and the businesses at Intel that participate in those ecosystems are now not only the processor business but the networking businesses and the communications and all of the other businesses of Intel. So the Lab's role and mission and competencies are the same. The universe that we apply them in is continuing to expand.[55]

Other managers agree that the expanded agenda positively affects IAL. Rick Yeomans, head of IAL's technical marketing group, argues that finding new avenues for investment and people interested in creating different products has opened up a new way to channel IAL's resources: "I think it has affected the Lab in that it gives you another outlet for some of the creative ideas."[56] Kinnie admits, however, that IAL's new responsibilities lead to new conflicts with some of Intel's product groups.

> [Job 3] is an interesting blend of those two [Jobs 1 and 2] where we were trying to make something new happen in the industry. There isn't an Intel business unit but we think there ought to be and we have an additional motive that . . . Intel needs to grow its business beyond its core business. . . . Actually, there's often more tension between Jobs 2 and 3 than there is between 1 and 2.[57]

There is more potential for internal conflicts, according to Mary Murphy-Hoye, director of IT strategy and technology, for several reasons. First, Intel top management in mid-2000 granted business units more autonomy to pursue "green" business areas and further the search for new, high-growth businesses that did not necessarily complement or depend on microprocessors. Intel's product group managers are still trying to figure out just how much authority they actually have to pursue their own agendas, however, and there is some concern that the company might become a "federation" of overly independent business units. A second, related issue is that, as different groups pursue new businesses, such as e-business solutions, they are beginning to see the world in terms of multiple platforms—not just the Intel-microprocessor-based PC. Some customers want Internet-based systems that accommodate a variety of equipment, including servers from rival Sun Microsystems. To develop these promising new businesses and provide broader customer solutions, Intel has to work with a variety of new partners. Third, as discussed briefly in chapter 3, Intel reorganized several groups in 2000 and created new units around solutions and platforms for different markets.[58]

INTEL CAPITAL: JOB 1 OR JOB 2?   Intel Capital is the other source of expertise and resources that Intel uses to move beyond the core business (Jobs 2 and 3) as well as to invest in complementors. Its portfolio in July 2000 had a market value of some $7.5 billion and included more than 450 firms, with approximately $2.9 billion invested directly by Intel.[59] The group's overall strategy is to "stimulate advances in computing" by investing in promising companies that could "establish new and innovative technologies, develop industry standard solutions, drive Internet growth and advance the computing platform."[60] Intel Capital also oversees investment organs with partner companies such as Compaq, Dell, HP, NEC, and Silicon Graphics. These funds include the Intel 64 Fund (July 2000 value of $250 million), which invests in companies planning to develop products using Intel's new 64-bit chip technology, and the Intel Communications Fund (July 2000 value of $200 million), which invests in firms developing Internet communication technologies, such as Internet telephony.[61]

Intel made these investments both to "expand the industry" by attracting new uses and new users or by removing technical roadblocks and to enhance Intel's own computing capabilities through improved products and faster time to market. Les Vadasz, a senior VP and Intel

Capital's director, recalled in our 1998 interview how Intel got into the business of investing in other companies:

> We have invested in various companies over a period of twenty years. There was nobody in charge of it right from the beginning. But, in the early 1990s, we really started to systematize this and we created an activity. That's when I got in charge of it, and then we started to learn. Initially we only invested in companies directly related to our business, helping us deliver products. Then, we started to venture out a little bit further to the complementors, to the point right now that we're mainly focusing on the complementors.[62]

Like the other venture initiatives, however, Intel Capital has the potential to be a source of internal tensions. Some Intel managers argued that it was a distraction because it forced Intel to compete with the Silicon Valley venture capital (VC) community—and on a very large scale. Intel Capital in the late 1990s was receiving hundreds of proposals monthly, and had some forty or more analysts reviewing proposals, talking to companies, and deciding which investments to make. Intel's investments have typically been in the $1 million to $10 million range, although it occasionally made billion-dollar deals. Vadasz counters that his group's mission is to cooperate rather than compete with venture capitalists (VCs):

> Cooperative business development is basically our venture— although venture is a bit too restrictive a word because generally it refers only to private companies. We invest in both private and public companies. Our investment philosophy is driven by a two-fold strategy. One part is to create new market segments—new markets for our products and for our technologies. For that, we invest primarily in complementors, people whose products on the market will help establish a total market capability. The other groups we invest in are people who can help us directly deliver products to our market segment. These can be companies such as those in the CAD [computer aided design] field and the equipment field, such as semiconductors and manufacturing equipment. We try to take certain market segment areas that we see are going to

become important for us, and see what's needed to accelerate the development of these new market segments.[63]

Graphics and visual computing provide a good example of what Intel Capital could do, especially when working in cooperation with other Intel groups. Vadasz revealed to us how Intel not only did some architectural work but also invested $15 million in outside companies such as Avid Technology to make the PC more competitive with the Mac in running multimedia applications. Intel later invested heavily in software start-ups skilled in technologies for viewing multimedia and graphics over the Internet. The idea, again, was to build up new segments, such as Internet-based visual computing, as well as send a signal to the industry that Intel is an "appropriate player to team with." Working with start-ups also benefited Intel by exposing its engineers to state-of-the-art technologies and applications that were potentially different from Intel's in-house expertise.[64]

Although Intel Capital plays the role of a VC, there are important differences between Intel and VCs. Intel primarily wants to promote complementary products for the PC platform or its microprocessor product line. It also explores new businesses areas or opportunities for profit. Perhaps most important, however, Intel's investments can give new companies instant credibility with VCs—an Intel "seal of approval."[65] For this reason, along with the technical or marketing assistance Intel can provide, Intel managers believe they are good partners for at least some VCs. Alex Wong, Vadasz's assistant, explains:

> Venture capitalists make investments, and their pure motivation is return on investment. They want to make money . . . Intel's role is somewhat different. We often don't invest without a venture capitalist. We're not in direct competition with them by any stretch of the imagination. We don't take a board seat, whereas a venture capitalist will almost invariably want to have that kind of control. We'd like to provide guidance to the company. Perhaps we can help with some technology that is in-house. Perhaps we can help with a channel, marketing. Sometimes there's a halo effect with an Intel investment—a lot of companies see that as being the case. A recent *San Jose Mercury News* article talked about the Intel "Good House-

keeping" seal of approval. One of the concepts was—and I don't know if this is true or not—that if Intel invests in a company, then it means that at least a certain amount of due diligence has been done. It says: "This is a reasonable company." . . . There are these things that Intel brings to the table that are very different than the venture capitalists, but we invest at the same time—usually about the second or third rounds. We'll invest in a seed-stage company all the way through companies that are public.[66]

Despite these obvious benefits to Intel and to the platform leadership mission, disagreements flare within the company whenever Intel Capital proposes investments that stray too far from Intel's direct experience. Intel Capital also has to be careful when investing in complementors that Intel groups might decide to compete against in the future. Vadasz acknowledges that Intel Capital sometimes walks a fine line:

In our business, the boundary has always moved because the interfaces between our customers and us have always changed as a result of the way the technology has evolved. While I recognize that it's moving and that it's always moved, it's very important that we don't get carried away with our own delusions of grandeur, that we stay in businesses that we know we can succeed in. . . . We have looked at our business more as a supplier of building blocks that others can build their business on, and that continues to be the majority of our business. But even there, we have skirmishes sometimes because the interface changes. When we first started to sell motherboards, there was a lot of paranoia amongst our OEMs. What's our intent? Why are we doing this? I think now it's more of a positive to the business than a negative. But anytime you do that, there are a lot of issues. Also, it's important that your complementors trust you because you need them, they need you, and you cannot just trample all over everybody's business willy-nilly. Those kinds of things have to be done carefully.[67]

Vadasz's solution to this dilemma is to focus on the context of the total market—the "ecosystem"—and make investments that accelerate the development of complementary products. Anything else can too easily become a distraction:

> The most important thing is that you develop a philosophy in the company to look at your business in the context of the total market segment, other than in the context only of your own capabilities. . . . It's all about complementors. When you go into a new area, you have to look at what's going to make up the market segment ecosystem. What are the various buttons I have to push in order to have something happen? Anytime you forget that, you are playing with disaster. We've played with disaster from time to time in our history. We'd say: "Gee, if we do this, look what it could be"— without recognizing who else has to play in order for the "could be" to happen? . . . Now, if there are complementors out there, the picture looks different. If there are no complementors, it may be different again. Given that the lifespan of a generation is relatively short, look at the benefit you get by being able to accelerate deployment. And the way you accelerate deployment is by engaging with the market, with all these complementors. You could argue that eventually they would happen anyway, that the market forces would take care of this. But given the relatively short technology cycle in new products, you are not getting the most out of any technology generation if you don't do something overt in accelerating deployment of a new generation.[68]

Internal Conflicts: What to Do about Them

Through trial and error, Intel managers learned not only to expect internal conflicts but also how to manage them. The following approaches seem to work most effectively:

1. *Acknowledge conflicts*: Senior executives found it useful to acknowledge openly that there were differences of opinion and that these could lead to serious internal tensions. Such acknowledgment sent a message to internal groups that it was okay to have debates and thus created a basis for resolving key issues.

2. *Manage conflicts*: Intel implemented management processes useful to resolve conflicts. The company established a formal planning process with scheduled review meetings once a year for the corporation and twice a year for business units, as well as formally communicated a set of common objectives every year for the entire corporation.

3. *Create a culture that encourages debate*: Intel relied on a corporate culture that encouraged debate to resolve conflicts and prevent tensions from escalating.

Economic Analysis of the Job 1–Job 2 Trade-Off

We believe that any platform leader that tries to do both Job 1 (selling their main product line) and Job 2 (profiting in complementary businesses) will encounter tensions within the firm if there are internal groups whose mission includes supporting outside complementors. So should a firm avoid pursuing these two seemingly conflicting goals? A simple solution would be to abandon Job 2 and not enter complementary markets directly. But this is not a good solution. Why not? First, any company, platform leader or not, needs to be on the lookout for potential new business opportunities because demand may diminish in its own market. Second, counting on external firms to produce all necessary complements is not always feasible (as we saw in the case of chip sets and motherboards with PCI). Last, a platform leader needs to be concerned about maintaining enough bargaining power vis-à-vis complementors. By relying exclusively on external provision of complements, the firm could lose its expertise in important technical areas—and gradually lose its ability to assess the quality or price of externally produced complements.

In economic terms, there is an issue of distribution of overall industry profits that is linked to the issue of bargaining power between the firm and its complementors. When external companies produce a complementary innovation, they can share in the returns on this investment if the platform leader buys their innovation (the complementor then becomes a supplier) and pays them a fair price and distributes this innovation with its core product. This is a win-win situation. But if the platform leader does not pay a fair price for the innovation, the outside company has no incentive to innovate. Conversely, if the complementor tries to capture too much of the profit coming from an innovation, the platform leader might have less incentive to invest in activities that facilitate third-party innovation.

We interpret Intel's decision to keep some complementary activities in-house (Lever 1) through this lens. By keeping some complementary expertise and possibility to commercialize complements in-house, Intel has a powerful bargaining chip: the ability to compete with its complementors. Though managers would indicate that they were likely or unlikely to enter certain areas, Intel reserves the right to enter any market. Intel's product groups (mainly concerned with Job 2) were the "meat" behind this warning. They represent a credible threat to enter a variety of markets because they have access to money, people, and technology, as well as the Intel brand name.

The bottom line is that Intel managers have generally preferred to have a smooth, collaborative relationship with complementors—but only when they behave in ways that Intel wants, such as making timely investments to support Intel's latest microprocessor lines. If complementors do not live up to Intel's expectations, however, they might very well see Intel enter their markets, even temporarily.[69]

The trade-off is the following: The price Intel pays to be able to send these powerful signals is the internal tension between profit-centered product groups and the "industry-enabling" units. Despite the frequent conflicts, it seems to be in Intel's best interests to have groups doing Job 2, even if their investments never amount to much. Their mere existence helps ensure that outside firms invest in a continuous stream of complementary innovations for fear that Intel would make these investments if they didn't, and would reap all the rewards for itself.

At the same time, there should be no argument that a platform leader must do Job 1, nor that Job 1 should include facilitating complementary innovations done inside or outside the firm, such as by creating new technologies or standards that promote sales of the platform. Intel tried to reduce this healthy tension between Job 1 and Job 2 (and Job 3) by making the organizational units within the firm independent of each other (a Lever 4 solution). IAL, for example, could have been part of a product division such as the chip set business, but it was not. It was our impression that this "neutrality" and tension with Intel product units helped IAL serve as a neutral and credible ally for outside firms.

Acknowledge Conflicts and Manage Them

Acknowledging tensions rather than ignoring them allows a company to manage them. Intel executives explicitly acknowledged that they expected internal conflicts of interest to emerge. Widely distributed company documents such as "Intel's Objectives" referred to these internal tensions. Executives did not expect people to resolve disagreements as soon as they appeared. Instead, the company relied on certain management processes to encourage formal debates on the issues underlying these tensions, where people could express dissenting views. These debates often took place under the guidance of executives such as Andy Grove, Gordon Moore, and Craig Barrett, who would make the final decisions in many cases.

This debating process allowed Intel's top management to review the pros and cons of controversial decisions, such as whether to keep certain information "open" or "closed." Managers or engineers who argued before top management clearly had an incentive to make the senior executives accept their point of view. Moreover, during the debates, Intel executives had a chance to clarify, redefine, and disseminate their corporate objectives. Aymar argued that internal conflicts were important to Intel's platform leadership strategy because they forced managers to decide which activities were Job 1 and what should be Job 2:

> Tensions between Job 1 and Job 2 happen all the time. We don't yet have a really good way of dealing with it, *but at least we accept it,* and we're trying to come up with a clear way of dealing with it. For example, one thing we know we want to do is make a given activity clear. Is it Job 1 or not? Is its primary purpose to support a microprocessor ramp and the growth of those technologies? If not, then it's really got to be a business that stands on its own. It has to behave like a profit center. A lot of times, if you're not clear up front with whether a given project is part of Job 1, people get confused. They're trying to make their profit center, but the microprocessor guys are telling them that, by doing so, they're not cooperating with the rest of the company.[70]

Grove sees that Intel has a fundamental Job 1 versus Job 2 dilemma. In our August 1998 interview, Grove argued that supporting Intel's large microprocessor business usually made more sense than using a complementary technology to diversify. The result of this logic, though, was that Intel had not diversified as much as some managers would have liked.

> These tensions exist. We argue about it. It happens all the time. Somebody who is doing videoconferencing wants to keep a [coder/decoder] proprietary to the videoconferencing product. The people who are responsible for microprocessors want to give those videoconferencing products away free. The internal terminology for that is that microprocessors are Job 1, and creating other businesses is Job 2. So, our shorthand is to call it a Job 1 versus Job 2 conflict. Depending on the strategic importance of the product and competitive pressures, we decide one way or another. We always lean towards Job 1 because so much more of our business is microprocessors. A little bit of help to the microprocessor business is much more important than any additional business that we can create with videoconferencing and chips sets and the like. This is not all good because the consequence over a long period is that we have managed to build a very strong and successful microprocessor business, but nothing else. That's not a good environment in which you can build new businesses because everything that the new business wants to create will get sucked away by the microprocessors and given to the new business competitors. Not everything, but almost everything—which is why, on the flip side, the world trusts us when we do that. *But they trust us because we have not created an additional business that was successful.*[71]

Grove believes internal disagreements over these issues of diversification and outside investments are important for the company in that although they may generate tensions, they also bolster creative thinking on the best strategy to follow.

> I think we need to lean toward new business creation more. It became too automatic to give everything away. We need to build back some more tension and contention for it. It became a little too easy to go with Job 1. *I don't think tension is bad. Tension focuses strategic thinking. It focuses people to figure out what's important and what's not so important.* It's a bit like the judicial process in that it

uses advocacy method to get at the truth. Here, the advocacy method and the arguments get the best results of strategy.[72]

Strategy Setting through Confrontation and Debate

While the first step may be to acknowledge the tensions between Job 1 and Job 2 (or Job 3), Intel also has to address them. Several formal mechanisms are useful for strategic planning and for managing disagreements.

STRATEGIC LONG-RANGE PLANNING MEETINGS   First, Intel holds strategy-setting meetings—called Strategic Long-Range Planning (SLRP) meetings—twice a year. According to many Intel managers, the level of confrontation at these meetings is quite intense. Leglise described these meetings:

> The [SLRP] meetings happen twice a year. Andy [Grove] will start with his view of the environment and the strategic issues facing the company. And we'll assign four, five, or six topics that various members of the executive staff will then drive. Then they form a working group of people who have some knowledge related to the subject matter, and about a month later the group will get together again—the executive staff and a lot of the senior managers of the company. Each working group presents its analysis of that particular topic, and what it believes is its best strategic recommendation for what Intel should do. That will be a month to six weeks later. It's an intense planning process. These officers do this in addition to their jobs. In the last two weeks before the meeting, there's a lot of work to do.[73]

A major task of the attendees is to analyze trends in the business and evaluate if their observations and plans from the previous year are still accurate. These meetings produce a new set of official corporate "objectives" for the following year. The objectives include initiatives to develop both the primary platform business and complementary areas. For example, in 1998, Intel defined Job 1 as "Strengthen the Number 1 position of Intel microprocessors in the ever-changing computer industry" and Job 2 as "Grow the Visual/Connected PC market and build successful businesses around the related technology." In 1999, company executives shifted the mission to become "the preeminent building block supplier to the Internet economy."[74] According to Leglise, the SLRP process allows Intel managers to define and refine Intel's strategy:

> We present our analysis of what's going on: Here's the trend; here's where we think it's going to go; and here's what we're going to do about it. The outcome can be one of many. It could be that we're on the right track, that we're just going to tweak a little bit what we're doing, and the road map continues. What we said a year ago is still valid and okay. Another outcome can be that the market segment has changed completely and so the track we were on is now totally irrelevant. In the worst case, they say it makes no sense whatsoever, and you have to go redo it. That happens practically every year: You forget something major, or you understand the market but your solution is harebrained. *It's a very intense, fairly confrontational process* because, at the end of the day, we have to have the absolute best answer. That's why it's good to have these things *regularly* because we indeed may need a major change. So, we do a regular checkup. What changed? What do we know?[75]

Encouragement of voicing alternative points of view is an integral part of the strategy-setting process:

> Our SLRP meetings . . . get pretty hot because that's the purpose. You want to put the best possible knowledge on the table, irrespective of someone's . . . grade level in the corporation, so that the best minds are applied to solving our problems. If all you do is agree with each other, then you get nothing done. People here are absolutely not afraid of talking. There are no sanctions. That's the point. If you can't tell Andy [Grove] that he's wrong just because he's the boss, then the whole thing falls apart.[76]

Grove and Barrett take a "hands-on" approach in managing the SLRP meetings. Aymar offers these impressions:

> Sometimes the proposals are pretty bizarre, so there's a lot of argument and discussion. Other times, they're smooth. It depends. But in general, they're pretty contentious, because we're talking about fundamental assumptions and strategies, and we're saying

what we should do. There are a lot of opinions. We usually come to consensus. But Grove and Barrett are very hands-on. They have very firm opinions and, in the end, they summarize what we're going to do and what the ultimate decision is. They have to be the tiebreakers if there is still dissension. They have to be the ones who say: "I've listened, and this is what we're going to do"—and get on with it.[77]

PRODUCT LINE BUSINESS PLAN MEETINGS Once a year, all Intel product groups hold strategy-setting meetings: the Product Line Business Plan (PLBP) meetings. As Aymar relates, these meeting deal with more division-specific issues and reflect Intel's efforts to focus on Job 1. This focus is important to keep the core business healthy:

> Once a year, we have a thing called Product Line Business Plan, PLBP. We come in with the specifics. We say: "Okay, here's what we're going to do. We're going to have this program to do the $2,000 home PC. This is the processor that's going to be in it. This is the work we're doing to do to enable the industry in hardware. This is the work we're doing in software. It's costing this much here, and it's costing that much there. Our returns from each of these are such and such." We paint the whole picture. We try to make it so that each investment is self-funding even though it's part of Job 1, but in the end we look at the whole picture. As you know, Job 1 is selling our next-generation processor and creating value to go with them, a reason people want to buy them—because they're worth something and they do something special. That's the process we use. So, these budgeting decisions are negotiated or discussed or shared in these venues: the strategic long-term plan, the product plan, the business plan. *We're a very focused company*. For a company as large as we are—$25 billion or so—we are incredibly focused on this one market segment, the PC market segment, and so we have *a lot of top-down priority setting in these two venues* I described.[78]

CORPORATE COMMUNICATIONS Once Intel managers make decisions in these meetings, they rapidly communicate the results throughout the corporation. Gerald Holzhammer, head of the Desktop Architecture Lab, attributes this fast communication to a tight group of senior managers: "Intel has a core of maybe 100 to 150 senior managers who are very well connected and talk to each other. New directions get disseminated to the corporation very, very quickly."[79] Leglise describes how Intel uses effective communication mechanisms to disseminate strategic decisions:

> Every so often we have what we call the BUM, the Business Update Meeting. Andy [Grove] or Craig [Barrett] will prepare a forty-five-minute to one-hour presentation on the state of the business. And it goes to every employee. We have a session where Andy or Craig will present to the senior managers, fifty to a hundred people. Then our assignment is to take that presentation and give it to all of our employees. So, in a matter of two weeks, the entire corporation, everybody, has heard the word about what's going on: revenues, profits, employees, how we're hiring, and a discussion of the strategic things—initiatives, success in the marketplace, failure in the marketplace, what we need to do next. For example, the last one was in the last thirty days, and a huge chunk of it was the output of SLRP. So, everybody in the whole corporation today knows what the direction is, what we are going to do for the next two or three years, until we change our mind.[80]

The other formal communication mechanism is the ubiquitous wall poster: "Intel Objectives," which lists the goals for that year. The poster provides a visible (they hang on every wall at Intel and in almost every cubicle) and concise formulation of corporate directions as defined through the SLRP meetings. Leglise explains:

> These Objectives are created through a bottom-up process, and then tweaked by the executive staff. Once it's all agreed, they're published. So, the whole company knows what we're trying to accomplish. The Objectives stem from the SLRP process. And then we post it on every bloody wall in the place ... every conference room and every office. Anybody from the top on down to the bottom or the other way around can know exactly what we're doing. This is what we're supposed to be accomplishing, and so you know what you're here for.[81]

Internal Culture: Tolerate Ambiguity and Encourage Confrontation

Intel is well known for having a corporate culture that tolerates ambiguity in goals and objectives and encourages open confrontation. In his 1996 best-selling book, *Only the Paranoid Survive*, Grove described this culture as promoting "strategic dissonance," which he defines as the divergence between actions and statements. Grove's argument is that diverging opinions allow important information to surface and help managers become aware of changes in their environment. He refers to external changes that require a reformulation of strategy as "strategic inflection points."[82] Several other Intel managers expressed similar points of view. Leglise, for example, emphasizes the importance of encouraging new employees to challenge what they hear from their superiors:

> Forty-three percent of our employees were not Intel employees two years ago. So, the critical issue is socialization: How do we make them understand our values and be efficient at using the assets and the resources of the corporation so they can accomplish their goals? They need to know this stuff. They need to know that if they hear a senior manager presenting something in a meeting that they know is blatantly false—because they have data that somehow the senior manager doesn't have—it is their duty as an employee and a shareholder to raise their hand and say "I object." That is not only acceptable, but it's expected.[83]

Intel people value the ability to tolerate ambiguity. Miller describes this aspect of the company culture:

> Intel's culture is one that rewards tolerance for ambiguity. When we hire people, we want them to be very comfortable with ambiguity.... The hierarchical line of reporting has some impact, but is not the only force in decision making. For example, the review process or the performance measurement process here is 360 degrees, which means that you get feedback from your peers. It is expected that, as part of the performance process, you get input not just from people in the organization that you functionally report to.... Careers are made cross-group. They are not made in a single, vertical group. Most projects that go cross-group create all sorts of visibility. This company prides itself on the ability to get results. And cross-group results

are infinitely more recognizable than results in one group because you're exposed to more people. You're exposed to new ideas.[84]

We believe that Intel's culture makes it possible for managers and employees to deal with the ambiguity and conflicts that characterize the Job 1 versus Job 2 dilemma. Managers continually face the choice of whether to distribute new technologies and information as aids to complementors or keep them for developing in-house products. Open debates help inform Intel managers about how new technologies could be put to use. Smith believes this perspective is important in helping managers decide whether they should be Job 1 or Job 2.

> There is what I would call creative tension. It's kind of natural. It's definitely not something that I would call a war or a big political fight. Usually, we come to some kind of agreement. We look for a pragmatic solution. We have this tenet of the Intel culture called *constructive confrontation*. We typically have a constructive confrontation and get everything on the table and collectively decide a course of action. The idea is to get every stakeholder in the decision together to at least have a voice.[85]

Internal Organization: Separate Groups Pursuing Job 1 and Job 2

Part of Intel's Lever 4 strategy is keeping Job 1 separate from Job 2. According to Kinnie, "keeping the Lab's agenda separate from the product's agenda" has worked internally as well as externally.[86] The PCI bus initiative illustrates this. Intel executives wanted graphics card producers and chip set vendors throughout the industry to adopt the new standard, which would help Intel sell new microprocessors. But executives also wanted their own chip set group, located within the Computing Enhancement Group (CEG), which had about 10 percent of the market, to continue having a viable business selling these same components. Schuler explains that Intel solved the PCI chip set problem by separating the relevant groups:

> The issue that Intel corporate faced was how to balance telling the other chip set vendors about this technology and, at the same time, make sure that we weren't seriously damaging [CEG's] business. The head of [CEG] was very outspoken, and he wouldn't have let that happen. How did the Intel politics internally decide between

enabling our competitors and making our own business grow? *We separated the two different groups.* The marketing group responsible for promoting the PCI specification was separated from the product group. The group I was in took on the role of industry evangelists, not reporting directly to [CEG], but parallel.[87]

The USB standard provides another example. Pappas recalled how keeping his platform initiatives group apart from Intel's product groups and attached to IAL was crucial to maintaining good relationships with external parties. This was true even though Intel product groups incorporated the USB technology into their chip set products. It also helped that Intel executives had agreed that developing the USB specification was a Job 1 activity rather than Job 2:

> Once we decided we were going to put [USB] in our chip set products, all of a sudden there were many people working on the design. But we had a *very clear separation.* We had a group that was defining the specification, and we had other groups implementing products. They would take our specification and implement the products, but we kept a sort of wall between the two. . . . Selling processors is Job 1, and *this [USB effort] was all done for a Job 1 purpose: Advance the platform so we sell more PCs.*[88]

Without this organizational separation from the product groups, we think IAL would have trouble convincing outside parties that it is neutral. Doing both Job 1 and Job 2 gave Intel the technical knowledge and general credibility to define the broader PC platform, including other hardware and software components that connected to the microprocessor. But the lack of a profit incentive made IAL the right organization to promote new standards for the industry. Grove commented:

> We are in a certain business and we are defining a platform upon which other people are going to plug in peripherals or other products. And we want competition in those areas. And yet we want to supply there, also. . . . We are defining the platform and we want to be a participant to build on the platform. It's a pretty common situation. *It is almost inconceivable that you can have the expertise, the momentum, and the market credibility to define a platform unless you are participating both above and below that platform.* Microprocessors

are below. You can't come and define buses if you don't know enough about chip sets and microprocessors. On the other hand, if you are in it, you obviously have a business interest for yourself. *The resolution of these tensions is crucial for repeated success.* That's where IAL came in. IAL, by and large, was created as an architecture lab, as its name implies. IAL has no profit-and-loss responsibility, and no products. Most of this work was done by IAL. *And IAL has achieved an extra measure of credibility.* It comes, first, from the fact that they are very good, and second, that they are not in a business. For the CEG organization to proselytize platform design and architecture was much more difficult than for IAL because CEG would be a supplier to that platform. Wherever possible, it is much better that the standards be done by a group that is not a profit-and-loss center.[89]

It is not enough simply for a platform leader to separate potentially conflicting groups. The platform leader also needs to make sure outside companies understand the structure. Kinnie emphasized this point:

To deserve the trust, a separation of roles inside the organization is an absolute necessity. And it has to be observable from the outside. There is a tension between the two perspectives: the Lab perspective and the product groups' perspective. We [IAL] advance their [the product groups'] thinking and pull it a little more forward, but they dampen our exuberance or naiveté into reality. The truth lies someplace in between. It also is important to keep that polarity for the sake of enrolling others on the outside. If the labs were buried inside of the product groups, the perceived neutrality and trustworthiness of the labs would go down.[90]

Keep Internal Tensions Alive: Keep Job 1 and Job 2

Intel's managers have developed a savvy way to resolve the Job 1 versus Job 2 dilemma. They acknowledge that Job 1 and Job 2 objectives conflict, but recognize that the company needs to pursue them both. Without the investments of internal profit-seeking product groups, Intel would never have successfully developed many technologies. The interest of internal product groups helps departments such as IAL get funding for complementary technologies, even though this interest creates tensions with both IAL and the outside firms with which IAL works closely. Interest from one of Intel's product groups was usually essential for Intel to follow through on the development of a new idea. The support of IAL alone is not enough. Schuler explains:

> If Intel comes up with an idea, the germ of the idea usually starts in one group. Whether it has to do with cable modems or whether it has to do with a new bus interface, whether it has to do with smart batteries or whatever—there's just a number of hurdles that you have to get over. The first hurdle is whether it makes any sense at all. Can you state your goal? Next, you have to find an Intel product group that will become the champion for that idea once it begins to establish itself. If you don't have a product group—especially if the idea comes out of one of the groups like the Lab that's not profit-and-loss-oriented—you run the risk of getting outside people "pregnant" and not being able to follow through on it. . . . So, there are some forces that keep you from taking ideas out that are half-baked. . . . If you can get a product group to feel like they're going to make money out of this idea, then you've really passed your first hurdle. Now you have somebody who can make some serious P&L decisions based on what you have to do. Of course, then you get into the second half of it: Once Intel as a corporation has decided that there's an initiative it needs to promote, what are the steps that are necessary to make that happen in the rest of the industry? [That's where IAL comes in.][91]

We already explained (under "Economic Analysis of the Job 1–Job 2 Trade-Off") the simple economic reason—maintaining bargaining power over complementors—that justifies keeping complementary activities in-house. This discussion resonates in light of the recent lawsuit against Microsoft, in which the U.S. Department of Justice in its first remedy proposal called for a complete separation of the "Applications" business (Microsoft's equivalent for Job 2 groups) and the operating system part of the company (Microsoft's equivalent for Job 1).

Conclusion: Platform Leaders Need to Balance Multiple Roles

We have seen in this chapter that Intel as a platform leader routinely faces external and internal tensions as it pursues multiple goals. It therefore needs to *play multiple roles* at the same time. This is one of the toughest challenges that Intel in particular, and platform leaders in general, face. First is the industry-enabler role, by which Intel has pursued broad long-term objectives aimed at expanding the pie for the whole industry. Then there is the neutral-broker role, whereby the IAL leads in promoting the "public interest." Meanwhile, other parts of the company play more conventional "profit-seeking" roles and aggressively compete in the marketplace. Sometimes this competition occurs with complementors that IAL or Intel Capital or other parts of the company are supporting. The results are tensions and sometimes conflicts of interest. Disagreements can be healthy, however, to the extent that they keep everyone, at all levels of the corporation, thinking about and debating the best courses of action.

We want to highlight two insights from the way Intel manages the conflicts it has faced in its pursuit of platform leadership. The first one relates to Lever 3 (relationships with external firms): *Assuming the role of industry negotiator seems to have helped Intel tremendously in its pursuit of platform leadership.* In any business environment, there are always gains from competition, as there are other gains from collaboration. A platform leader is aware of both gains, and is careful about the trade-offs involved. As we saw, Intel was concerned with conveying its desire to promote collaboration at the industry level to external parties. Neutrality in this context means being careful about pursuing its own interests at the expense of complementors. We saw different Intel departments restrict the scope of their competitive activity to augment their chances at cooperative behavior with external companies. IAL and the Content Group, for example, avoided the software applications business, despite their knowledge of critical technologies.

The second insight concerns Lever 4 (internal organization and culture): *Separating groups pursuing Job 1 and Job 2 is a powerful strategy.* Intel managers decided to separate groups organizationally if they had potentially conflicting agendas or objectives. Here, organizational design can be an important strategic tool both internally, by keeping certain groups distinct, and externally, by communicating a level of neutrality to outside partners. Intel used both of these approaches to signal to complementors that it could act for the good of the industry and not only for itself.

Chapter Five

Alternative Strategies for Platform Leadership

Microsoft and Cisco

As we noted in chapter 1, there are many high-tech markets where companies want to establish their products as the platform of choice. Companies that believe they are competing in platform markets range from established firms like Microsoft in "old" technologies such as desktop PC software to start-up firms like Palm in new areas such as handheld computing devices and NTT DoCoMo in services for Web-enabled cell phones. In between are a wide variety of high-tech markets and competitors. Firms that make data-encryption technology for Web-based publishing, for example, want their technologies to be the platforms of choice for electronic publishing around the world. Firms that make application servers and tools for developing Web sites or caching Internet content have similar ambitions. The main requirements to be in a platform business seem to be that a company develops and sells a core product that is (1) part of a system that is itself evolving and (2) not valuable itself without complementary products or services. The platform product also needs to have interfaces to the outside world so that other firms can make complements to complete the system.

Most platform leaders and platform-leader wannabes do many of the same things Intel has done for the past decade. They try to build communities of customers and third parties who are interested in building complements or offering complementary services. Many propose new interface standards or join with other firms and organizations to create standards that enable their platform or core product to connect to other products. Most, if not all, have to reveal some of their proprietary technology to these potential producers of complements so that they can make their products compatible and easy to interconnect. Many, but not all, invest in R&D that explores potential complements or applications. Some of these firms will make at least a few complements or enabling tools themselves.

In this chapter, we discuss two prominent companies that are well-known platform leaders in high-tech: Microsoft (PC operating systems and related technologies) and Cisco (Internet-based networking technology). Both companies resemble Intel in many ways but compete in different contexts with somewhat different leadership strategies. As we will see in this and the following chapter, platform leaders all need to manipulate the same four levers. But they may choose to use these levers in different ways, depending on their particular market and technological situations. In the cases of Microsoft and Cisco, for example, we can see some clear differences with Intel that make a lot of sense in their contexts:

1. *Scope of the firm*: Intel relied mainly on outside companies for complements to the microprocessor component and the broader PC platform. Its expertise was limited primarily to hardware design and microprocessor programming. Moreover, the enormous investments required to design and mass-produce each new generation of microprocessors left Intel vulnerable to support from complementors (especially PC manufacturers and software applications and operating systems companies). Microsoft, too, partnered with third parties and stayed close to its core technical competence in software, but had the resources to make many of its own software complements (i.e., software applications for the Windows operating system) and thereby

ensure that new generations of its platform would be successful. Cisco partnered with third parties as well, but tended to *acquire* companies that provided either complementary technical skills or new alternative technologies, either in software or hardware or both.

2. *Product technology*: Intel relied mainly on open PC interfaces that many companies, including Intel and Microsoft, helped to establish and evolve. In contrast, Microsoft had a more dominant position with its Windows operating system and established interfaces that were mainly proprietary. Cisco's networking technology relied primarily on open Internet or other industry standards. This strategy prevented Cisco from introducing much proprietary technology and opened the company to severe competition, although Cisco had the ability to influence the direction of these open standards by championing particular technologies and incorporating them into its software platform.

3. *Relationships with external complementors*: Intel had limited skills outside of microprocessor design. Therefore, establishing trust with complementors, especially software companies and PC vendors, was a key part of its strategy. Although Intel showed restraint in invading the territory of complementors, it sometimes moved into specialized complementary markets such as chip sets and had to manage conflicts of interest with these partners. Microsoft, too, limited the scope of its business but always made it clear that it might compete with its software and even hardware complementors. Its strategy for software applications was to enter any "horizontal" business of large market potential. Its strategy for Windows was to ward off potential competition by enhancing the operating system with numerous features or technologies that complementors often sold as separate products. Cisco, perhaps more like Intel, worked on establishing good relations with its complementors, but, more so than Intel or Microsoft, the company was likely to try to acquire any firm that made an important complementary technology or potentially threatening substitute technology.

4. *Internal organization*: Intel tried to establish a "Chinese wall" to separate internal product and R&D groups that might have

conflicting interests among themselves or with third-party complementors that relied on Intel microprocessors and the PC platform. In contrast, Microsoft long maintained that it did *not* have such a wall between its operating systems groups and applications groups. Microsoft also insisted that "integration" of different applications, systems, and networking technologies (such as embedding an Internet browser in Windows) was central to its strategy and good for customers. Microsoft had the market power to push its choices forward, although antitrust litigation in the United States and Europe was forcing Microsoft to make some adjustments to its behavior. Cisco had a de facto separation of many product groups because of their histories as independent firms acquired through acquisitions. Nonetheless, the trend in Cisco as well was to integrate as many product technologies as possible and offer comprehensive "solutions" that required breaking down the organizational separation of different product groups.

Make Your Own Complements: The Microsoft Strategy

In many ways, Microsoft functioned as the alter ego to Intel since the launching of the IBM PC in 1981. It dominated the software side of the PC platform with MS-DOS (Microsoft Disk Operating System), introduced with the IBM PC in 1981, and then Windows, which was introduced for the mass market with version 3.0 in 1990. Indeed, the high-tech press often referred to the combination of these two companies as "Wintel," referring to the dual dominance and mutual interdependence of Windows and the Intel microprocessor. The operating system was as essential as the microprocessor in that it allowed a PC to run an almost infinite variety of software applications. As we noted earlier, Windows also contained APIs (the code routines that activate functions in the operating system and are necessary to write applications programs), and special programs, called drivers, that operated components of the PC system such as the video screen, the keyboard and mouse, and memory storage devices.

PC users demanded what has been called "backward compatibility" (the ability to read files made using older versions of their applications). As a result, no one company could easily change any of the hardware or software standards that made up the PC. (This was not as true in the early days of the PC industry, when various companies competed to set the software and hardware standards that came to define the PC architecture.) Microsoft in 2001, for example, could not make radical changes to Windows even though it owns the interfaces because this would destroy compatibility with existing software assets and applications, hardware platforms, and complementary peripherals. Were Microsoft to attempt such changes, it would likely alienate a large portion of the 400 or so million PC users and the 4.5 million software engineers who wrote Windows programs.[1] Former Microsoft VP Brad Silverberg, who headed Windows 3.1 and Windows 95 development, pointed to compatibility as a key reason why his group did not improve Windows earlier:

> [Windows] 3.0 was pretty big and pretty slow; 3.1 made a lot of improvements. . . . [But] at some point you can't break compatibility, either. It's the interfaces. Some of them define the APIs through the applications. In some ways, if we could do them over again, we know how we could do it so we could write the system faster. But once you have those interfaces, you're pretty much locked. You can't just change them and break applications. A system like we have, we don't own it. The ISVs [independent software vendors] own it. We [the Windows/MS-DOS group] exist for one purpose, which is to run applications. And if you break an application, you don't have a reason for being any more.[2]

When Silverberg said that the Windows/MS-DOS group existed to run applications, he did not mean that Windows itself generated no sales or profits for Microsoft. What he meant is that Windows by itself has little or no value without applications. It was in this area—*complementary applications*—that Microsoft's strategy for platform leadership departed most notably from Intel's.

Unlike Intel, Microsoft early on in its history moved aggressively into making its own complements—applications such as Word and Excel, later joined in the Office suite. Other major Microsoft applications included Outlook, an e-mail, scheduler, and information manager embedded in Windows; Exchange, a workgroup server; and enterprise products such as the BackOffice suite of servers and programming tools, and the SQL Server database system. In fact, of Microsoft's $23 billion in fiscal 2000 sales, almost half ($10.47 billion) came from applications and developer support tools like programming languages and compilers. The remainder of Microsoft's sales came from Windows ($9.38 billion) and consumer products, including services sold through the MSN Web site ($3.11 billion).[3] The scale and importance of Microsoft's applications business distinguished it from Intel, which made a relatively small (though increasing) number of complements to the microprocessor. In 2000, only 20 to 30 percent of Intel's revenues came from non-microprocessor products and services, including investment income.[4]

Despite this difference, there were similarities. Like Intel, Microsoft dominated a key part of the PC platform (the operating system) with a mainly proprietary technology (MS-DOS, and then Windows). Also like Intel, Microsoft worked hard to evolve its operating system and shared the interface specifications openly with potential complementors (such as PC hardware and peripherals manufacturers, software applications companies, and, increasingly, consumer electronics and telecommunications companies). Microsoft also resembled Intel in that it continually added features to its software platform that were once separate products sold mainly by complementors. But where Intel did this incrementally (such as by adding features to its microprocessors to make them handle graphics or mathematical processing better and thereby eliminate the need for complementary chip sets), Microsoft added a broad range of functions to its operating system platform. The result was a blurring of once-traditional distinctions among operating systems, applications programs, and networking or communications programs.[5]

This extension of the software platform functionality into what were once complementary applications has been a general trend in the software business. Operating systems built not only by Microsoft, but also by Apple, IBM, Hewlett-Packard, Sun Microsystems, and others increasingly bundled small applications (e.g., calendars, screen savers, and file management utilities) as well as sophisticated communications and networking features, such as for dialing into computer systems from remote locations, communicating across networks of computers, and accessing and browsing the Internet. The most well-known application of this type is Internet browser software.

Microsoft made international headlines when it began bundling its Internet Explorer browser with Windows 95 "for free," and then strong-armed PC manufacturers to accept this bundle in order to preserve their Windows licenses. The potential illegality of some of Microsoft's practices, as well as the negative impact of these moves on Netscape—a company that first introduced its Navigator browser in 1995 as a complement to Windows—became the focus of the 1998 antitrust case against Microsoft. (Microsoft lost the case, but the remedies were still under debate during late 2001.) The reason for Microsoft's aggressive response to Netscape was that the Navigator browser could also be a foundation for using Web-based applications, making Windows less valuable or even unnecessary for many PC users and potentially harming Microsoft's desktop applications business as well. In this section, we discuss the evolution of Microsoft's software foundation, its applications business, and the effort to merge Windows and applications with the Internet in order to create a new software "platform" (called Windows.NET) for the future.[6]

Platform Evolution: From DOS to Windows

When Bill Gates and Paul Allen founded Microsoft in 1975, they did not conceive of their company as a platform leader. Rather, they planned to make BASIC (initially designed for minicomputers) and other programming languages for the new PCs that were just starting to hit the market. They saw programming languages as the major software business of the time. There were no PC operating systems or applications programs available before the Apple II, introduced in 1977. The few hundreds or thousands of PC users that existed during the mid-1970s had to make most of their own software, and for this task they needed programming languages. As the market expanded and the need for "packaged" or standardized and ready-to-go software programs emerged, Microsoft moved deftly into new businesses. Eventually, Gates and his lieutenants adopted the strategy of trying to dominate desktop PC software, from operating systems to other "horizontal" applications such as word processing and spreadsheets.

INCREMENTAL EVOLUTION AND TECHNOLOGY BUNDLING Microsoft has always chosen to evolve its operating system (or "software platform" as Microsoft calls it) incrementally. It gradually offered multiple versions of the software platform (i.e., for individuals, groups, and corporate users). Microsoft has paid special attention to maintaining the ability of its operating systems to run applications written for previous versions. This commitment to backward compatibility succeeded as a business strategy because users valued the ability to run or at least use data from their old applications, but it made Windows somewhat awkward to develop, evolve, and use—thus locking Microsoft into a mode of incremental evolution and innovation.

A critical event in Microsoft's emergence as the PC software platform leader happened in 1980. IBM executives asked Gates to develop an operating system for its new PC, the IBM PC, for which Intel was designing the microprocessor. The story is well known: Microsoft acquired a rudimentary operating system (modeled on the primitive CP/M operating system) from Seattle Computer for $75,000, and this became the core of DOS. At the time, IBM saw itself—not Intel or Microsoft—as the platform leader for the PC. IBM had patented the basic input-output (BIOS) program code, a virtual bottleneck in the system that controlled key functions between the hardware and the software. But Compaq, with the help of Microsoft and software companies such as Phoenix Technologies, legally cloned the IBM BIOS code in 1983. Thereafter, Microsoft quickly emerged as the most powerful provider of software products and programming standards for IBM-compatible PCs. Microsoft continued to enhance DOS through a half-dozen new versions introduced through the mid-1990s. These new versions added various features, special programs, and networking functions to the original DOS core, although Windows became the mass-market operating system of choice for PC users after 1990.

Windows originated as a graphical user interface, patterned after Apple's Macintosh operating system (introduced in 1984), that sat on top of DOS. Microsoft began developing Windows even before Apple released the Macintosh, but not until 1990, with Windows 3.0, did it have a commercially viable version. Later versions of Windows (Windows 95, 98, and ME) still included some old DOS code to run DOS applications. But these products were fully integrated operating systems, not merely graphical layers. Each version of Windows came with an increasingly full set of API.

Microsoft also designed a new version of Windows from scratch in the early 1990s, initially for corporate users and servers. This was Windows NT, first introduced in 1993 and later renamed Windows 2000. Microsoft planned to use this product to replace the original Windows code base for mass-market users, which had evolved somewhat clumsily from Windows 3.0 through Windows 95/98 and Windows ME, introduced in 2000. Microsoft also had another variation of the operating system under development and scheduled for release in late 2001 called Windows XP (initials that supposedly stand for "experience"). Microsoft based this version on the Windows NT/2000 code base. The company also hoped to use a consumer version of XP as an "always-on" operating system for the home, controlling multiple PCs simultaneously, cable TV set-top boxes, and programmable home appliances such as clock radios, music systems, and wall panel displays.

Windows XP was Microsoft's first major revision of the mass-market operating system since Windows 95. It demonstrated Microsoft's powerful position as a platform leader and its tendency to become a target of critics and antitrust agencies in the United States and Europe—again. In the antitrust case litigated initially during 1998–1999, the U.S. courts found Microsoft guilty of inappropriately using its market power with Windows to persuade companies not to support Netscape's Navigator browser and inappropriately integrating Microsoft's Internet Explorer browser with the Windows code base. An appellate court in 2001 overturned the government's proposal to break Microsoft into two separate companies. Microsoft also made policy changes to allow PC manufacturers to load more non-Microsoft software on new versions of Windows, such as XP.[7] The courts left it somewhat unclear, however, to what extent it was legal for Microsoft to continue bundling new features into future versions of Windows. The courts were likely to evaluate challenges on a case-by-case basis, trying to weigh potential harm to competitors versus potential benefits to consumers.[8]

The problem with Windows XP was Microsoft's decision to include various Internet-related technologies within the new operating system. Gates and company hoped these new technologies would then become industry standards—dominated, of course, by Microsoft. The bundled technologies included Microsoft's version of instant messaging (incompatible with AOL's technology, which was the market leader) and its multimedia player (incompatible with RealNetworks' technology, another market leader in this area). Windows XP also contained services to support e-commerce shopping and personal identification. Users could input their credit card numbers, home addresses, and e-mail addresses once, and then Microsoft's Passport technology would transmit this information directly to any Web site the user visited. The browser embedded in test versions of XP also contained a button that brought users directly to MSN, Microsoft's Web portal, with access to services for instant messaging, Internet mail, e-mail alerts, shopping, digital photo processing, ad infinitum. There were potentially enormous synergies across the services accessible through Windows XP: The MSN Web site had more than 50 million users each month; their free Internet-based e-mail (HotMail) had some 100 million users; the instant messaging service had about 30 million users; Passport accounts numbered more than 150 million. All these numbers could increase dramatically as Microsoft shipped an expected 160 million copies of Windows XP on new PCs in 2002. Microsoft used the code name "Hailstorm" for the array of Web services it hoped to offer using Passport as a base technology. These services ranged from automatically updating calendars when a user purchased tickets and made appointments online to notifying users of specific events or purchase opportunities.[9]

PC manufacturers generally did not want more government interference in the industry and preferred to have Windows XP come out on schedule; they viewed it as an essential driver of sales for new PCs in a period of flat or declining revenues.[10] Antitrust experts and Microsoft critics, however, voiced many concerns. Should Microsoft be allowed to continue pushing its own technologies and services? Was it wise to let one company collect sensitive shopping and identification information on individuals?

Microsoft's decision not to include Sun Microsystem's Java technology with Windows XP, for example, was controversial. Java is a neutral programming language that enables the PC to run on different operating systems, making computers less dependent on Windows to run applications. But, because many Web sites already used Java for animation and other small applications, lack of support for Java in Windows XP meant that users would have to go to a special site to download a utility to view Java-enabled Web sites properly. Or Web masters might decide to use a

Microsoft alternative rather than Java in the future—striking a major blow against Sun.[11] The Java controversy continued a long-standing dispute between Sun and Microsoft. Microsoft had licensed Java in the mid-1990s and modified it so that programmers could write applications that ran better on Windows. These modifications violated Sun's licensing terms. Sun sued Microsoft in 1997. In the final settlement, reached in 2001, Microsoft ended up paying Sun $20 million. Microsoft executives, in turn, decided not to work with Java anymore.[12]

Microsoft provoked another dispute with Kodak with regard to technology in Windows XP for editing and printing digital photographs. Microsoft initially decided to adopt as its default a standard incompatible with Kodak's technology and to make it a nine-step process for a user to switch to a competing technology, such as Kodak's. In addition, Microsoft planned to include a feature in Windows XP that would direct users who wanted to buy prints of their photographs to companies that paid Microsoft to be listed in Windows and agreed to pay Microsoft a fee for each print. Kodak felt betrayed because its engineers had worked with Microsoft for a year on the technology and then found themselves "frozen out" of Windows XP, while Microsoft seemed to be leveraging the knowledge it had acquired from working with Kodak to exploit a new business opportunity for itself. Microsoft relented and in a later beta version of Windows XP changed the feature to allow users to select the photo editing software of their choice without making the Microsoft technology the default selection. This disagreement over digital photography technology is another example of how a platform leader can exert its power—and potentially abuse its position—to make or break the business models of other companies, including potential partners.[13]

Some critics expressed concern about a feature in beta versions of Windows XP called Internet Explorer Smart Tags. This feature automatically scanned Web sites that a user visited and inserted links beneath key words that brought the user directly to Web sites of Microsoft's choosing. To some people, the technology not only gave Microsoft undue power to influence how people surfed the Web, but violated the open nature of Internet browsing.[14]

These examples show Microsoft's enormous power over the desktop PC platform as well as the Internet browser. Competitors, customers, and complementors had little choice but to rely on Microsoft's judgment as well as government oversight to make sure Microsoft did not push its advantage too far.

Despite its power, Microsoft faced stiff competition in both business and newer consumer markets. Some businesses preferred competing operating systems UNIX and Linux. Windows NT far outstripped versions of UNIX in unit sales since NT's launch, first for use on corporate PCs and later for enterprise servers. Servers running Windows 2000 had an estimated 41 percent of the market in 2000.[15] For large server applications, however, most companies still preferred to use versions of UNIX and powerful non-Intel workstations sold by Sun Microsystems, IBM, HP, and Compaq. As we discuss in chapter 6, the open source Linux operating system, available free over the Web as well as through companies such as Red Hat and VA Linux, was slow to catch on with mass-market PC users because it was difficult to install and had few applications. However, many corporate back offices used Linux to run Web server software. In the Web server market, Microsoft bundled its Web server software with both Windows NT and 2000, but the leading product was another open source program, Apache, distributed free over the Internet as well as through some companies. Firms such as IBM also offered support services for Apache.

In newer consumer markets, the Palm operating system (Palm OS) dominated the PDA business with an 80 percent market share in 2000. It dwarfed sales of Microsoft's Windows CE/Pocket PC, which had about 14 percent of the market, although one source predicted Pocket PC could have a 35 percent market share by 2004.[16] In Europe, the Symbian joint venture—backed by Ericsson, Motorola, and Nokia, the three leading makers of cell phones—provided another operating system for cell phones and presented fierce competition to Microsoft's Stinger operating system, which was only in the trial stage. Microsoft's forays into various consumer electronics markets, too, faced stiff competition. These efforts included the Xbox video game player (shipped November 2001) and Ultimate TV (Microsoft's latest entry for cable TV and satellite TV control boxes, launched in spring 2001).[17]

"OPEN BUT NOT OPEN" PLATFORM INTERFACES   Unlike in these newer consumer markets, Microsoft had more influence over home and business customers who had already invested in buying or building software products to complement Windows. Thanks to applications compatibility, these customers continued to use Microsoft's software assets as Windows evolved. Even Microsoft's Pocket PC could run cut-down versions of Office and read files from many standard Windows programs; some customers found this a compelling reason to buy PDAs running Pocket PC rather than Palm OS, even though new software extensions made it possible for Palm devices to read Windows applications. Moreover, customers who had invested in buying or building DOS and then Windows applications were reluctant to switch to alternative operating systems for their desktop needs. This technical "lock-in" was essential to Microsoft's continued domination of the desktop PC software platform. Intel benefited from the same technical lock-in since customers generally could not switch hardware platforms and run the same applications software, unless they were using applications written in a cross-platform programming language such as Java or deploying Web-based products hosted on servers and accessed through a platform-neutral browser.

Like Intel with its programming interfaces for the microprocessor, Microsoft considered the DOS and later the Windows programming standards as open. It broadly distributed specifications and programming information for free or a minimal charge to companies that it considered complementors. Even competitors could get this information relatively easily from the open market.

Nonetheless, as with the Intel microprocessor, the Windows programming interface standards were *not open* in the sense that Microsoft—not any group of companies or a standards body—controlled their design and future evolution. Furthermore, like Intel, Microsoft would sometimes withhold technical information from firms that it considered competitors, as it did on occasion, for example, with Netscape and IBM. Unlike vendors associated with the open source software movement, including Netscape with its Navigator browser, Microsoft did not give away the actual source code to its products. Thus, applications developers outside the company were at a disadvantage in creating products that worked well with Windows versus Microsoft's applications product groups, which had access to source code and could easily consult the Windows developers and sometimes even include former Windows developers on the applications teams.[18]

LEVERAGE BETWEEN THE PLATFORM AND COMPLEMENTS   Microsoft used its Lever 2 strategy (control platform interfaces and technical information) to gain market advantage in those complementary markets that it had decided to enter (Lever 3). Not surprisingly, the possibility that Microsoft used these levers to create an unfair advantage in applications development was a major issue in the antitrust trial. Some competitors complained, for example, that Microsoft applications programmers had access not only to Windows engineers but also to "undocumented calls" or low-level APIs found in Windows, which they might use when writing applications.[19] Although it was not clear how useful undocumented APIs were, the combination of the software platform and applications software groups within one company granted some technical advantages to Microsoft when creating complementary applications.[20]

Moreover, even without considering potential technical advantages such as undocumented APIs, Microsoft clearly leveraged its position as the PC software platform leader when it came to the complements business. It frequently made investments and commitments, as well as adopted particular standards and policies, that mutually reinforced both businesses. For example, in the late 1980s and early 1990s, Microsoft managers committed to Windows as their new standard environment and quickly authorized graphical versions of Microsoft's main applications. These products successfully challenged Lotus (later acquired by IBM) and WordPerfect (later acquired by Corel) in the spreadsheet and word-processor markets. Both of these competitors had been the market leaders by far when Windows 3.0 first appeared. But both companies fell behind Microsoft in adopting Windows as the new software platform and delayed introducing graphical versions of their products. One reason for this delay was their decision to invest in applications development for IBM's OS/2 (which Microsoft had publicly supported but abandoned in favor of Windows), in part due to the limited memory capabilities of earlier versions of Windows.[21]

When Netscape (founded in 1994) introduced its Navigator Internet browser in 1995, this was a new and highly promising complementary application to Windows as well as other operating systems such as UNIX and Macintosh. Because the browser posed a potential threat to both their software platform and applications businesses, Microsoft executives and senior engineers quickly decided to embed the browser in Windows 95 and head off this threat. Navigator's share of the browser market dropped from a peak of 90 percent or so in 1995 to about 15 percent in 2000.[22]

Microsoft also designed its Office suite and other applications to work well with the Windows interface—an integration between the software platform and applications that Microsoft management believed was in the best interest of consumers.[23] Not surprisingly, Microsoft was revising Office to work especially well with the new version of Windows, and planned to rename the applications suite "Office XP."[24] The company intended to build more applications for stand-alone PCs and the Internet (including products as part of the .NET initiative) that took full advantage of features in the latest versions of Windows. Microsoft would most likely continue this blurring of boundaries between its software platform and complementary applications and Internet standards.

In a sense, Microsoft "forced" its customers to upgrade their applications because of how it manipulated the standards that defined some areas of compatibility. Essential to Microsoft's business model was that it receive not only revenues from new sales of Windows and applications but also from "upgrade" sales as users moved to new versions of Windows and applications. Like Intel and PC manufacturers with the hardware platform, Microsoft faced the challenge that the PC and software programs were so powerful by the late 1990s that few users felt a pressing need to upgrade.

How did Microsoft reconcile its commitment to applications compatibility with its need to generate revenue from upgrade sales? Microsoft maintained "backward compatibility" but did not always guarantee "forward compatibility." For example, users of programs written for Windows 95 or later versions could generally read files and run programs written for Windows 3.1 or DOS. However, users who were still running DOS or even an old version of Windows, such as 3.1, could not run applications designed for Windows 95 or newer versions. Similarly, if a user wrote a report using Office 97, a colleague using Office 95 could not read the report unless the Office 97 user had saved them in the old file formats.

Another problem was that older computers might not be able to run new versions of Windows very well, requiring that people buy a new computer. Microsoft (along with Intel, PC manufacturers, and many software applications producers) depended on this "upgrade cycle" phenomenon as central to its business model, even though it was also committed to maintaining backward compatibility to enable users to retain their software assets. In Microsoft's case, it had a special ability to influence users because it dominated both the software platform and highly popular applications.

Microsoft's Applications Business

Just as it did not invent the BASIC programming language or the core of the DOS product, Microsoft did not invent its first applications for the PC—games such as Flight Simulator (which Microsoft bought in the early 1980s), or office and personal productivity products such as the spreadsheet and word processor (which Microsoft copied). Again, it pursued a strategy of following other firms and incrementally introducing innovations. Microsoft made many acquisitions (though usually of small companies) to buy new software products, ranging from DOS to Power-Point (a graphics presentation program) and FrontPage (a tool for designing Web pages), and invested billions of dollars in complements producers and infrastructure providers, including AT&T and various cable TV and satellite companies. The April 2001 acquisition of Great Plains Software for $1.1 billion illustrated Microsoft's plans to move aggressively into applications for small businesses, a $19 billion market, including customer-relationship, human-resource, and supply-chain management software.[25]

Microsoft's personal productivity products for word processing (Word) and spreadsheet analysis (Excel) were most important in terms of sales and market awareness. They originated in applications programs written years before for mainframe and minicomputers as well as for the Xerox Alto PC prototype and the Xerox Star workstation. The launch of innovative products by other PC software companies prompted Microsoft to introduce various competing products during the 1980s, such as personal finance software, a market dominated by Intuit and its Quicken product.

Once the IBM PC and PC-compatible markets began taking off after 1981, Microsoft began introducing "good enough" competing products and marketed them aggressively throughout the rest of the decade. We can see the extent of Microsoft's ambitions in a 1991 quote from former executive VP Mike Maples, who headed operating systems and applications development during the late 1980s and early 1990s: "If someone thinks we're not after Lotus and after WordPerfect and after Borland, they're confused. My job is to get a fair share of the software applications market, and to me that's 100 percent."[26]

EARLY AND AGGRESSIVE MOVEMENT INTO APPLICATIONS   Microsoft entered the applications market deliberately, shortly after its entrance into operating systems. Company programmers began work on spreadsheets in 1980 by studying the two products that had started the market—VisiCalc, introduced in 1979 for the Apple II by Software Arts (later acquired by the Lotus Development Corporation, founded in 1982 and now a division of IBM), and SuperCalc, developed for 8-bit CP/M machines by a company called Sorcem (later acquired by Computer Associates). Microsoft released the first version of its spreadsheet, dubbed Multiplan, in August 1982 for the Apple II, followed by versions for CP/M computers and the IBM PC.[27] Lotus 1-2-3, introduced by Lotus in 1983, provided the main inspiration for Excel, introduced in 1985 as Microsoft's successor product to Multiplan. Lotus had as much as 80 percent of the U.S. spreadsheet market in the early 1980s and was the number-one PC software company in annual sales until Microsoft took over the lead for good in 1988.[28] In the 1990s and early 2000s, particularly by bundling Excel with Word and PowerPoint in the Office suite of applications, Microsoft Excel far outstripped Lotus 1-2-3 in sales and ultimately captured some 90 to 95 percent of this market.[29]

The story was similar in word processing, one of the most important complementary applications for the PC. The MicroPro company started the market in 1979 with their WordStar product, written for CP/M machines.[30] Because it was difficult to use, there remained an opening for other early entrants such as the former WordPerfect Corporation (founded in 1979) and Microsoft. Using some technology inherited from employees who joined from Xerox PARC, Microsoft launched Word in 1983 for the PC and in 1984 for the Macintosh. The Macintosh versions of Word and Excel helped lay a foundation for Microsoft to design graphical applications products for the new Windows software platform. PC Word did not receive as much attention from Microsoft as the more advanced graphical applications and it soon fell far behind WordPerfect in sales for DOS machines. But later versions of Word competed head to head and then surpassed WordPerfect in sales for Windows machines and eventually for total word-processor sales.

Microsoft followed its spreadsheet and word-processing programs with a host of other applications, such as for presentations, database management, project management, e-mail, personal scheduling, desktop publishing, home finance, video games, and enterprise applications, usually for both the Macintosh and Windows PCs.

In the personal productivity area, which generated the bulk of Microsoft's applications sales, the company initially concentrated on stand-alone products, like Word and Excel. It soon found that it could attract more customers by bundling products together and dramatically lowering prices. As a result, after 1990, when the Office suite first appeared, Microsoft gradually replaced most individual desktop applications sales with Office, and priced the bundle at about the same level it used to sell just one individual application. The Office suite became so commonly used that U.S. Department of Justice documents proposing remedies for the Microsoft antitrust case dubbed it an "applications platform" in its own right because many companies build applications that depend on features in Office, particularly from the Excel spreadsheet program.[31]

NO "CHINESE WALL"   Another issue discussed frequently during the antitrust trial was that Windows gave Microsoft at least an indirect advantage over its competitors—other complementors of Windows— in developing and marketing applications products. In this sense, Microsoft relied on complements made in-house not simply to drive sales of its software platform product but also to generate enormous revenues and profits. Microsoft designed Windows as well as MS-DOS, and its developers understood the intricacies and idiosyncrasies of these operating systems better than anyone else. Since the late 1980s, one executive has usually headed both the systems and applications divisions. Gates and other executives openly encouraged the movement of people and sharing of technical knowledge across the different product groups. (Gates openly admitted in a March 1995 interview published in the *Wall Street Journal* that "There is no Chinese wall" between the applications and systems groups, and that "We don't block input going in either direction."[32])

The Windows teams had a large incentive to ensure that popular applications ran properly on new versions of Windows. Therefore, it was common for Windows developers to help even competitors such as Lotus and Netscape get their products running properly. It was also common, however, for Microsoft to deliver key technical information late to these same competitors in order to give its own applications groups an advantage. For example, beta versions of Windows 3.0 omitted the documentation for 32-bit mode applications support on the Intel 386 microprocessor until just before the product shipped.[33] Microsoft also was late in providing both IBM and Netscape with important technical information on Windows 95.[34]

Not all of Microsoft's relationships with complementors were adversarial. Microsoft had a long history of working closely with certain hardware vendors and no doubt had intimate relationships with these companies. Microsoft's contacts with Compaq, for example, dated back to 1982, when this PC vendor, with Microsoft's help, introduced the first IBM PC "clone."[35] But we must conclude that Microsoft, compared to Intel, placed a lower priority on gaining and maintaining the trust of its complementors, particularly software applications complementors. A major reason would seem to be Microsoft's ability to create its own software complements, if necessary. Its recent venture into home game machine design with the Xbox (a $20 billion market) also indicated that Microsoft had the resources to create a new hardware platform that would rely on Microsoft software, even if this move might create tensions with Sony, a partner for its PC business. The Xbox competed not only with Nintendo machines (e.g., GameCube, Nintendo 64) but also with Sony PlayStation, and it boasted a much more powerful microprocessor than either rival's machine. Sony was a major producer of PCs that utilized the Windows operating system and was not likely to be happy with Microsoft's entry into the game machine market.

Apart from the technical advantages of combining Windows and applications developers with an intimate knowledge of its programming interfaces in one company, Microsoft also seemed to have had a marketing advantage: The company developed close relationships with many hardware vendors, who bundled Microsoft applications along with Windows on their PCs. Microsoft also had close relationships with retail software stores, which gave prominent space to Windows applications. And, thanks to agreements with hardware vendors, millions of customers saw the Microsoft name every time they started up their computers. These marketing relationships developed brand awareness and helped Microsoft sell its products—both the very good ones such as Excel and Word and formerly unpopular or new applications such as Works, PowerPoint, Mail, and Access.

We should note that bundling applications together (for retail sale or on the PC hardware), lowering prices, advertising the Microsoft name, and selling aggressively to retail stores were not enough in themselves to guarantee a vibrant complements business. Products had to be close to or as good as the market leaders in their categories *and* they had to be relatively early to market. The low market penetration of Microsoft Money (introduced in 1991) compared to Quicken (introduced around 1985) attests to this reality. Microsoft succeeded in a wide range of applications because it had usually been early to market (it rarely has been necessary to be first) and it strived to match or surpass competitors in product features and prices. Microsoft groups developed many award-winning applications products, even though they usually took three or four versions of a product to "get it right." Versions 3 and 4 of Internet Explorer, for example, were widely believed to have matched and then surpassed the Netscape Navigator browser in features and reliability.[36]

ENABLING TOOLS AND TECHNOLOGIES   Like Intel, Microsoft was active in promoting standards that would be beneficial to it as a platform leader: first the DOS standards and then the Windows standards. This ensured that new computers and new applications programs continued to be available and compatible with new versions of Windows. Microsoft did not rely on a central laboratory, like the IAL. But the DOS and then Windows product groups engaged in a similar set of activities. Microsoft developers held annual development forums for applications developers to demonstrate how the Windows programming interfaces were evolving. The company shipped SDKs with programming tools and sample code to help applications developers. Microsoft also worked closely with hardware component vendors like Intel as well as PC manufacturers like Compaq, Dell, IBM, and HP to make sure they understood how to design computers that could use the latest versions of its operating systems.

Like Intel, Microsoft provided enabling technologies to applications developers. Examples include the Object Linking and Embedding (OLE) technology for sharing functions and data (which benefited from prior work done at Lotus and Novell), a newer version of OLE for distributed Web objects, called Active-X, and the Visual Basic programming tool. Microsoft made beta versions of these technologies available to outside developers and held specification reviews and developers conferences before releasing new versions to the public. Microsoft also published volumes of detailed technical information on these and other tools, and continued to hold conferences for developers to discuss the future evolution of these technologies. Nonetheless, over the years, Microsoft appears to have been the most enthusiastic and expert user of these enabling technologies, in both its operating systems products and in its applications.

Once more, as the provider of the software platform *and* key enabling technologies, Microsoft seemed to possess an advantage in applications development, even if it shared all details of the specifications and volumes of documentation with other applications developers.[37] To be fair, however, one could also argue that Microsoft provided the software industry with a software platform for applications and useful development-support tools. In addition to Microsoft, thousands of applications companies have effectively used Microsoft technologies for many years. Microsoft stimulated a huge complements business as well as fed this market directly.

INTERNAL AND EXTERNAL CONFLICTS OF INTEREST   Like Intel, Microsoft's dual role as both a platform leader and a complements producer generated tensions within and outside the company. Managers and programmers who worked on operating systems and related technologies, for example, were primarily interested in making Windows work with different applications and hardware combinations, whether they were Microsoft applications or products from other companies. Microsoft applications groups, however, primarily wanted to take advantage of their special understanding of Windows. At the same time, Microsoft product groups that made versions of their applications for the Macintosh preferred to be more neutral. As a result, Microsoft had to deal with numerous internal as well as external disagreements. The antitrust trial provided ample evidence of this, as Microsoft executives clashed internally over strategy and angered long-term customers and partners such as Intel and IBM.[38]

To make matters worse, Microsoft executives made some decisions over the years to improve efficiency in their software platform and applications businesses that exacerbated problems among company personnel and customers. For example, Microsoft policy since the mid-1990s was to merge the code bases of Windows and Macintosh products and, if there was a choice to make, favor designs that made the code run especially well on Windows—Microsoft's largest applications market. This was a business and technical decision that saved Microsoft from having to develop, test, and support two sets of applications products. One problem, though, was that the code-merging often hurt the performance of Macintosh applications such as Word. This created internal tension between applications groups who made products for the Macintosh and those working on Windows and created external tensions with Apple and Macintosh users. Microsoft also standardized many features across different products, often with considerable opposition from internal product groups that felt they had to compromise too much on their designs.

Microsoft addressed these internal conflicts by manipulating Lever 4—the internal organization. Most important, Gates placed well-respected executives (such as Mike Maples and later Paul Maritz) at the top of both the software platform and applications businesses and got directly involved in resolving disputes when necessary.[39] Having a common enemy, such as Netscape or the threat of the Internet, also helped marshal Microsoft's product groups to overcome their disagreements and adopt common goals, such as developing a browser or reorganizing product plans along the new .NET initiative.

Gates and other Microsoft executives, such as CEO and President Steve Ballmer and former Group VP Maritz (who left Microsoft in September 2000), did not completely succeed in resolving internal conflicts. Prior to deciding on .NET, a number of senior Microsoft executives wanted the company to introduce a fully Web-based operating system, such as one that relied on the cross-platform Java programming language. This would have competed directly with Windows. Gates vetoed the proposal and several key executives and engineers left the company during 1998 to 2000.[40] These departures of talented people did not bode well for Microsoft's future, although the organization seemed to be rallying effectively around the .NET strategy.

As for conflicts with its complementors—a Lever 3 problem—the Microsoft antitrust trial cited numerous instances where Microsoft attempted to protect the exclusivity of its Windows software platform.[41] The most prominent examples involved Netscape, Intel, Apple, RealNetworks, IBM, and Compaq:

- *Netscape.* Microsoft clashed with Netscape over APIs included in the Navigator browser. These interfaces made it possible for applications developers to bypass the Windows APIs and utilize the browser as the software platform for launching Web-based applications. Microsoft executives, in a series of meetings during 1995, tried and failed to dissuade Netscape from including extensive APIs in Navigator.

- *Intel.* Microsoft clashed with Intel in 1995 when the microprocessor producer tried to introduce programming tools that bypassed Windows. As noted in chapter 4, Intel developed its own Native Signal Processing (NSP) technology to help developers build applications with advanced video and graphics capabilities without the use of special signal processing chips. Intel engineers also thought Windows was behind in tapping the potential of the Intel microprocessor. In addition, NSP interfaces were platform neutral—which meant that developers could more easily port their applications to different operating systems. Microsoft pressured PC manufacturers not to install NSP software on their computers. Ultimately, Intel gave in and agreed not to promote its NSP technology and to curtail its software development efforts. In turn, Microsoft incorporated some of the NSP features into Windows.

- *Apple.* Microsoft clashed with Apple in 1997–1998 when Apple decided to create a Windows 95 version of its technology for editing and playing multimedia content, called QuickTime. Previously, the technology worked only on the Macintosh platform, and Microsoft, as well as other companies, had proprietary products for Windows. Apple executives did not agree with Microsoft's proposal that Apple adopt the Microsoft standards for multimedia playback on Windows.

- *RealNetworks.* Microsoft clashed with RealNetworks, the market leader in streaming audio and video playback technology, when it established an alternative standard that was not based on Windows. After failing to get RealNetworks to adopt Microsoft programming interfaces, Microsoft acquired a company and invested substantially in developing its alternative technology.
- *IBM.* Microsoft clashed with IBM repeatedly over the years, such as when IBM attempted to promote OS/2 as an alternative operating system to Windows, and when it promoted its own applications (Lotus 1-2-3 and the SmartSuite of office applications). As a major PC producer, however, IBM also had to purchase millions of copies of Windows. To pressure IBM, according to the Department of Justice documents, "Microsoft punished the IBM PC Company with higher prices, a late license for Windows 95, and the withholding of technical and marketing support."[42]
- *Compaq.* Microsoft even clashed with its long-time partner Compaq, the largest PC manufacturer in the world during the 1990s and a preferred Microsoft customer (it purportedly received the lowest prices for Windows), when the PC manufacturer decided in 1996 to continue featuring Netscape Navigator on the Windows desktop and to remove the Internet Explorer and MSN icons. Microsoft threatened Compaq with a discontinuation of its Windows license. Compaq relented.

And these are only recent cases. There are many others. For example, in another incident that made national news, Microsoft was sued by Stac Electronics for copying the company's disk compression software during the early 1990s and shipping its own compression technology with version 6 of MS-DOS. Microsoft lost the case.[43]

Merging Windows, Applications, and the Internet: Microsoft.NET

Microsoft took on the challenge of the Internet as an alternative computing platform by bundling a browser with Windows and aggressively pursuing deals with PC manufacturers, AOL, and other distributors and customers to make Internet Explorer their default browser.[44] But the Internet presented a larger set of challenges to the Windows software platform and Microsoft's applications business. First, it was possible for users to access the Internet through non-Windows PCs and workstations, as well as through non-PC devices, including Web-enabled cell phones and PDAs. Second, it was possible for companies to host application products on large servers and allow users to utilize these applications through browsers running on either PCs or non-PC devices—thus potentially eliminating the need for Windows and Microsoft's desktop applications. This did not present a happy scenario for Microsoft, especially when combined with the prospect of declining sales of PCs, a trend against which Intel and PC manufacturers were also struggling.

THE NEW PLATFORM STRATEGY   As a result of this broad threat to its businesses, Microsoft in mid-2000 announced a five-year plan to evolve the Windows software platform, server products, applications, and MSN in a way that would make Internet browsing and applications hosting capabilities available as Windows "services"—that is, special programs hosted on remote servers that were available to Windows users by accessing them through .NET features. All applications and devices enabled with the .NET technology would also be able to communicate with each other, making, for example, an individual user's e-mail or data files accessible from multiple devices and locations. These elements formed the basis of Microsoft's .NET initiative, which also included a set of enabling tools for applications developers. Microsoft executives hoped that the millions of Windows developers and the thousands of applications software companies around the world would follow their lead and elevate the .NET technologies into a new industry standard for using the Internet. Microsoft described its new strategy in a June 2000 white paper:

> Microsoft is creating an advanced new generation of software that melds computing and communications in a revolutionary new way, offering every developer the tools they need to transform the Web and every other aspect of the computing experience. We call this initiative Microsoft.NET, and for the first time it enables developers, businesses, and consumers to harness technology on their terms. Microsoft.NET will allow the creation of truly distributed Web Services that will integrate and collaborate with a range of complementary services to serve customers in ways that today's dot-coms can only dream of. Microsoft.NET will drive the Next

Generation Internet. It really will make information available any time, any place and on any device.[45]

Microsoft.NET also required a new business model, at least for its applications business. Microsoft hoped that users who did not buy application programs for their PCs would at least subscribe to the online .NET versions of Microsoft products, such as Office.NET, and pay monthly rental fees. Microsoft was already experimenting with this fee-based usage model in Internet cafés, where customers could pay for using Office by the hour.[46] It also entered into an agreement with MobileStar Network and Starbucks to provide Web access to customers in Starbucks cafes.[47] In addition to these new sources of income, Microsoft also planned to sell many copies of Windows.NET and earn revenues from traditional software license fees and retail sales. Gates commented in a recent interview how he viewed .NET as an evolution of Windows and not as another "free" Internet technology: "The .NET is a Microsoft software platform. We haven't decided that Microsoft is a zero-revenue company."[48] To make the new software platform more compelling, Microsoft engineers were designing .NET applications that would work particularly well if a user accessed the Internet through a device running Windows.NET.[49]

THE NEW PRODUCT AND TOOLS PORTFOLIO   There were three core components to the new Microsoft initiative:

1. .NET software platform infrastructure and tool set for building applications (Visual Studio.NET, .NET enterprise servers, .NET Framework, and Windows.NET)
2. .NET services for users (Office.NET, Passport.NET for user authentication, and services under the Hailstorm banner for file storage, preference management, calendar management, and other functions)
3. .NET services or Web-based applications that Microsoft expected partner companies to provide

In the case of .NET, we can clearly see Microsoft trying to evolve its approach to using Lever 2. For example, unlike Windows, the .NET products, tools, and services relied heavily on open standards. These standards included Internet communications protocols and XML. The latter is an open-standard programming language defined by the World Wide Web Consortium that allows Web applications to exchange data and instructions much more easily than with other technologies such as HTML (Hypertext Markup Language), the original programming tool for the Internet.

The .NET initiative also affected Microsoft's plans to evolve its existing tools and product offerings. For example, Microsoft was designing the successor to Windows 2000 (Windows.NET) so that users could customize or personalize information, services, and applications offered from Microsoft and from third-party complementors. A redesign of the MSN online service would enable users to have a "single digital identity." The benefit was the ability to use "smart" services that would automatically deploy advanced ("smart") search and network technology to access their personal information or Web sites, from any device, through the .NET server and browser infrastructure. Microsoft planned to have Office.NET work as a service hosted from large servers and accessed through browsers. The new product would include a new natural language interface and a "smart" architecture to help users access information or collaborate over the Web. Microsoft was also building services for small businesses such as to deliver e-commerce and collaboration solutions through .NET, redesigning its server and database products, and rewriting development support tools such as Visual Studio to enable developers to design applications that could communicate more easily with each other, again, over the Web and through the .NET infrastructure.[50]

Despite these new activities, Microsoft did not abandon its attempts to "embrace and extend" the Internet and draw it closer to the Windows software platform. For example, while Microsoft wanted in-house and outside developers to use XML for .NET applications, it also encouraged developers to use Microsoft's new Java-like programming language—C# (pronounced "C sharp"), bundled with Visual Studio 2000 and Visual Studio.NET. The new language worked with an interpreter, much like Java did, and converted applications written in different languages so that they would run in the new .NET environment and work especially well with Windows.Net. Microsoft based C# on the standard C and C++ programming languages, but, unlike Java, made it a proprietary language that only ran on Microsoft operating systems—not the UNIX-based servers that power many Web sites. Microsoft executives expected their new development tools to reduce the use of Sun Microsystem's Java programming language (which had some 3 million users in 2000 and could run on any software platform) and encourage applications developers to write or rewrite programs specifically for the .NET software platform, whatever programming language they preferred.[51]

With the .NET initiative, Microsoft departed somewhat from past practices, where it often set its own standards and expected the industry to follow. This time, the company proposed new standards to the neutral World Wide Web Consortium. Microsoft submitted for review its SOAP (Simple Object Access Protocol) Contract Language and SOAP Discovery specifications, both tools to facilitate the development of .NET services. SOAP is a common communications format that allows programs built on different communications standards (such as the industry-defined CORBA standards and Microsoft's DCOM standards) to work together.[52] IBM and its Lotus subsidiary decided to support the SOAP standards after Microsoft incorporated some IBM suggestions.[53]

Microsoft's timeline for implementation of the .NET initiative was ambitious: .NET Enterprise Services and Windows 2000 Datacenter Server had already embedded the core components of the .NET software platform. Microsoft made the Visual Studio.NET and the .NET Framework available by the end of 2001, and company executives expected Microsoft and third parties to be delivering .NET products and services by 2002.[54]

Future Prospects for Microsoft's Platform Strategy: Success or Failure?

To implement the .NET initiative, Microsoft announced in August 2000 a major restructuring and shuffling of executives.

- The *Platform Products Group*, headed by Group VP Jim Allchin, was building Windows.NET (as well as other new versions of Windows) and enterprise server products (SQL server, Exchange, Biztalk).
- The *Platforms Strategy and Developer Group*, initially led by Group VP Paul Maritz until he left Microsoft in September 2000, focused on tools such as Visual Studio.NET and tried to persuade outside software developers to build applications for

.NET and other Microsoft software platforms. Microsoft did not replace Maritz, although Sanjay Parthasarathy, VP of strategy and business development, took over responsibility for the .NET strategy and evangelizing this initiative to outside developers. Like the other Group VPs, Parthasarathy reported directly to CEO Ballmer.

- The *.NET Services Group*, headed by Group VP Bob Muglia, oversaw development of the .NET architecture, user interface, and related technologies such as speech recognition.
- The *Personal Services and Devices Group* (formerly the Consumer Group), led by Group VP Rick Belluzzo, was integrating .NET services with Microsoft's MSN, TV, games, and wireless efforts.
- Finally, the *Productivity and Business Services Group*, led by Group VP Jeff Raikes, a marketing and sales veteran, supervised Office and other business tools and applications.[55]

The .NET initiative required an enormous investment by Microsoft and involved considerable risks.[56] Microsoft began pushing its new vision for .NET at the July 2000 Microsoft Professional Developers Conference, which had 6,000 attendees, mostly from applications development companies. The company was also devoting much of its $3 billion-plus in annual R&D expenditures to the effort. But, despite its powerful position as the PC software platform leader and the major producer of PC software applications, and despite some early support from companies such as eBay, the online auction firm, there was no guarantee that the 4.5 million Windows developers around the world, the thousands of applications producers that worked with current versions of Windows, and the several hundreds of millions of Windows customers would follow Microsoft's lead.

Alternative technologies posed another risk. Sun Microsystem's JINI, for example, was a new standard and networking software, based on the cross-platform Java language, that enabled any device connected to a network to communicate with other devices to complete similar types of Web tasks as .NET facilitated. The Internet itself remained full of browser-based applications that did many of the same things Microsoft was promising.[57] In addition, Sun as well as several other companies had their own .NET-type initiatives for Web services. Sun One, for example, provided Web services through a combination of Sun's UNIX operating system, Java and other "middleware" code, and the Sun–Netscape iPlanet server software. HP had a competing technology for creating Web-based services through its UNIX offering and OpenView management software. Oracle's Dynamic Services, application suites, and database products, and IBM's WebSphere application server and database technology, provided similar capabilities.[58]

To gain followers, Microsoft tried to make it relatively easy for developers and customers to convert. The .NET framework allowed developers to transform their Windows applications programs into Web sites that could share information and other services with various applications, even those running on different operating systems. Complementors and users, however, had to agree to enter into Microsoft's new environment and use C#. The .NET tools that Microsoft proposed worked within the new Windows environment only, at least for the moment. Nor was it clear that the .NET servers would be able to communicate easily with other servers that were not ".NET enabled."

More than once, Microsoft has tried to "force" the industry to adopt its "open but not open" standards. The company did this with DOS and Windows, and tried again with its own variant of Java with Windows-specific features for the Internet (as discussed earlier, they were stopped by a federal lawsuit from Sun Microsystems).[59] .NET had the same ring to it. Complementors had to adopt Microsoft's unique specifications for applications and services to be fully compatible and talk to each other "seamlessly," which the company touted as the big promise of .NET services. Some critics claimed that what Microsoft had proposed amounted to no less than a new Microsoft-centric version of the Internet. What is more, .NET made Microsoft's product development agenda enormously ambitious: Co-opting the Internet and making all devices talk to each other is an R&D project of gargantuan proportions. Despite vast experience in software development, it was by no means certain that Microsoft would be able to carry out all its plans on schedule, even if it spent its enormous cash horde of more than $20 billion solely on .NET development work.

We will not know the fate of .NET until at least 2002, when Microsoft expects .NET applications and Hailstorm services to become widely available. In the meantime, like Intel, Microsoft executives seemed to understand the importance of Lever 3: that any new platform initiative would succeed or fail depending on how complementors reacted. Without the proper development tools, applications companies would not create new applications or rewrite old ones to use the .NET infrastructure. We discussed how Microsoft was addressing this issue with its new tool sets. Without the proper technology infrastructure, such as fast wireless connections to the Internet, consumers would find it difficult to use .NET products and services from any device. Microsoft chose to address this area with investments in cable TV companies such as AT&T, which provided broadband Internet access services. Also as part of .NET, Microsoft and Intel teamed up to support the Bluetooth wireless standard developed by Nokia, which could link computing devices and peripherals through radio signals.[60] In his Forum 2000 speech, Gates acknowledged that Microsoft depended on hardware and communications infrastructure providers to make the .NET strategy work:

> We're making some very exciting assumptions about what our partners, who do hardware breakthroughs, will be doing in parallel. We're not assuming that the PC or the Internet network capabilities will be standing still. We're assuming that broadband becomes more pervasive. . . . We're also very bullish on wireless. . . . We think that authentication advances will be very important to this. Passwords are the weak link today in security systems. . . . The PC that we're thinking about is obviously much more powerful than what we have today. . . . The small screen devices are also something where there will be incredible innovation.[61]

Microsoft CEO Ballmer seemed convinced that Microsoft would prevail. At a conference launching the .NET initiative, he proclaimed that, as with Windows earlier, the company intended to succeed, however long it took. He assured developers and customers from around the world that Microsoft was doing what it could to ensure that its own product groups, as well as third parties, created the necessary pieces to make the .NET vision a reality:

> We have a commitment to doing not only the [software] platform, but services that support the [software] platform. People often ask, what was the key to Windows' success? Well, one of the keys certainly to Windows' success was our investment in Microsoft Office.

And we're investing in, we're putting our money where our mouth is, doing services built on the .NET [software] platform: MSN, Office, bCentral [Web-based products and services for small businesses], a personal subscription service. . . . We have great customer reach, through our run times [interpreters for the C# programming language], through MSN, through Office. I think that will be important. We're committed to third-party success. I've said it before . . . but it is absolutely critical that we be open, that we involve third parties. And we'll show the kind of patient long-term approach that is required.[62]

With .NET, Microsoft potentially faced even more tensions with outside complementors than Intel experienced. Unlike Intel, Microsoft did not have the reputation of making sure its complementors had successful businesses. Microsoft aggressively entered the domains of many applications companies that were once key partners and drivers of demand for the PC—Lotus, WordPerfect, Novell, Netscape, AOL, Oracle, and many others. It was by no means certain that .NET would generate outside cooperation and investment in complementary products and services of the magnitude that Gates and Ballmer expected. Nonetheless, it was hard to bet against Microsoft because of its Lever 1 strategy: It has the money and technical resources to produce enough complements to .NET, including development tools, applications, and services, to ensure that this latest platform initiative will have at least some success.

Acquire and Assimilate Complements and Substitutes: The Cisco Strategy

Cisco Systems became well known during the late 1980s and 1990s as the market leader in networking technology for the Internet. Its main product initially was the *Internet router*, a specialized computer that relied on software instructions to disassemble data into "packets," direct these packets over the best possible "route" on the Internet given the state of traffic, and then reassemble the packets when they reached their destinations. Cisco also produces *packet-based switches*, another type of specialized computer that sends packets of data over fixed routes from one point to another. In addition, Cisco provides a variety of other communications equipment and software that enables these devices to work with routers, switches, and other networking products. The company calls its basic software IOS for "Internetworking Operating System."

The dramatic growth of the Internet after 1995 provided the basis for Cisco's remarkable growth. When John Chambers, a former IBM salesman, joined the company in 1991, Cisco had annual sales of $70 million. When Chambers became CEO in 1994, annual sales were $1 billion. For the fiscal year ending July 2001, Cisco revenues reached $22.2 billion. Even with an expected drop in revenue for 2002, this was an astounding performance, and Cisco did not do it alone. Much of Cisco's growth was tied to the existence of complements such as Internet browsers (introduced by Netscape and Microsoft in 1994–1995) and high-powered server computers (led by Sun Microsystems since the 1980s). Cisco also benefited from e-commerce applications and communications products that took advantage of the Internet. In addition to external complements, Cisco added to its product portfolio networking products that complemented the basic router. In fact, 61 percent of Cisco's sales in 2001 were from nonrouter products, compared to only 20 percent in 1985.[63]

We think of Cisco as a platform leader because it provided much of the infrastructure hardware and software behind the Internet. In addition, with a market share of some 80 percent for its core router products, Cisco was to Internet-based networking as Intel was to microprocessors and Microsoft to PC software. A key difference with Intel and Microsoft, however, was that Cisco championed open standards. Industry-standard communications protocols formed the basis of its platform technology. Though Cisco remained distinctive because of the breadth of protocols it supported, its primary strategy was to enable *interoperable networking* between Internet routers and a wide variety of other types of networking and communications technologies.

Compared to Microsoft's position in PC software or Intel in microprocessors, Cisco faced more competitors. 3Com, an early router producer and pioneer in commercial local area networks (LANs) based on Ethernet technology (developed initially at Xerox PARC in the 1970s) was one, although it had become a second-rate vendor of routers by the 1990s. Companies such as Lucent, Nortel Networks, Siemens, and Fujitsu entered the router market, but they came late or through acquisitions, and this proved not to be their main emphasis. Nonetheless, in the early 2000s, Cisco was losing sales to upstart companies such as Juniper Networks, which had more advanced router and switching technologies useful in niches such as ultra-high-speed routers. Established competitors Nortel and Lucent also dominated fiber-optic networking equipment and large-scale telecommunications switches, both used to build high-speed and high-capacity telephone and data line systems. New types of switching technologies that might replace routers posed another threat to Cisco. This and the commoditization of the basic router market during the late 1990s prompted Cisco to diversify into router complements and to vary the kinds of networks it built for customers.

Like Microsoft, Cisco tried to sell more complete solutions than Intel did. In Cisco's case, we are referring to networking solutions that usually centered on routers but also might include switches for LAN or wide area networks (WAN) or switches for large-scale telecommunications applications. To provide broader networking solutions and stave off competitors, Cisco had to fill many gaps in its product lines. To do so, it invested heavily in in-house R&D (which totaled some $3.8 billion or 17 percent of sales in fiscal 2001). Like Intel and Microsoft, Cisco also became a major venture player and spent some $200 million in 1999 alone on start-up investments.[64] Cisco manipulated Levers 1, 2, and 3 simultaneously. It chose to plug product gaps by making a dozen or more acquisitions per year. It aggressively acquired firms that sold substitute technologies. In addition, Cisco acted like platform leaders in other industries by pursuing alliances to drive industry standards and to develop new applications and services that used Cisco's routers and other products.

In this section, we discuss the origins and evolution of Cisco's platform technology as well as its strategy and process for acquiring companies that made complements to the router or potentially substitute networking technologies.

Origins of the Router Platform

Cisco's origins go back to the late 1970s and Stanford University.[65] A former graduate student turned network systems director in the business school (Sandra Lerner) and the systems director in the computer science department (Leonard Bosack) wanted to exchange e-mail and data files easily across their departments and the rest of the university. They couldn't because Stanford's departments were all on different computer networks. The Internet, then called the ARPAnet system (short for Advanced Research Project Agency network and funded by the U.S. Department of Defense) existed, but it was very clumsy to use. Computers on a network in one department (a LAN) had to go through special and expensive computers to access another set of computers that connected computer clusters at different universities. What Stanford and other organizations needed were specialized computers that could communicate with the different LANs and "route" communications traffic between them without having to go through the elaborate ARPAnet system.

Others at Stanford were working on creating "bridges" and then "routers" to link the departmental networks, but Lerner and Bosack, with some other Stanford engineers, took the project a step further. They created a system of routers and servers (the latter were mostly DEC minicomputers), wired up the networks with coaxial cable used in cable TV systems, and wrote a primitive network operating system for the router boxes. The software contained interfaces to the various local networks, servers, and the ARPAnet system. The routers worked well. Lerner and Bosack in 1984 decided to create their own company based on the router technology, and began shipping products in 1986 to other universities and a few large companies. Software engineers who joined Cisco during these years incrementally added new features to the router software, enabling the device to handle growing varieties of communications protocols.

Cisco received venture capital funding in 1987. This was also the year when the U.S. government decided to open up the ARPAnet system to users beyond the government and federally funded universities and research centers. The public Internet emerged, and demand for routers and servers began to rise rapidly. John Morgridge, an experienced manager who had worked at Honeywell and a PC manufacturer, joined Cisco as CEO in 1988. He took the company public in 1989. Lerner and Bosack found themselves at odds with their new boss and investors. They left the company a year or so after it went public, but Cisco continued to grow rapidly, along with the Internet.

Strategy Evolution: Interoperable Networking for the Internet

A founding principle of Cisco's corporate strategy was to be a "customer-driven" rather than "technology-driven" company. The basic vision of

Lerner and Bosack was to provide networking systems based on the Internet. They started with a specific problem and used their understanding of networks and computer technology to solve it. Cisco executives, from Morgridge through Chambers, continued this customer-driven, networking-centered philosophy. It proved invaluable in the early years of the Internet as technology rapidly evolved and customers encountered many different types of problems. Cisco could not sell one technology as a "black-box" solution that serviced everyone's problems. Its sales, marketing, and engineering people had to probe the networking requirements of various types of organizations and figure out how to meet their needs, often using an eclectic approach of software and hardware. Cisco management exhibited the same philosophy in 2001, as the company Web site explained:

> Cisco Systems is the worldwide leader in networking for the Internet . . . Cisco offers the industry's broadest range of hardware products used to form information networks or give people access to those networks . . . Cisco is unique in its ability to provide all these elements, either by itself or together with partners . . . In contrast to many technology companies, Cisco does not take a rigid approach that favors one technology over the alternatives and imposes it on customers as the only answer. Cisco's philosophy is to listen to customer requests, monitor all technological alternatives, and provide customers with a range of options from which to choose. Cisco develops its products and solutions around widely accepted industry standards. In some instances, technologies developed by Cisco have become industry standards themselves.[66]

Although Cisco routers quickly became the products of choice for Internet-based communications systems during the late 1980s and 1990s, comprehensive networking solutions usually required Cisco to bring together different types of communications equipment. This was relatively easy to do if routers were the core of the network because the interfaces were open—they consisted of the basic Internet communications protocols. It required additional software to connect Internet systems to LANs, such as for Ethernet-based systems, and to the voice and data networks of the large telephone companies, although many of these interfaces were also in the public domain.

By the early 1990s, Cisco had learned a lot about the strengths and limitations of the router product line and the value of connecting routers to other types of communications gear. But Morgridge and other Cisco executives concluded they did not have the R&D resources to develop a full slate of networking technologies and keep pace with the level of inventions going on in and around the Internet. Hence, Cisco management decided to acquire the *complementary technologies* they needed to implement their vision of providing broad networking solutions to customers and to continue fueling growth. They also decided to acquire companies with *competing technologies* that potentially could displace routers in some network applications.

A recent study broke down Cisco's strategy in the early 1990s into the following four key elements.[67]

1. Provide "complete solutions" for customers and become a "one-stop shop for networking," whether or not Cisco made all the necessary products.
2. Acquire the products they needed for complete solutions but "make acquisitions a structured process" to offset the high failure rates of acquisitions in most industries.
3. Define and drive industry standards for networking protocols that would allow different networks to communicate more easily and thereby help Internet usage to grow.
4. Form alliances and partnerships with complementors and even competitors, not only to provide complete solutions but also to get access to new markets and new technologies.

Cisco executives had no trouble distinguishing between complementary and competing technologies, and they wanted to acquire both. Cisco's response to the threat of competing technology in the early 1990s provides an example. New telecommunications switches from companies such as Crescendo had evolved to the point where they competed directly with routers. Customers could build sophisticated networks by using the advanced switching hardware with large Ethernet LANs, rather than building lots of smaller clusters of networked computers connected by Internet routers.

Although switches could do the job of routers, the two technologies were not equivalent. Switches simply received and passed on data to different locations using preset instructions and defined circuit pathways, whereas routers enabled more efficient use of the network capacity because they could read addresses on packets of information and send these packets over the Internet to their destinations using the fastest available pathway given the state of traffic. Switches were "dumb" in comparison; they worked only from one point to another and could not find alternative or best-available routes for the data they were transmitting. But they could be faster and cheaper than router-based networks for some applications. Furthermore, by using special-purpose microprocessors, Crescendo and other firms designed new switching equipment that could route incoming data packets—perhaps not as well as dedicated routers, but faster and cheaper and often "good enough." For point-to-point data transfer lines, inexpensive switches could substitute directly for routers. Some customers wanted both kinds of technologies in their networks.

When Cisco executives realized they were losing sales to Crescendo, they acquired the company in 1993 for a very large premium ($97 million for a start-up with just $10 million in sales) and quickly leveraged the switching product line into a major new area of revenue growth.[68] The Crescendo acquisition also made it possible for Cisco to offer customers a broader array of state-of-the-art networking products and let them choose exactly which combinations of equipment they wanted. This approach—offer a total solution using more than one networking technology—rather than simply selling routers, became Cisco's strategy going forward.

Another important development occurred during the mid-1990s. Telephone companies generally bought switches from Lucent, Nortel, and other traditional switch vendors, and had not purchased Cisco equipment. It is surprising that Cisco had not courted potential customers because telephone companies had always been essential to Internet access for residential customers as well as most corporations; they provided the linkages to the Internet backbone. As telephone companies became increasingly interested in providing Internet access services to their customers, Cisco pursued a whole new set of applications for routers, such as data transmission and telephony over the Internet. These applications attracted a new set of customers, including telephone companies, for Internet switching equipment as well as high-end routers.

After taking over as CEO in 1994, Chambers moved aggressively to market total solutions to a larger group of companies with a broader set of product lines and technologies. He began by decentralizing Cisco into relatively independent business units organized around the company's main product lines. Initially, these divisions were workgroups (LAN switching, ATM [asynchronous transfer mode] workgroups, and adapter products), ATM high end (large-scale switches), network access (stand-alone Internet routers), core (high-end routers, switching technologies, and telecommunications services), and IBM internetworking (routers compatible with IBM computer networks, LANs, and WANs).[69] Each group had its own marketing and engineering groups, though Cisco kept most sales support centralized to provide better service to customers.

Cisco continued to modify this organizational structure as its product lines and customer needs evolved. In 1996, the company reorganized around three lines of business: enterprises, small/medium businesses, and service providers. The idea was to target specific markets. The enterprise line was the center of the company, with high-end routers and WAN technology. The small/medium business group developed cable-modem and high-speed connection software. The service provider group worked on products that merged networking with telephony, and it targeted as customers telephone companies, Internet service providers, cable companies, and wireless companies.

This structure had some problems, however. Not every business group sold routers; indeed, some sold alternatives to routers that competed with each other, creating some internal conflicts. Most Cisco products interconnected through the IOS software, however, and were able to form part of a total communications solution with routers or router-like switchers. Some marketing groups organized around hybrid solutions, which made it easier to sell products from different areas of the company, though the engineering teams were generally dedicated to particular product lines.

In an effort to reduce overlaps across different divisions and ease development of comprehensive solutions in particular areas, Cisco announced in August 2001 a reorganization into eleven new groups. These are based on key technologies, led by Internet switching, optical networking, and wireless products.[70]

Acquisitions of Complements and Substitutes

Between 1993 and 2000, Cisco acquired seventy-one companies, spending more than $20 billion. It made an astounding twenty-three acquisitions in 2000 alone (table 5–1). Acquisitions helped Cisco grow revenues roughly 50 percent each year for the previous decade. Each acquisition also made the company less dependent on the original router product line. In 2001, Cisco had revenues from switches, mostly for LANs ($10.6 billion or 47 percent of total revenues) that were larger than its router revenues ($8.7 billion or 39 percent).[71]

Under Chambers, Cisco became famous for its acquisitions process, the steps of which are summarized here.[72]

1. *Evaluate the acquisition target*: Acquisition teams used a fixed set of strategic, cultural, and economic criteria to identify companies likely to blend well with Cisco's culture as well as add state-of-the-art technology to the product portfolio. Cisco's extensive experience with acquisitions enabled it to refine these criteria to a considerable degree.

2. *Sell the target company on the idea of being acquired by Cisco*: Leaders of the acquisition team as well as executives, managers, and engineers from related groups usually met with acquisition candidates and talked about the advantages of becoming part of Cisco.

3. *Conduct a formal appraisal and offer*: Cisco's stock remained very attractive until late 2000, and the offers were usually generous—making it easy for Cisco to close deals, at least prior to 2001.

4. *Integrate the acquisition*: This final phase was the most difficult, and included measures to retain key managers and employees.

In general, Cisco did well in integration and retention of key people, and with its acquisitions strategy more broadly. Historically, some two out of three acquisitions end up as failures.[73] Cisco had a much better record, despite paying high prices and diluting the value of its stock. Cisco's vast experience in acquisitions, its aggressive sales staff, and the efforts of its engineers to integrate the products of acquired companies into Cisco's product portfolio and IOS software platform were likely factors in Cisco's success rate.

Table 5-1 Cisco's Acquisitions in 2000

COMPANY	MONTH	PRICE (IN MILLIONS OF DOLLARS)	TECHNOLOGY
ExiO Communications	December	$155	Wireless for corporate networks
Radiata	November	$295	Chip set for high-speed wireless networks
Active Voice	November	$266	IP-based unified messaging solutions
CAIS Software	October	$170	Software for broadband Internet services
Vovida Networks	September	$185*	Networking protocol software
IPCell Technologies	September	$185*	Broadband access software
PixStream	August	$369	Digital video
IPmobile	July	$425	Third-generation wireless software
NuSpeed Internet Systems	July	$450	Software for storage networks and IP networks
Komodo Technology	July	$175	Voice over IP for analog phones
Netiverse	July	$210	Content-aware switches
HyNEX	June	$127	ATM and IP solutions
Qeyton Systems	May	$800	Optical networking software
ArrowPoint Communications	May	$5700	Content networking
Seagull Semiconductor	April	$19	Silicon for terabit routers
PentaCom	April	$118	Metro IP networks
SightPath	March	$800	Software management of Web content
infoGear Technology	March	$301	Software to manage information appliances
JetCell	March	$200	Wireless telephony
Atlantech Technologies	March	$180	Network element management software
Growth Networks	February	$355	Internet switching technology
Altiga Networks	January	$567	Consulting services, virtual private networks
Compatible Systems	January	NA	Virtual private network solutions

Source: Cisco Systems, "Acquisition Summary," <http://www.cisco.com/warp/public/750/acquisition/summarylist.html> (accessed April 2001), and Sonny Wu, "Strategic Management of Cisco Systems," unpublished paper for MIT Sloan School of Management, Subject 15.902, Fall 2001.

Notes: * = estimate; ATM = asynchronous transfer mode; IP = Internet protocol; NA = not available.

As implied by Step 1 above, Cisco's acquisitions were strategic, focusing on different areas to complement and then extend its networking business as well as to counter competition from substitute platforms. The first diversification effort involved telecommunications switches. After the initial acquisition of Crescendo in 1993, Cisco bought six more switching companies over the next three years, including the $4.4 billion acquisition of StrataCom in 1996. After 1996, Cisco's focus shifted to cable boxes and Internet-access equipment, including products such as digital subscriber line (DSL) gear, Internet phones, and home modems for telephone companies. More recent acquisitions have been in the wireless networking arena (table 5–2).

The ten companies Cisco acquired between 1993 and 1996 laid the base for its expansion into switches and other areas of networking, many of which complemented router-based networks or could serve as router-like platforms. Here is a sample of the technologies Cisco acquired from eight of these companies:

- Crescendo: low-cost telephone line switches
- Kalpana: Ethernet switches with interfaces for routers located on remote networks
- Lightstream: ATM technology for both switches and routers
- Combinet: high-speed ISDN products and applications for telephone companies
- Internet Junction: "gateway" software that connected PC users with the Internet
- Grand Junction: digital switches that increased the speed of Ethernet networks
- Network Translation: Internet firewall systems
- TGV Software: software products that connected computers on different types of network systems[74]

ATM is a good example of a new networking technology that competed with both routers and circuit switches. The traditional telephone system depended on circuit switching, less efficient in many applications than "packet switching" used on the Internet, many local- and wide-area networks, and ATM equipment. The ATM technology also broke up data from either phone or data networks into 53-byte bunches and then sent

Table 5-2 **Cisco Product Debuts**	
YEAR	PRODUCT
1986	Routers
1992	Dial-in access servers
1993	LAN switches
1994	WAN switches
1995	Hubs, firewalls, caching engines
1996	Cable boxes, cable head-ends
1997	DSL head-ends
1998	Internet phones
1999	Home modems
2000	Wireless LANs

Source: Based on Andy Serwer, "There's Something About Cisco," *Fortune*, 15 May 2000, 126.
Notes: LAN = local area network; WAN = wide area network; DSL = digital subscriber line.

these packets over a network of switches or routers. Another important advantage was that the ATM switches could connect traditional phone networks with modern data networks.

In the mid-1990s, connecting ATM switches to Internet routers or using ATM switches in place of routers was clumsy and expensive. But, to handle the booming traffic on the Internet, telephone companies (which purchase billions of dollars of equipment every year) began pondering a move to packet-switching technology and wanted to create hybrid networks combining ATM with other technologies. Equipment vendors scrambled to find ways to make the ATM switches work with non-ATM routers.

As usual, Cisco management wanted to offer a complete solution and ensure that ATM technology did not make routers obsolete. Toward these ends, Cisco joined with AT&T and StrataCom in 1993 to define ATM standards and develop products and services for this technology or ATM–router combinations. Cisco bought a small-scale ATM product in the Lightstream acquisition, but this was no match for products from companies like StrataCom and Cascade, which sold heavy-duty ATM switches using a similar technology called frame relay. Cisco also had to compete with the established switching systems vendors, led by Nortel and Lucent, which added Internet protocol or "IP on ATM" capabilities to their switches during the mid- to late 1990s. (These companies also used major acquisitions to expand their portfolios and move into newer technologies. Nortel, for example, acquired a leading Internet switch manufacturer, Bay Networks, in 1998 for $9.1 billion, and Lucent acquired Ascend, the market leader in ATM switches, in 1999 for a staggering $24 billion.)

Cisco also acquired and developed the Fast Ethernet networking technology as a substitute for ATM switching. This worked well for LANs, but not for WANs. For WAN applications, customers wanted frame relay and ATM switches. Thus, to enter into the ATM market, Cisco followed its usual strategy of acquiring the market leaders, including StrataCom—Cisco's largest deal until it bought ArrowPoint Communications in 2000 for $5.7 billion. With these acquisitions, Cisco was able to provide both router and ATM solutions. Moreover, Cisco *redefined its Internet networking platform* as containing either or both non-ATM routers and ATM technologies.[75]

By 1997, other technologies had appeared, making alternatives to routers even more attractive: for example, Layer 3 switches (routers that combined more traditional switching functions) and Gigabit Ethernet (which worked a thousand times faster than regular Ethernet). Although smaller competitors introduced these new products first, Cisco patiently worked on *incorporating interfaces and operating code for the newer technologies into its IOS software.* Then Cisco *introduced products with the newer technologies, not as replacements for its basic router line but as add-ons.* In this way, Cisco sold hybrid networking solutions to customers that wanted high-end equipment, with switches at the core of the systems and routers at the perimeters, directing traffic. Customers could keep their old and expensive (but "smart") routers, buy the latest switching technology from Cisco, and use IOS (which relied on open industry standards and had no forward or backward compatibility limitations) as the software operating system.[76]

The Crescendo and StrataCom acquisitions provided a beachhead for Cisco to sell more equipment to telephone companies, but Cisco still needed more robust products. The company's experience with switching technology prior to 1996 had been limited to relatively small-scale packet switching in computer networks. Cisco's strategy was to target innovative small companies that had leading-edge technology in the new areas and either introduce similar products through in-house R&D or, if that was too slow, acquire the market leaders.

Following this approach, Cisco acquired another dozen or so companies in 1997 and 1998 to move into new technologies of interest to telephone companies: DSL equipment, which enabled high-speed Internet access over conventional telephone lines; multiservice equipment, which handled both voice and data; and fiber-optic switching equipment, used in networks built of fiber optical cables that normally did not connect with Cisco equipment. Again, all these products diversified Cisco away from routers and provided the company and its customers with different technology options.

Unlike in routers, however, as of 2001, Cisco was not a market leader in any of these new areas. Cisco struggled, for example, to enter the fiber-optic switches area. It finally brought a product to market in late 1998 after two years of R&D and $8 billion in acquisitions.[77] Cisco badly trailed firms that specialized in optical equipment, such as Nortel, though by 2001 it had made headway in connecting routers with high-speed fiber-optic, cable, and wireless systems to enable voice and video over the Internet.

Incremental Platform Evolution: IOS Software as "Glue"

Most of Cisco's networking products complemented the basic router by connecting different types of networking equipment. Even substitute technologies, such as ATM switches, played a role in hybrid networks that included routers and other devices. At least indirectly, even hybrid networks helped keep demand high for Cisco products because they contributed to overall use of the Internet. The Cisco "platform" by 2001 had evolved from the Internet router, a specific combination of hardware and software technology, to the broader *concept of interoperable networking*, which usually began with Internet routers, but could also include ATM and frame-relay switches, LAN and WAN systems, and connections to Internet telephony systems, cable-TV Internet access and DSL equipment, and wireless communications servers. Cisco managed to link or "glue" together most of these different networking technologies through its operating system software, IOS, which worked alongside Cisco's Network Management Software. CiscoFusion, first introduced in 1994, was an architecture or high-level set of technical guidelines for how IOS would combine router networks with new technologies such as ATM, WAN and LAN workgroup switches, and other types of networks (figure 5–1).

In 2001, IOS was probably more important as the de facto Cisco platform than the Internet router because the software was at the foundation of all of Cisco's networking solutions. Cisco management seemed to share this view; the Web site touts IOS as "the platform that delivers network services and enables networked applications . . . [and] runs on the majority of Cisco networking equipment, including routers, access servers, and switches. Cisco IOS Software seamlessly links heterogeneous media and devices across the broadest set of protocols."[78] Cisco licensed and sold IOS by packaging different sets of features, depending on the user's requirements. Its two main flavors, Basic and Plus, varied depending on the hardware combinations. Cisco also offered a version of IOS with encryption technologies.[79]

IOS, however, was not without its drawbacks. The software had evolved somewhat haphazardly from Cisco's early days and, after twelve versions through mid-2001, remained a hodgepodge of code from different products and networking protocols. It had some modular, layer-like characteristics but was not a top-down-designed operating system such as Windows NT/2000 or UNIX. Some people believed that IOS was little more than a set of concepts used as a marketing tool. To make it easier to sell customers a complete networking solution, however, Cisco engineers had to make IOS into a "one-stop" software package containing all the software than ran on Cisco's hardware equipment as well as interface software for connecting to the outside world. It took until 1997 to make IOS a working system for multiple products, not only routers. From this point on, IOS enabled Cisco to offer broad networking solutions that connected Internet routers with routing hubs, ATM and frame-relay switches, computer-based file servers, and other equipment.

Like Microsoft's Windows platform, IOS is an "open but not open" platform technology.[80] The specifications that defined the interfaces for connecting with IOS are open—available in the public domain as Internet, LAN, or WAN standards. IOS itself, however, is not an open system

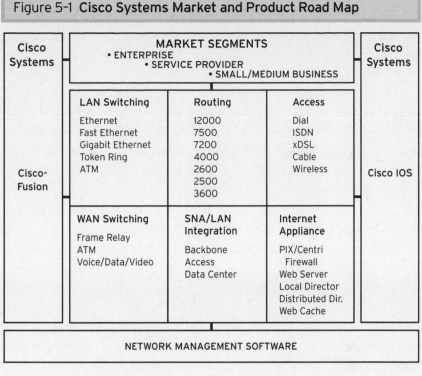

Figure 5-1 **Cisco Systems Market and Product Road Map**

Source: <http://www.i-gensolutions.com/partners/Cisco.htm> (accessed August 2001).

such as Linux or Apache. It consists mainly of proprietary software code that enabled Cisco products to operate alone or with each other. On the other hand, Cisco licensed IOS broadly to other networking equipment companies, including competitors, which enabled them to build systems that more easily integrated with Cisco equipment. Cisco also designed the software so that it was easy for customers to extend or update their networks with Cisco equipment.[81]

In the late 1990s and early 2000s, IOS became a common software platform for Internet networking because Cisco routers were so prevalent. Vendors of other equipment usually had little choice but to license IOS from Cisco and test their code with it to make sure their products worked properly with Cisco's products. Cisco worked actively with industry groups to set new networking standards and was often among the first companies to add these protocols to its operating system software. In addition, Cisco claimed there was enough proprietary code within IOS (about 1 percent of the total system) to allow Cisco products to "work better when they talk to each other, rather than with machines made by rivals."[82]

In response to Cisco's near-monopoly in networking technology in the mid-1990s, competitors tried to take their momentum away. In 1995, 3Com, Bay Networks, and IBM formed the Network Interoperability Alliance (NIA). The agenda was "to promote a common set of open specifications for building integrated networks" and test products from the three companies to ensure that they worked together. Several smaller companies also endorsed the NIA standards.[83]

Cisco responded to NIA in 1997 with several measures that contributed to the collapse of the alliance within a year, heavily using Levers 2 and 3 from our framework. First, Cisco licensed IOS aggressively to powerful companies such as Compaq, HP, Cabletron, DEC, NEC, Microsoft, Alcatel, Ericsson, and GTE (Lever 2, as it is sharing technology). To these and other firms, Cisco promoted IOS as the equivalent of Windows in the PC software world. Marketing promotions described the software as the "glue" that every major networking equipment vendor should rely on to make sure their products operated with each other and, of course, with Cisco's systems. Cisco did not allow licensees to change the software code, keeping it a proprietary system despite the open interfaces. But licensees had full information on how the interfaces worked and were able to adapt their products to run on IOS. This meant that their equipment would interconnect with other IOS-compatible equipment, whether or not Cisco was the manufacturer. In this sense, IOS served as an effective software platform for Internet infrastructure equipment and hybrid networks.

Cisco launched a marketing campaign promoting "Cisco-Powered Networks" as a second measure to counter NIA. The effort involved media ads as well as forums for communications services providers and equipment resellers. Instead of selling or giving away SDKs like Microsoft and Intel, Cisco sold advertising kits to customers that had networks with at least 70 percent Cisco components. The arrangement allowed these customers to use the "Cisco-Powered Network" logo in their own advertising and claim that networks using Cisco equipment were superior to those of competitors—similar to what Intel did with its "Intel Inside" campaign. Because IOS used standard communications or Internet protocols to connect even its own products, this claim was largely marketing propaganda, but it was persuasive for many customers.

Cisco also pushed the idea of a "community of Cisco users and partners" and in 1996 launched the "Cisco Connection Online" Web site, which provided the latest information on Cisco products and facilitated technical support and Q&A sessions. Through the Web site and its networking technology conferences, Cisco created a "virtual culture" around its products. This culture reinforced Cisco's branding and licensing campaigns and, with the aggressive price cuts, helped maintain Cisco's position as the platform leader for Internet infrastructure equipment. Third, Cisco cut prices on its equipment—by as much as half in some cases. Most competitors could not compete with Cisco on pricing because of its scale economies and lean operations.

We should reiterate that IOS did not provide much of a technical advantage to Cisco because it relied so heavily on open interfaces. Unlike Intel and Microsoft, or Palm, Cisco did not really control the "architecture" of its platform—which the Internet defined. Other companies also had superior equipment in some market segments (such as Juniper Networks in high-end routers) that customers could use interchangeably with Cisco equipment, with no degradation of performance.[84] Nonetheless, as long as customers valued interoperability, IOS and Cisco hardware were good choices. The concept of interoperable networking thus proved to be a powerful and successful platform strategy for Cisco, particularly when combined with the acquisition of so many leading-edge companies and bolstered by Cisco's world-class engineering, sales, and marketing capabilities.

Partnerships with Complementors and Competitors

Forming alliances with complementors—Lever 3—was a key part of Cisco's strategy. Morgridge recognized that Cisco did not have the same influence over the industry as a Microsoft or Intel and thus needed partnerships. He, and Chambers after him, also recognized that there were limits to their Lever 1 strategy: Cisco could not acquire all complementors and potential substitutes. Even if Cisco had the financial resources, managers were reluctant to make acquisitions that strayed too far from their core of technical expertise. Some partnerships were useful only for marketing because Cisco did not have the capabilities in the early and mid-1990s to sell and service its routers and other equipment in all global markets, where demand was rising rapidly. Early marketing and service partners included most major Japanese electronics, Internet, and telecommunications firms (NEC, Hitachi, Fujitsu, and Softbank, among others), as well as HP and IBM.[85]

In the 1990s, Cisco began to ally with manufacturers of *hubs*— devices that relay or retransmit communications signals. Cisco's goal was to enable producers of these hubs to combine them with Cisco routers. DEC (now owned by Compaq) signed on as a partner for workgroup routing systems in 1992. Hewlett-Packard was an important partner since 1994 for hubs and later for ATM and LAN products. Hewlett-Packard and Cisco combined efforts to catch up with the leaders in these markets, and more recently with UNIX-based computer networks. HP also resold and serviced Cisco products since 1995. IBM became a major partner in 1992, when it began selling Cisco equipment and linking it to its own networking and computer products. IBM eventually abandoned making its own networking equipment and became a reseller of mostly Cisco equipment.[86]

In the switching market, Cisco's strategy was to license IOS broadly at minimal cost to users to push IOS as a standard, and then use a deeper knowledge of its own technology to build superior routers and switches or make stronger marketing pitches to customers.[87] The goal was to sell equipment to phone companies, which traditionally relied on the switching vendors. In the early 1990s, Cisco licensed IOS to Cascade and twenty other companies to handle routing on telephone switches, and then it acquired StrataCom, which made equipment for the switching market. But it needed partnerships with telecommunications service and manufacturing companies to make more headway. In 1993, Cisco joined with MCI to market Cisco products with MCI's WAN product line. Cisco also allied with NEC for ATM switch development and with Nortel for access to Ethernet LAN switching technology, and then made acquisitions in these areas.[88]

During the late 1990s, Microsoft and Intel moved into the low-end networking market through their software and hardware products, such as Windows NT and new Intel-based servers. Chambers reportedly was not eager to enter into an alliance with these potential competitors, but he saw some sort of cooperation as unavoidable. The three companies joined together in 1997 to form the Networked Multimedia Connection (NMC), with a new lab based at Cisco headquarters, to promote high-end applications such as videoconferencing for networked computing.[89] Conflicts quickly emerged, however. Cisco's IOS software, Intel's ProShare videoconferencing system, and Microsoft's NetShow application (bundled in Windows 95/98) all overlapped to some extent. Cisco and Intel also directly competed with their hardware networking products, especially as Intel moved more into PC server-based switching systems. Intel dropped out of the alliance about a year after it started, though Cisco and Microsoft continued to cooperate in areas such as multimedia, security, and network directory services.[90]

Cisco also worked with other types of partners that helped it implement custom networking solutions. In 1998, for example, it established a new Internet Business Solutions Group. This group worked with consulting companies such as Cambridge Technology Partners, Ernst & Young, and KPMG (which helped Cisco set up its own intranet system in 1993) to advise clients on how to build Internet-based systems. Later, in 1999, Cisco purchased a 20 percent stake in KPMG.[91] In 2000, Cisco bought a 4.9 percent stake in Cap Gemini, the French software and consulting firm. A joint venture of the two companies focused on network design and consulting.[92] Cisco had other alliances with AT&T for value-added networking solutions; Cap Gemini Ernst & Young for broadband services, network management, and customer relationship management tools; and PeopleSoft for network-based enterprise applications.[93]

Cisco formed many other partnerships in the late 1990s and early 2000s and was an active member of industry groups that set standards incorporated in IOS, such as the Internet Engineering Task Force (IETF), the Institute of Electrical and Electronic Engineers (IEEE), the Optical Internet Working Forum, the ATM Forum, the Frame Relay Forum, and the DSL Forum.[94] Like Intel and Microsoft, Cisco entered many corporate relationships to try to direct industry standards in ways that benefited Cisco products. A sample of these alliances:

- *BMC Software, Compaq, Intel, and Microsoft (1998)*: to devise standards for allowing network administrators to use any Web browser to manage different types of networks, computer systems, and applications. The group proposed its Web-based

Enterprise Management (WBEM) standards to the IETF and the Desktop Management Task Force (DMTF).[95]

- *EDS and HP (1998)*: to provide "a single source for establishing a Web-based business." The partnership combined EDS consulting and system integration skills with Cisco's networking solutions and HP's servers and software.[96]

- *Motorola (1999)*: to invest $1 billion and cross-license technologies to develop and deliver wireless Internet access across the globe. The two companies were designing "an open Internet-based platform for integrated data, voice, and video services over cellular networks." The system was intended to work across existing digital wireless systems.[97]

- *Motorola, Broadcom, Texas Instruments, Samsung, Toshiba, Pace Micro, Bechtel Telecommunications, KPMG, LCC International, and EDS (1999)*: to drive open standards for broadband wireless Internet devices. The goal, from the company press release, was: "Cisco is leading the formation of this open system ecosystem of partners to stimulate the rapid development of innovative consumer devices and appliances based on cutting-edge technologies."[98]

- *Akamai Technologies (1999)*: to integrate Akamai's content delivery technology into Cisco's networking technology. Akamai was a start-up firm that specialized in delivering rich Web content for customers such as Yahoo! through a global system of mirror sites. The two companies also planned to study how to enable next-generation switches to adapt to changing network conditions.[99]

- *EMC and Oracle (2000)*: to facilitate development of e-business infrastructures, called the "ECOstructure (EMC/Cisco/Oracle) Initiative." The focus was on tools development and integration of different technologies, such as for networking, mass data storage, and software solutions that support e-business applications. KPMG planned to offer consulting services to companies using the new ECOstructure framework.[100]

Cisco's partnerships did not go unnoticed. Like Intel and Microsoft, Cisco was investigated by the Federal Trade Commission (FTC) for potential antitrust violations in 1997 after discussions of potential partnerships between Cisco and rivals Lucent and Nortel. The agency cleared Cisco and the other companies of any wrongdoing. Cisco also came under frequent scrutiny by the FTC and U.S. Department of Justice because of its many acquisitions. It apparently learned how to stay clear of antitrust violations and work well with regulators, although, with such a large market share, Cisco always had to be careful how it treated partners, rivals, and customers.[101]

Future Prospects for Cisco's Platform Strategy: Success or Failure?

Although Cisco remained the market leader in Internet-based networking equipment, it faced several problems. First, vast numbers of acquisitions had not been enough to keep the company at the leading edge of key networking technologies. For example, a recent start-up, Juniper Networks, led in technology for high-end routers, used mainly by telephone companies as the backbone of the Internet infrastructure. Juniper had about 35 percent of the $2 billion market in late 2000, compared to about 65 percent for Cisco, a drop of some 15 percent within a year or so.[102] Cisco retained about 80 percent of the market for basic routers used in corporate networks, a $3 billion market. But Cisco had merely 3 percent of the $25-billion market for optical switching equipment—a key networking technology of the future.[103]

Second, how far could Cisco continue to push its acquisitions strategy? Cisco's acquisitions generally benefited the company and increased sales dramatically for products that it bought, no doubt because of its sales force, integration expertise, and reputation. Some analysts believed, however, that acquisitions were too expensive. The acquisition of ArrowPoint Communications in May 2000 prompted sharp criticism. Cisco bought the company with shares then worth some $5.7 billion, even though ArrowPoint had a negative book value, no history of ever earning a profit, and an annual sales run-rate of about $40 million at the time. U.S. accounting standards that allowed for stock purchases of companies and a "pooling of interests" rather than taking charges against earnings made this type of acquisition possible. U.S. companies did not have to account for such acquisitions in their profit and loss statements under rules in effect prior to 2001. Such acquisitions, however, diluted stock value.[104] Thomas Donlan's now-famous critique in the May 2000 issue of *Barron's* began the downward spiral in Cisco's stock price:

> Unfortunately for Cisco, the success bred by its acquisitions carries with it the seeds of self-destruction. As the company bids higher and higher for its targets, it drives up the market for all telecommunications-equipment companies—including Cisco itself. Acquisitions come harder and higher. Once upon a time, takeover artists looked for companies with shares trading far below the value of total corporate assets. Today's takeover artists at Cisco and other such companies are not buying products. They are not buying profits and they are not even buying revenues. They are buying people and half-formed technology that the people may someday turn into products generating revenues, profits, and assets. Cisco's takeover specialists run a risk: They must buy the right companies, with the right people, developing the right products for a market that may not exist for years after the deal is done.[105]

A third problem was internal tensions due to Cisco's strategy of providing complete networking solutions and acquiring or partnering for most of the technology it needed. In our view, Cisco was still struggling with Lever 4 (internal organization). Its business units consisted largely of formerly acquired companies. There was integration through a common sales force and technical support. But it seems unlikely that Cisco's business units always worked well together, especially when they sold potentially competing technologies or consisted of recent acquisitions that had yet to become integrated with the rest of the company. Many Cisco groups could sell their components (such as an ATM switch or optical switch) without making modifications to accommodate the requirements of other Cisco business units that, for example, wanted to build a hybrid system or a customized solution.

What intensified internal tensions was a fourth problem that Cisco faced: The basic Internet router was no longer the dominant or even the only networking technology that Cisco sold. Furthermore, even the basic router used mainly by corporations ceased years ago to be a single type of product. Different Cisco business units (as well as competitors) offered different routers, for high-end, medium, and low-end applications. It was not unusual for a platform leader to segment the market. Intel had microprocessors of different capabilities for different customers. Microsoft had different operating systems for different customers and markets as well. But the variations in Cisco's routers, and their varied origins (mostly through acquisitions), were large enough to make them seem like different products, and some versions potentially competed with one another. More seriously, Cisco in 2000–2001 received approximately 40 percent of its revenues from nonrouter devices, including ATM switches, some of which could serve as substitute products. Different Cisco business units sold these competing and complementary technologies to the same customers. Senior executives at the line of business level and Chambers at the CEO level were there to mediate any disputes between business units, although it would have been easier for Cisco executives and Cisco customers to make decisions if the company had a less eclectic platform strategy.

Finally, and most important, was the problem of the technology that has served as the glue for Cisco's networking hardware: IOS. To the outside world, IOS was a powerful common platform for Cisco equipment and the equipment of many other vendors. The software contained the standard interfaces that outside companies needed to link into networks and make their products work together. It was a convenient way to link diverse products. But IOS was not a product in itself, like the Intel microprocessor or Microsoft Windows. Cisco licensed IOS as part of the bundle with specific hardware products. Furthermore, IOS did not have a proprietary or internal set of APIs that made it easy for Cisco business units to create special links among their products. Consequently, Cisco had little control over its own platform technology because it was committed to following open standards. IOS by the early 2000s had also become extremely large and cumbersome because of all the products and interfaces that Cisco had tied into the system. Making changes or additions to the software was complex and slow, requiring hours to change even one line of code.[106]

Conclusion: Platform Leaders Need to Manage Platform Evolution

In some ways, Microsoft and Cisco could not be more different. Microsoft relied on proprietary technology for its software platforms;

Cisco did not (Lever 2). Microsoft invested heavily in in-house R&D to evolve its platform and complementary applications; Cisco relied on acquisitions (Lever 3). However, the two companies shared common problems. Both relied heavily on complements to make their platforms more valuable and did whatever was necessary (acquisitions, partnerships, in-house R&D) to make these available in the marketplace. More striking, however, is how both companies struggled to manage platform evolution. In Microsoft's case, the PC software platform evolved from DOS to Windows and then to the .NET system. In Cisco's case, the networking platform evolved from basic routers (a hardware and software system) to interoperable networking, based on software that linked together a variety of technologies through open standards.

Microsoft probably faces the greater task. Much of the company's resources, as well as considerable goodwill and cooperation from its myriad of partners and customers, will be necessary for Windows.NET to become the next dominant software platform. Because Microsoft makes many of its own complements, we are reasonably certain that there will be incentives for at least some users to move to the new platform. These incentives might not be enough, however, to create a new platform standard or replace revenues lost from Microsoft's traditional systems and applications businesses. In addition, a future breakup of the company (a possible, albeit remote, outcome if Microsoft violated terms of the antitrust settlement) could put a dent in Microsoft's ability to deliver the .NET platform and applications products, although there is no legal, technical, or strategic reason why two or more "Baby Bills" could not continue down the same .NET path. The key uncertainties, we believe, are Microsoft's ability to execute on its own ambitious R&D agenda and to overcome potential conflicts with outside partners. Microsoft has to progress in both areas to deliver a new infrastructure as well as applications and services sufficiently compelling to replace conventional versions of Windows and applications with .NET.

Cisco is likely to have difficulty protecting its market share because its platform consists of relatively little proprietary technology. It is not clear, though, what other strategy Cisco might have followed to become a platform leader in interoperable networking. The technology changed quickly and somewhat unpredictably. Cisco might have concentrated on routers, like Intel concentrated on microprocessors, and tried to push proprietary technology that would keep it state-of-the-art in all segments of this market. But, if the company had refused to move beyond routers, its sales and growth rates probably would have been half (or less) of what they were in the early 2000s. Acquisitions, though expensive, clearly helped Cisco expand its product offerings quickly and remain competitive, despite many technical challenges. In many ways, we can say that Cisco managed a remarkable evolution: It redefined the concept of "platform" for Internet-based networking from the router to a set of software-based communications standards that worked with routers and other types of networking equipment. It broadened the set of networking technologies that fit into the category of platform. And it provided the glue—the IOS software, imperfect though it was—to make disparate networking technologies work together. Cisco remained the market leader in Internet-based networking, though its position was clearly somewhat fragile.

In chapter 6, we turn to platform-leader wannabes that would do well to learn from the examples of Microsoft, Cisco, and Intel, though we need to emphasize that every industry and technology has its own characteristics. We will see, again, that there is no one formula for platform leadership.

Chapter Six

Platform-Leader Wannabes

Palm, NTT DoCoMo, and Linux

Intel, Microsoft, and Cisco are among several companies that have succeeded in becoming platform leaders (at least momentarily) in their industries—but many more are struggling to get there. We call them platform-leader wannabes. This chapter describes the challenges and obstacles that wannabes are likely to face.

We present the cases of Palm, Inc. in the area of handheld computing, NTT DoCoMo in the area of wireless content, and Linux in the area of open source software. Each case captures a key challenge that many wannabes must encounter. Palm illustrates how a new entrant can fight a giant (Microsoft) by playing a platform game—and the difficulties of doing so. DoCoMo illustrates the challenges inherent in internationalizing a successful local platform formula. And, Linux provides an opportunity to delve deeper into the power and limits of relying exclusively on external development and open standards to create complements to a platform. We see that wannabes can manipulate the same four levers as established leaders. These three chose to use the levers somewhat differently, however, depending on their external environment, resources, and some initial structural conditions and strategic choices:

1. *Scope of the firm*: Palm started off by designing a device (the Palm Pilot) that could function on its own, minimizing dependency on external firms. After succeeding with this product, however, Palm changed its strategy and started to move strongly in the direction of an operating system decoupled from applications, for whose development it started to rely more and more on external firms. NTT DoCoMo, on the other hand, created from the start a business model in which external complementors provided most of the content that DoCoMo users could access through their cell phones. Finally, the open source movement that gave birth to the Linux operating system is an extreme case of external development: Linux's structure made it impossible to do any complements development in-house—as there was no "house" to speak of. The open source movement was a network of mostly independent software developers who decided to collaborate in the creation of an operating system that would follow radically different rules (for design, testing, diffusion, and further innovation) than those of conventional commercial software development. Almost everything became outsourced, except functions of coordination and guidance, in which individuals such as Linus Torvalds played a major role.

2. *Product technology*: Like Intel and, to some extent, Microsoft, Palm relied mainly on internal proprietary technical choices for its operating system and on stimulating external innovation for most complementary applications. Also like Intel, their technical architecture is modular and therefore facilitates external development. NTT DoCoMo managers decided to follow mostly open standards for data transmission (CDMA [Code Division Multiple Access] technology), but they created a slightly different version of CDMA than the standard variety. Their version both facilitated external development for their i-mode phone and erected a barrier to imitation. Linux was developed with an attachment to open standards almost akin to religious commitment. Linux developers even created a new type of technology license (the General Public License) that prevented making proprietary any piece of software designed following the rules of the open source movement.

3. *Relationships with external complementors*: Once it adopted a platform strategy, Palm treated its complementors in a way quite similar to Intel: It actively invested efforts toward developing communities of software developers and users, launched developers forums, and facilitated technical training and even marketing for complementary developers. NTT DoCoMo entertained more classic business relationships with content developers, with a pricing contract that extracted a fixed percentage commission for all user transactions, on top of a fee for content developers. The Linux community of user–developers, however, entertained different types of relationships. Not devoid of self-interest, they nonetheless expressed strong attachments to ideals of software development, such as glory linked to technical prowess, and other intangible dimensions of merit less easily translatable into financial terms.

4. *Internal organization*: Palm went through several organizations, was bought up by 3Com, and then was spun off. In 2001, Palm decided to separate the group responsible for the handheld operating system from the rest of the company . NTT DoCoMo management decided from the start that applications (here, content) would always be done outside NTT DoCoMo. And the Linux movement, as stated earlier, had no significant "internal" development organization to speak of, as it was mostly a network of independent individuals.

From Device Vendor to Software Leader: The Palm Strategy

With approximately 12 million handheld devices sold through early 2001, a number expected to grow to nearly 34 million by 2004, the market for PDAs was ripe for a platform war.[1] The PDA device and its operating system (Palm OS) made up the platform. The platform needed complements such as software applications and wireless services to be anything more than a lifeless piece of hardware. And thousands of firms were beginning to create software applications, offer services, and create attachments that complemented the basic functions of the PDA device. In 2001, three main contenders led the PDA market, although Palm had more than a 70 percent global share for its hardware devices (table 6–1).

Table 6-1 PDA Global Industry Sales and Company Market Shares

	1999	2000	OS PLATFORM
UNITS SOLD:	1,347,185	3,515,414	
MARKET SHARE:			
Palm	77%	72%	Palm
Handspring	–	14	Palm
Casio	11	6	Microsoft
HP	3	2	Microsoft
Compaq	–	6	Microsoft
Other	9	–	

Source: NPD Intelect, quoted in K. Gerard, "The Palm Phenom," *Business 2.0*, 3 April 2001, 78.
Notes: PDA = personal digital assistant; OS = operating system.

Palm was also, by far, the fastest growing company in the industry: Its revenues rose from $1 million in 1995 to hundreds of millions of dollars per year in the late 1990s and reached $923 million in 2000.[2] The company suffered from excess inventory and declining sales, but it had sold over 11 million PDA units as of early 2001.[3] Palm was thus established as the market champion in both PDA hardware and software, especially with Handspring, the second leading vendor of PDA devices in 2000 with about 14 percent of the market, also using Palm OS.[4] The other leading contenders in the PDA space, competing primarily for leadership in operating systems, were Microsoft (with its Windows CE/Pocket PC software) and the Psion/Symbian consortium (with its EPOC software).

Like Intel, Palm did not start out with a specific strategy to become a platform leader in either hardware or software. That strategy emerged gradually, once Palm had a comfortable lead in the PDA device market. What Palm executives focused on during their critical formative years, that is, between 1995 and 1996, was to create a device that would sell and demonstrate the viability of the PDA market. This was a segment of the computing business that Apple, AT&T, Microsoft, and a host of other wealthy firms had failed to develop before Palm came along.[5]

Palm executives started to talk openly about a platform strategy in 1998, after they had sold a million or so units. By then, the Palm Pilot had become the de facto industry standard. Confident of their early lead,

Palm executives reformulated their strategy and decided to promote Palm OS as the industry software platform for handheld computing. For Palm, that meant both growing the market for handheld devices in general and trying to license Palm OS as broadly as possible. To achieve these objectives, Palm executives pursued two related but distinct activities: (1) They began to facilitate complementary innovations at outside firms by providing interface information, technical assistance, and some financial assistance, with the goal of helping thousands of external software developers write applications that enhanced the value of Palm's hardware and operating system software. And (2) they tried to grow the market for devices running Palm OS by licensing the operating system to competitors as well as partners, with one of the key licensees (Handspring) emerging from within its own ranks.

In early 2001, there were some 145,000 software developers (2,000 were signing up each week) at a variety of companies making some 8,500 applications that ran on Palm OS.[6] The battle for handheld computers was far from over, however. Handspring had at least 14 percent of the device market after starting business only in 1998. Its success helped Palm dominate the software platform side of the PDA business, but Handspring also had the potential to steal sales from Palm, which, in 2000, made more than 98 percent of its revenues from selling hardware. Furthermore, Microsoft was finally getting it right on its sixth attempt with the Pocket PC. There was no guarantee that Palm OS would continue to dominate as the software platform for PDAs. Nor was it certain that Palm would remain the hardware leader, especially as potentially lower-cost manufacturers like Handspring or consumer electronics companies moved into this space.

And this was not the whole picture. The PDA arena faced potential competition from players in a different industry that had its own ongoing platform battles. Nokia, Ericsson, and other makers of "smart phones" (Web-enabled cell phones) were beginning to offer PDA-like features. Some PDA makers, including Palm, countered with wireless connectivity features similar to Web-enabled cell phones. This competition was bringing both devices—PDAs and cell phones—somewhat closer together in terms of the underlying software and product features. Tackling the cell-phone makers was not a pleasant prospect for Palm and other PDA producers because the cell-phone makers had large-scale economies in manufacturing as well as distribution. The worldwide market for cell phones in 2000 exceeded 400 million units, of which Nokia alone made about one-third.[7]

As the platform leader (so far) in PDAs and as one of the few firms to beat Microsoft in a major market, Palm probably had the best chance to remain the platform leader in the PDA field. In this section, we discuss the evolution of Palm's strategy and how it achieved such a dominating position so quickly. We also examine the competition Palm encountered from Microsoft and Handspring in the United States and Psion and Symbian in Europe.

The Early Years: Establishing a Market for the Palm Pilot

Palm was founded in 1992 by Jeff Hawkins, an engineer who had worked at Intel and at a small manufacturer of portable computers, and Donna Dubinsky, a Harvard M.B.A. who had helped Apple launch its Claris software subsidiary.[8] Their initial goal was to create a firm that would develop software applications (in particular, handwriting recognition programs) for the fledgling handheld device market. That market had started with a resounding flop: Apple failed in its attempt to sell the Newton, introduced in 1993, to the mass market, largely because of software problems and other limitations.

In the same year as the Newton debacle, however, Palm introduced a product called the Zoomer, which it built in collaboration with Casio (for the hardware), GeoWorks (for the operating system), and Tandy (for the distribution). Palm engineers wrote the applications. The Zoomer, offered at $700, and with inadequate writing recognition software, sold a mere 15,000 units, but Palm learned much from that experience. The company started over from scratch, since it could not find any partners willing to try again, and focused on a few key goals that would soon define the essentials of the PDA platform: simpler features, a lower price, better handwriting recognition software, and connectivity with the PC through a one-button synchronization function with a cradle.

Palm made its brilliant "second debut" in 1996 with the launch of the Palm Pilot 1000 and Palm Pilot 5000. These devices integrated the hardware and software with a proprietary architecture, and were hugely successful with consumers. By the end of 1996, Palm had sold thousands of units and owned 51 percent of the nascent PDA market—surpassing

Sharp, Casio, and Apple as well as IBM and Microsoft, which had their own entries. Although Palm seemed to be on the road to success, the Palm Pilot, in Dubinsky's words, was little more than an "accessor[y] to PCs."[9] In other words, Palm management had positioned their product to be a complement to the well-established PC architecture, dominated by Intel and Microsoft. The Palm Pilot certainly was not a substitute for the PC. This positioning allowed Palm to avoid attracting too much of Microsoft's attention in the handheld space.

In their book *Judo Strategy*, David Yoffie and Mary Kwak argued that Palm's early philosophy was to keep a low profile so that Microsoft would not see them as a dangerous competitor. Contrary to Netscape, which had boldly (and provocatively) positioned Navigator as an alternative platform to Windows, Palm's early effort did not strike at the core of Microsoft's business—PC operating systems and the Office suite of applications. In fact, Palm defined its product as a device, not a platform. Dubinsky explained: "We always said: 'Look, if Microsoft had a decent platform we would consider it.' We are first and foremost a device company." And "of course," she added, "they didn't have a decent platform, so that was sort of a moot point." Hawkins elaborated: "We are not about the operating systems . . . we are about a highly integrated product that delivers an end user results. . . . In all honesty, if Microsoft walked in today with a great environment that we could build great products on, we'd absolutely consider it."[10]

In reality, however, the Palm Pilot was not simply a device. Palm OS had the potential to become a platform for independent software developers. Fundamentally, the architecture of Palm OS allowed for add-ons and extensions—a critical element for a platform. Nevertheless, according to Yoffie and Kwak, Palm executives waited almost eighteen months before holding their first developers conference and bringing Palm OS out into the open as a potential software platform. Ed Colligan, VP of Marketing at Palm, explained the thinking behind this low-key approach:

> It was very, very much our strategy to underplay the whole platform side of our business in the beginning because we wanted to focus our message on selling units. It hurts us a little bit in the industry. People said, "You're proprietary. You're a closed platform,"

because we didn't go out and promote that a lot. But you know what—it didn't matter, because in the end we knew if we sold millions, all that would come around. And that's exactly what happened.[11]

Palm executives were aware of the deep disappointment that previous failed efforts in the PDA field had caused among investors, consumers, and complement producers, of which Palm had been one. For Palm managers, the lesson was clear. "We are not having a developer conference until we sell a million units," Dubinsky recalled saying over and over at the time. "This was like a mantra. We are going to prove it to developers. We are not going to ask them to trust us."[12]

In retrospect, it seems wise that Palm managers did not advertise the platform capabilities of their product before a PDA mass market emerged. But a look at the design of the Palm OS architecture, with its capacity for adding third-party software and hardware, reveals that Palm engineers must have viewed their operating system as a potential platform from the beginning. The company Web site also made it clear that Palm expected outside developers and partners to help it evolve the operating system: "From the start, the flexible, extensible Palm OS has been designed to grow and evolve in response to user needs. The open, modular architecture allows our more than 50,000 developers, licensees, alliance and OEM partners to develop innovative new products and applications for a rapidly expanding global market."[13]

As seen in figure 6–1, the Palm OS architecture in 2001 consisted of five primary components:

1. Palm OS kernel software
2. Reference hardware design
3. HotSync conduit data technology for one-button synchronization
4. Platform component tools including an API that enabled developers to write applications
5. Software interface capabilities to support hardware add-ons

Palm OS contained various components designed to facilitate the external development of complements. It explicitly accommodated third-party applications and libraries (collections of special programs or sub-

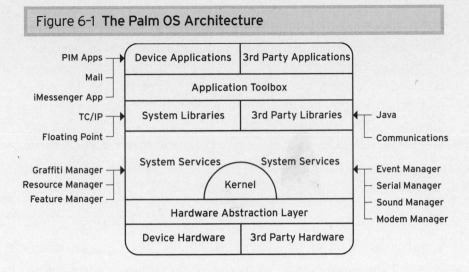

Figure 6-1 **The Palm OS Architecture**

Source: <http://www.palmos.com/platform/architecture.html> (accessed November 2001).

programs that developers can use when creating new applications). The system libraries let developers easily extend the functionality of Palm OS. An internal software map showed how the hardware worked, and a hardware abstraction layer gave developers the flexibility to modify Palm OS without having to rewrite code each time a change is made. Localization architecture made it easy to localize an application (i.e., create support for another language). Finally, an application interface made it easy to access a function or launch an application by pushing a clearly labeled on-screen button instead of navigating through a menu.

Device versus Platform: Palm Conflicts with 3Com Management

Once they had sold their first million units, Palm began to look attractive as either an initial public offering (IPO) or an acquisition. In September 1995, modem manufacturer US Robotics acquired Palm and began to operate the company as an independent subsidiary. Two years later, in June 1997, 3Com bought US Robotics. Fairly quickly, however, problems emerged. In particular, 3Com executives did not want to spin off Palm as an IPO or allow the unit to operate too autonomously. There were major disagreements over Palm's pricing policy for the Palm Pilot.

A low price, Dubinsky insisted, would allow deep penetration of Palm Pilots into the marketplace and encourage "network effects"— essential to establish one's product as a platform. 3Com management wanted to pursue more of a premium pricing strategy and go for the high end of the market. We believe that this pricing issue reveals a profound misunderstanding by 3Com management of Palm's potential as a platform—a misunderstanding that lasted until 1998. Dubinsky believed that the Palm Pilot's business model had to fit the economics of network effects (penetration, then installed base, then profits), rather than commanding a high price right away. But 3Com executives were used to selling modems—devices with short life cycles and no significant network effects—and accustomed to making high margins in the early phase of a product life cycle. Dubinsky recalled her arguments:

> We are a platform business. The idea in the beginning of a platform business is to get as much market share and installed base as possible, to draw as many developers as possible. And when we get high barriers to entry and lots of support, the network effect kicks in. Over time, we can have a product line that supports higher margin products, and we'll be protected against the competition. US Robotics and 3Com management didn't understand network effects; none of that was meaningful to them.[14]

3Com executives eventually got the point, but not before Hawkins and Dubinsky departed in 1998, mainly because 3Com would not approve an IPO, which 3Com later did anyway in March 2000.[15] The story does not end here, however. Hawkins and Dubinsky founded Handspring, a company that sold Palm Pilot look-alikes, all operating on Palm OS. We discuss Handspring in more detail under "Expanding the Pie."

Platform Competition Emerges in the PDA Segment

The Palm Pilot sold some million units in 1996 and 1997, demonstrating that the PDA mass market was a reality and that there were potentially large profits in this business. Profitable businesses attract attention, and real competition entered the PDA arena at about this time. Microsoft decided to push a cut-down version of Windows as the software platform for this market and to develop relationships with various hardware makers. Palm executives decided to go more decisively for a software platform strategy rather than just try to sell devices.

Hawkins and Dubinsky understood that attractive software applications would augment the value of the Palm Pilot. Therefore, like Intel, they quickly came to see external developers as a precious and scarce resource—to be cooed and wooed. But, as Yoffie and Kwak point out, Palm could not pursue external software developers too aggressively without attracting even more attention from Microsoft. So, without much fanfare, Palm began to provide developers with software tools useful in creating complementary software applications that ran on Palm OS. Palm's strategy was similar to Intel's: facilitate external complementary innovation by developing and distributing platform-specific tools to external software developers.

Palm released its first SDK in early 1996, with the Palm Pilot. Palm published the source code for the bundled applications with the SDK (the calendar, to-do list, address book, memo pad, and others). Two years before Palm OS as a platform really took off, Palm had found a way to make it easier to create complementary applications by providing access to the application source code already on the device, which developers could then use as a reference for building other applications. Dubinsky recalled:

> This [application] source code was in the SDK, so was under a license, but a royalty-free license. We found many developers that took advantage of this. Some would just use the source code for specific elements, such as picking up the code for a scroll bar. Others looked at it as sample code, and others yet took a whole application and created an enhanced version (such as the advanced calendar app that is now bundled in the [Handspring] Visor, which we licensed from its developer).[16]

Microsoft's Challenge: Trial, Error, and the Pocket PC

Microsoft executives noticed Palm's success in the handheld market and renewed their efforts to improve the cut-down version of Windows, then called Windows CE. Microsoft had released CE in November 1996 but then added new features that Palm did not offer, such as a voice recorder and the ability to support a color screen. Years and multiple software versions went by before Microsoft made much progress. But Pocket PC, the latest incarnation of Microsoft's operating system for handheld devices, introduced in spring 1999, was and remained in 2001 a serious threat to Palm. Customers had real choices because the technical approach that Palm and Microsoft followed in designing their operating systems differed considerably.

Palm went for a focused operating system, optimized for PDAs. Microsoft set much broader goals. Handheld devices containing the Pocket PC operating system ran a version of Windows and therefore could use modified Windows applications as well as offer the familiar Windows user interface. The Pocket PC devices both complemented and occasionally substituted for the desktop PC. Applications developers could use many of the same user interface code and programming techniques as they did for regular Windows applications—a feature attractive to complementors. Pocket PC also included a media player, useful for music or game applications. Microsoft worked closely with computer makers such as HP and Compaq to put out elegantly designed devices and cut-down versions of Windows applications that demonstrated these capabilities.

In mid-2001, Palm and Microsoft were locked in a battle to entice software applications developers to adopt their respective operating system platforms. Microsoft should have had the advantage here, given its huge resources and years of experience cultivating Windows applications developers around the world. Palm executives realized they were fighting an uphill battle against Microsoft, at least in terms of resources. Colligan described Microsoft's approach: "They'd offer funding for the initial development. They held all the development kitchens. They always put on a big dog-and-pony show, and we did our little nothing thing."[17] What's more, Microsoft's reputation as a fierce rival carried a lot of weight. When Microsoft released Windows CE, Colligan recalled that "People did have to say, 'Hmm, is Microsoft just going to kill Palm?' . . . And for a small point in time, a lot of people started going to the Microsoft product."[18] But the momentum behind the new Microsoft offering did not last. "In the end," Colligan concluded, "all the schmoozing and all the tools and all those things really don't matter if the products aren't selling."[19]

Palm's Response: Continue to Act as the Platform Leader

In a sense, Palm (headed by Sony and Reebok veteran Carl Yankowski [who resigned from Palm in November 2001] after Hawkins and Dubinsky departed) reacted to Microsoft's new entry by not reacting—by refusing to acknowledge that Microsoft might become the PDA platform leader. Company executives continued to act as if they—Palm—would sustain their position as the industry leader. In particular, Palm executives were determined to convince their troops of the danger of trying to play catch-up with Microsoft. They insisted on the importance of resisting the temptation to match every feature that Microsoft announced it would offer on its handheld OS.[20] This was a game that Netscape, Lotus, WordPerfect, and Novell had all lost in their respective head-to-head battles with Microsoft in browsers, applications, and networking software.

Microsoft's latest entry into the handheld market may have helped Palm executives be more resolute about their claim to industry leadership and more aggressive in their determination to establish Palm OS as the software platform. This is our interpretation of Dubinsky's comments in her interview with Yoffie and Kwak: "We were the clear leader by every measurement out there."[21] In Dubinsky's words, acting like the leader meant that Palm had to "set the agenda and drive the industry" as well as avoid a feature war with Microsoft.[22] Like Intel, Palm was about to take the higher ground, a position not so different from Intel's goal for IAL to be "the architect of the industry."

How does a platform-leader wannabe "set the agenda" and "drive the industry"? Certainly, a large market share, even of a nascent market, is a good start. A successful product can define the nature of design competition and make it easier for the market leader to become the platform leader in terms of architecture, features, and technology. Two other ingredients seem essential to channel the innovative capabilities of external developers in a direction that benefits not only the end user but the platform leader as well: (1) an open architecture that allows external, complementary innovation and (2) relationships with external developers to stimulate these innovations.

But this is not enough. From Intel, we learned that long-term success as a platform leader requires vision: a user-centered vision for the future of the complete product as well as a vision for the evolution of the whole industry and its particular platform. This vision, furthermore, should lead both customers and complementors along a path that, in the end, benefits the platform leader more than its competitors. Intel did this. It took the lead in shaping interfaces that partitioned complementary innovations and in promoting interfirm cooperation. At least through

IAL, it also tried to be a neutral broker, exploring new interface standards and applications on behalf of the whole PC industry—albeit with the understanding that what was good for the computing industry was especially good for Intel. Even Microsoft, since its founding in 1975, pushed a grand vision of the future—a PC on every desktop, running a variety of software that did everything from entertaining us to enhancing our productivity in the office. The Microsoft vision evolved from DOS and Windows programming technologies to the all-embracing concept of Windows.NET, which may or may not become a dominant platform. To attain their positions, both Intel and Microsoft had to invest extensively in evolving their platforms as well as in creating consensus among external players to support innovations.

Palm, too, worked hard to mobilize complementors and to suggest new uses for its platform—suggestions that fit how Palm management saw the future for its industry. The wireless Internet connections available on Palm VII and the "Palm.net" service are noteworthy examples. Palm devices had been getting closer functionally to wireless phones, with attachments that enabled sending and receiving e-mail as well as making phone calls. At the same time, wireless phones were evolving to resemble PDAs by including calendars and address books. Palm VII was essentially a Palm III with an antenna. It offered e-mail and used Palm's proprietary Web Clipping technology to enable users to perform limited functions over the Internet using a small monochrome display. Palm also established a proprietary wireless communication network, outsourced from BellSouth and named Palm.net, specifically to support Palm VII.

Introduced in August 2000, an improved version of the Palm VII, Palm VIIx (priced initially at $449) offered a fourfold increase in memory to 8 megabytes and bundled forty Web Clipping applications, nearly double the wireless content of the original Palm VII.[23] The Web Clipping technology eliminated the need for content developers for the Palm Pilot to design specific Web pages or use proxy servers to translate Web pages to the small PDA screens—a big advantage over the wireless application protocol (WAP). As of early 2001, Palm.net covered 260 major U.S. metropolitan areas and was offered in service plans starting at $9.99 per month and going up to $49.99 per month. It represented a bold move by Palm to gain expertise in the wireless world and sent a clear message to end users and partners that the Palm Pilot could serve as a platform for full-fledged wireless communications services.

Palm's Strategy for Facilitating External Innovation

Like Intel, Palm did not try to make all the complements for its platform itself. Instead, it encouraged outside companies to do most of these innovations. In March 2001, Palm boasted that it had some 145,000 external software developers writing applications, and over 500 hardware developers creating add-on accessories—from keyboards and voice recorders to digital cameras and global positioning system (GPS) wireless connection systems. The Palm Web site claimed there were also thousands of other applications available for Palm OS.[24]

A sample of software and hardware complements announced for the Palm platform as of 2001 was truly impressive: More than a dozen e-reading (electronic book reading) programs and thousands of e-books; spreadsheet programs that can read and edit Microsoft Excel files; document-editing programs that let users read and edit Microsoft Word files; online shopping from Amazon.com, eBay, and other companies; full-function database programs; enterprise software tools that let users fill out forms, check inventory, take orders, and even make job offers through a wireless connection. There were also hundreds of games such as SimCity and Tiger Woods Golf, financial management programs such as Pocket Quicken, drawing and painting programs, and tools that allow users to customize their own Palm OS programs "in minutes" (according to the Palm Web site). Other software programs included two Web browsers, an MP3 player, GPS receivers and mapping programs, and cell phones that were also fully-functional Palm-compatible handhelds. An electronic camera let users view pictures on their Palm handheld or check the weather online from Weather.com, sports from ESPN, and news from ABC, *The New York Times*, and the BBC. Another application offered a voice memo recorder.

The term "Palm Economy" captured the idea that a successful platform creates complementary markets and business opportunities. The company used the term to refer to the set of players and the arena of opportunities for applications developers, partners, licensees, and OEMs who adopted Palm OS. Palm management understood the pull that such opportunities exerted on profit-seeking entrepreneurs. Like Intel, Palm's goal was to convince outside companies to invest their skills, talents, and energy into creating products optimized to the Palm OS platform. Some 2,000 participants from 560 companies and 30 countries attended a recent Palm developers conference, suggesting that the Palm Economy was indeed large.

To entice complementors, Palm management also made heavy use of the company Web site to communicate their message. They advertised that Palm OS covered 78.4 percent of the global handheld computing market, citing International Data Corporation statistics. They touted the 4,000 applications created by external developers and the speed of market development to get the bandwagon of developers going.

Like Intel, Microsoft, and Cisco, Palm sought out agreements with potential complementors. For example, it announced an alliance with Nokia, the Finnish phone maker, in September 1999, and another with Japanese consumer-electronic giant Sony in October 1999. A deal with Motorola came in December 1999, licensing Palm OS for future devices. These deals provided the partners with Palm technology for their cell phones and other handheld devices, existing or in development. Alliances were created with Handspring, IBM, QUALCOMM, Supra, Symbol Technologies, and TRG Products to create devices based on Palm OS. Other new product development alliances were set up with phone and appliance makers Nokia and Sony and with enterprise software vendors Oracle, SAP, and Sybase.

Like Intel and Microsoft, Palm provided a full set of software development tools to outside companies to help them build applications. Palm's goal was to provide a programming interface (API) for the key technologies in Palm OS (e.g., its "conduit" technology) so that developers could create applications that would work with PCs as well as Macintosh computers.[25] The APIs hide the details for making the applications work on the different platforms.

Like Intel, Palm created both formal and informal mechanisms to stabilize its interface standards and facilitate technical exchanges and business dealings among the growing community of complementors. For example, Palm's Web site listed the business development resources that it offered to its community of developers, ranging from joint development and marketing to bundling and other types of programs to strengthen product offerings. Palm also provided financing information to help firms secure funding, and advertised that its software development forums (SDF) helped external developers start and grow their own businesses. The SDF offered "venture capital advisory meetings, entrepreneurial business seminars, workshops, and networking."[26] The company also offered Palm OS development classes (five-day seminars) regularly in California, New York, Texas, and Hong Kong.

Palm was also encouraging activities among its "community of users," who exchanged information and had similar interests. For example, PalmGear H.Q., a Web portal and e-commerce site, brought shareware developers and users together as a resource for the Palm OS community. The site—from the same-named privately owned company that claimed to be the leading Internet source for Palm OS—offered software, hardware, accessories, news, and information.

In another move reminiscent of Intel, Palm launched in September 2000 a $50 million venture unit, dubbed Palm Ventures, to aid complementary firms.[27] Palm management stated that it hoped to forge alliances with companies that it funded. It also declared that Palm wanted to boost the development of application programs for Palm OS so it could keep the lead in the handheld market. Robert Hayes, Director of Palm Ventures, explained Palm's goals: "[There are] companies out there that fill the gaps which we don't fill and provide the solutions we don't provide—they have really contributed to the success of Palm. . . . We want to accelerate that and invest in companies that are going to help this Palm phenomenon to continue to grow."[28] Palm Ventures was planning to make approximately twenty investments, including ten to fifteen in its first year, with an average investment of $1 million to $5 million. The initial fund of $50 million was only "the first of multiple rounds" of funding that Hayes expected Palm to provide.

Finally, as another part of Palm's strategy to facilitate external innovation, the company worked with other firms to evolve key interfaces to its platform. The synchronization protocol is a good example. It allowed users to transfer and update data between their PDAs and desktop computers and other devices, such as smart phones. In June 2000, IBM, Lotus, Nokia, Palm, Psion, and Starfish Software founded the SyncML Initiative (SyncML stands for Synchronization Markup Language). The group's goal was to develop an "open industry specification for universal data synchronization" that enabled users to exchange information across various types of networks, software platforms, and computing devices.[29] The initiative fit with Palm's goal of creating a thriving complements market and reflected their commitment to an open interface.

Expanding the Pie: Handspring and the Palm Economy

Ironically, it was after Hawkins and Dubinsky left 3Com in 1998 (and probably as a direct result of it) that 3Com finally decided to implement many of the moves they had proposed when they were still on board. The new platform strategy began in October 1999 when 3Com announced it would spin off its Palm Computing subsidiary as an IPO, leading to the creation of Palm, Inc. Coincidently, this announcement came one day before Handspring announced its Visor product, a low-priced version of the Palm Pilot that used Palm OS. The new Palm, Inc. soon started to license Palm OS to firms other than Handspring, including consumer giant Sony. Handspring itself went public in June 2000 and saw its share price more than double before falling back with the rest of the market by spring 2001. Nevertheless, as of mid-2001, Handspring was still a leader of the emerging Palm Economy—the group of firms building complements to the Palm Pilot or licensing Palm OS for their own PDAs or Web-enabled cell phones.

After its founding in June 1998, Handspring adopted a platform approach to product design. Unlike Palm, however, Handspring engineers designed the hardware around this concept in a bold move to make modules or peripherals as easy as possible to connect. The expansion modules literally snapped into the expansion slot on the back of the Visor PDA. Palm devices lacked such a simple mechanism for expansion when Handspring introduced this innovation. Handspring called its hardware platform SpringBoard. The company sold a full line of Spring-Board expansion modules and accessories, in addition to its Visor line of handheld computers.[30] But Handspring also encouraged external companies to develop products that acted as accessories or modules to Visors. Table 6–2 lists a sample of modules available for the Handspring Visors as of March 2001.

For example, IDEO designed a digital camera (Eyemodule), and a radio module (CUE). The Eyemodule sold for $150 and captured either color or black-and-white digital images.[31] Users could beam images from their Visor's infrared port to another Visor or to any other Palm OS–based handheld. With HotSync, another technology developed by

Table 6-2 Third-Party Modules for Handspring Devices

MODULE	VENDOR	PRICE	FUNCTION
PowerOne Finance	Infinity Softworks	$50	Cartridge for math calculations such as profit margins, depreciation, interest rates, currency exchange rates
Gameface	Handspring	$40	Plastic faceplate that adds buttons and a joystick for playing games
Minstrel S Wireless Modem	Omnisky	$299	Wireless modem that works with Omnisky's content service. Content can be saved on the Web into a memo pad or address book.
VisorPhone	Handspring	$299	Module that fits on the back and converts the Visor into a mobile phone with wireless modem
MiniJam MP3 Player	InnoGear	$259	Player and storage device for music as well as electronic books and images
GoType! Keyboard	LandWare	$70	Portable keyboard with word-processing program
Total Recall Digital Voice Recorder	Targus	$100	Voice recorder
Eyemodule Digital Camera	IDEO	$150	Camera that beams pictures to other PDAs
CUE Radio Module	IDEO	N/A	AM-FM radio and wireless device for e-mail, traffic alerts, personal messages
Geode GPS Module	GeoDiscovery	$289	Electronic city guide
Presenter-to-Go	Margi Systems	$300	Digital projector

Source: Compiled from J. Lardner and K. Girard, "Hawkins Talks," *Business 2.0*, 3 April 2001, 86; and <http://www.cue.net> (accessed November 2001).

3Com, users could also transfer these images to a PC to edit, e-mail, or print. The CUE radio module allowed users to listen to music on their favorite radio station as well as receive e-mail, traffic alerts, and personal messages. The latter two were sent over CUE's FM subcarrier network, which covered over 95 percent of the United States and Canada.[32]

Handspring engineers also worked hard on designing interfaces to the SpringBoard platform, a move that we believe was essential to establishing platform leadership. For example, SpringBoard allowed users to synchronize data with their PCs via a USB connection, rather than through a cable plugged into the serial port on the back of a PC which was an older approach that Palm used. (Hawkins and Dubinsky had pushed for this design change in the Palm Pilot while the company was still part of 3Com, but they failed to convince 3Com management.)

Newer Palm devices could accommodate similar types of modules, but with more cumbersome connector technology. A major disadvantage of the original Palm hardware architecture (especially in contrast to SpringBoard) was the lack of an expansion slot or standard connector that made it easy for third parties to add on modules or peripherals. Palm rectified this with its newer models. Its revamped Palm V line introduced in 2001 included two models (the m500 [$399] and the m505 [$449]) with expansion slots and Palm's new Universal Connector. The new models also came with software by the DataViz Corporation that allowed users to edit Microsoft Word and Excel files—a feature that Microsoft's Pocket PC already had. The m505 was also a color unit—another feature of the Pocket PC and Handspring models.[33] These new features were introduced late in the PDA race, but they made Palm's offerings more competitive with models from Handspring and Microsoft Pocket PC vendors such as HP and Compaq. Palm also cut prices on its products to match Handspring's lowest priced models—suggesting that Handspring had taken the lead in defining price points for PDAs as well as hardware design.

Although Handspring was helping to build broader acceptance of Palm OS as a standard platform, the company seemed to be doing more than Palm to drive forward the PDA architecture and functionality. This raised an interesting question: Was there a part of the Handspring Visor that might become an industry platform? There are two main possibilities: First, there might be room for more than one platform, as in the PC business. In a multiplatform scenario, Palm OS could emerge as the dominant software platform and the Handspring Visor SpringBoard as the dominant hardware platform. Microsoft's handheld operating system might remain as a second standard, much like the Macintosh operating system continues on in the PC world. Second, Palm OS might not be the ultimate software platform after all. Microsoft or some other vendor might win. Handspring seemed prepared for this scenario. Since the hardware platform was its main selling point, Handspring could potentially develop its own operating system or switch to another vendor, such as Microsoft.

But, for Palm executives, Handspring's ambitions for platform leadership made us question who really controlled the Palm Economy. As we saw with Intel, offering one piece of a system was not enough to guarantee platform leadership. Platform leadership is weakened, for example, if external innovations do not reinforce demand for the product or if the product loses its edge over a competing product. Also, after Hawkins and Dubinsky left Palm, the company did not introduce any new breakthrough products; they instead only incrementally added features (i.e., wireless capabilities and Palm.net services) to the Palm series. It remains to be seen whether these initiatives will be enough to keep Palm ahead of Handspring, Microsoft, and other competitors, such as those in Europe.

Competition from Europe: The EPOC Operating System

If Palm only had Microsoft and Handspring to worry about, its task would be easier. But another challenger in the space for handheld operating systems loomed: the Symbian consortium in Europe, initially formed around the Psion company. This group is particularly strong in software technology for wireless devices.

Psion is a British maker of handheld computers founded in the early 1980s. It is one of Europe's last remaining computer companies. As of 2001, Psion owned about 28 percent of the London-based Symbian consortium. Nokia, Motorola, Ericsson, and Matsushita were the other major investors. Symbian was trying to make Psion's operating system (called EPOC) a platform for Web-surfing handheld computers and cell phones—a market expected to reach 1.3 billion units by 2003.[34] Symbian planned to charge $5 to $10 per device and eventually grow to become a billion-dollar software company in its own right.

Symbian members licensed EPOC from Psion, which designed the software specifically to control portable computers with wireless access to phones and other information services. More than any other PDA operating system, EPOC seems well positioned to be the operating system of choice for the converging worlds of handhelds and wireless phones. A complicating factor, however, is that Psion faced competition not only from Palm and Microsoft, but also from Symbian partners such as Nokia, which was not locked into EPOC as the only alternative for an operating system. Nokia preferred an "open" or "decentralized" platform approach, with different kinds of platforms and coalition partners for different types of applications.[35] Microsoft, in contrast, was trying to make Windows and its multiple versions a "centralized" platform covering multiple devices and applications, ranging from PCs to mobile phones to handheld computers.

In general, which European or American firm was committed to which operating system for handhelds remained a confusing subject. For example, although Psion was not well known in the United States, it successfully established relationships with Sun Microsystems and IBM in order to target the corporate market. Psion hoped that its Web-surfing "palmtops" would be in much demand among mobile professionals such as sales staff and become the preferred device to link users to their corporate intranets. It also teamed up with Motorola to target the consumer market with plans for a "mobile surfer" design that included a color screen, a speakerphone, and a list of contacts that the user could dial up with the touch of a stylus. In Europe, not all Ericsson and Nokia devices ran on the EPOC operating system. In March 2000, for example, Ericsson demonstrated a prototype for a color Web surfer that used non-EPOC operating system software similar to the product Psion was building with Motorola.

In December 1999, Motorola signed a memorandum of understanding with Palm to license Palm OS for future wireless devices. "The market is showing us that the Palm and [the Symbian EPOC operating system] are the two platforms to go after," said Motorola spokesman Bott Ikeler.[36] He then claimed the company had no plans to offer devices based on Microsoft's Pocket PC operating system. But Ericsson declared in December 1999 that it would support Microsoft's operating system and use Symbian's operating system, too. Then, in a joint declaration by Palm and Symbian in October 1999, the two companies announced they were working together on a new platform that would combine the EPOC operating system core with the graphical user interface of Palm OS.

What was afoot among the cell-phone and handheld computer manufacturers in Europe and to a lesser extent in the United States was a scramble to hedge platform bets. No one was sure which software standard was likely to emerge the winner, if indeed there would be only one. Companies might continue to use different operating systems for different devices and wait to see what happened in the future.

Future Prospects for Palm's Platform Strategy: Success or Failure?

The Palm case suggests several do's and don'ts for a platform-leader wannabe to maximize its chances of success. First, be patient. It may not be a good idea to try to be a platform leader before one's product has gained mass-market acceptance. It takes a lot of effort and public relations to attract, license, support, and possibly subsidize partners and complementors. It seems wiser to maintain a low profile in the early days of market development and focus on designing a product that people want to buy. It also takes time to earn the trust of applications developers. A highly publicized failure such as Apple experienced with the Newton can make it very hard for a platform leader to regain the trust of software developers and other complementors who need to make large investments tied to the platform.

The lesson here? A platform strategy is not a substitute for a product strategy. For a platform strategy to work, the market has to adopt the product in large numbers, and this depends, at least in part, on having features and prices suitable for the mass market. The platform winner need not be superior to the competition in all features or dimensions of the product. It is difficult to claim, for example, that Windows, particularly versions from ten years ago, was superior to the Macintosh operating system, or, in the realm of home video recorders, that VHS was ever superior to Sony's Betamax standard. But the platform products were comparable. And, in those cases, platform strategy won out. An inadequate product, however, does not make an attractive platform.

Second, it is possible to evolve from leadership in hardware or product design to leadership in software. Cisco, for example, started in router hardware, but its platform became the IOS operating system, which could link many types of networking equipment. Palm decided to license its operating system to competitors in the hardware space such as Handspring and Sony. Management bet that Palm could make more money from software and services, such as through Palm.net, rather than from hardware, at least in the long run.

Software licensing, of course, is the business model Microsoft pursued with great success. The danger is that, unlike Microsoft with Windows for the desktop PC, Palm has not yet won the software platform battle for handheld devices. As discussed in the Microsoft antitrust trial, the software platform leader is somewhat protected from competition by third-party complements—the so-called applications barrier to entry. Palm did not yet have such a strong position with its operating system. Microsoft's Pocket PC and Symbian's EPOC operating systems remained viable competitors, particularly because the market for PDAs was still in an early stage. Palm's 80 percent or so market share meant little if the market was truly only at the beginning stages of growth. Palm executives should recall, for example, that Sony once had 90 percent or so of the home VCR market—when the market was still in its early stages and Matsushita and Japan Victor had not yet mass-produced or broadly licensed VHS-standard machines.[37] In 2001, it was also unclear which direction Palm would go. Company executives were hedging their bets by trying to do everything—continuing with a large hardware design staff, a large software effort, and a portal effort for wireless services. Not even Microsoft tackled so many avenues at once.

Third, a platform leader should maintain architectural control over its platform. At times, Handspring seemed to be the leader in hardware architecture, even though Palm did control the interfaces to its operating system. However, despite an aggressive policy of licensing Palm OS even to competitors, Palm might not have created enough barriers to entry in its own core business to be able to survive the competition. Challenges were coming both from within its ecosystem (Handspring and Sony, which licensed Palm OS but sold competing devices) and from other software platform producers (Microsoft and Symbian, which had competing operating systems and hardware). In addition, Nokia and other cell-phone giants were entering the PDA battlefield as well with hybrid cell phones.

Fourth, when the future of a platform battle is very uncertain, managers need to prepare for multiple scenarios and develop an aggressive strategy to promote the outcome they favor. In Palm's case, the possibility that cell-phone producers (rather than Palm, Microsoft, or Symbian) might determine which software platform dominates made the future especially uncertain. Three possible scenarios are the following:

1. Convergent devices would win out over single-purpose devices; that is, people would prefer to carry one device that was both a PDA and a cell phone. PDAs did not make comfortable telephones, although cell phones could serve reasonably well as PDAs with calendars, address books, e-mail, and other functions

readily accessible. Therefore, if convergent devices were to win out, the operating system that best handled Web phone functionality would probably become the dominant software platform. Symbian's EPOC software seemed to have a technical and strategy edge here, given the support it had from cell-phone giants such as Nokia, Ericsson, and Motorola.

2. Users would prefer handheld devices that substituted for their PCs and performed other functions, such as wireless telephony and PDA-like tasks. In this scenario, Microsoft's Pocket PC probably had the edge because Microsoft designed the software to act like a small Windows PC.

3. Users would prefer specialized devices. In other words, people would continue to carry separate cell phones, PDAs, and small PCs. This is the outcome we thought most likely, in part because convergent devices generally involve design compromises. This is why specialized video game machines remained more popular than PCs running video games. In this scenario of specialized devices, we might well see multiple platform leaders: Palm for PDA software, Handspring for PDA hardware, Symbian for cellphone operating systems, and Microsoft for handheld PC-like devices.

The Palm case also evokes this question: How do you challenge and beat the giant in your industry, or a giant that wants to move into your industry? Palm might prevail over Symbian simply because Symbian is a consortium of companies with conflicting goals. They might never come up with one coherent strategy. Microsoft, however, is a relentless competitor with extremely deep pockets. Moreover, Microsoft executives and engineers generally learned from their mistakes. Pocket PC, Microsoft's sixth attempt at a handheld design, was a good example of this process of trial and error, and persistence. Microsoft CEO Steve Ballmer expressed concern over the limited potential profit in handheld computing, but he was unwilling to give up: "We can't afford to give up a potential choke point on our core platform."[38] In other words, Microsoft feared losing control over the software that dominated the computing world—if Palm or another firm were to establish a truly dominant position in handheld computing.

Integrating Wireless and Content:
The NTT DoCoMo Strategy

Although wireless services and Web content were available over PDAs, Web-enabled cell phones were by far the dominant device for mobile Web access. In this market, Japan's NTT DoCoMo was the most powerful player. In 2001, DoCoMo was both the world's largest provider of Internet-based mobile wireless services and Japan's largest company in terms of market capitalization.

Nippon Telephone and Telegraph (NTT), Japan's largest telephone company, spun off DoCoMo in 1992 as part of the Japanese telecommunications industry deregulation and retained two-thirds ownership of the company. NTT DoCoMo quickly became the largest cell-phone operator in Japan, with a market share in 2001 of approximately 60 percent, which translated into some 32 million Japanese users.[39] The Japanese company used its base in cell phones to launch a new service in February 1999 that pioneered wireless data transmission over cell phones with an instantly accessible and always-on mobile Internet service called "i-mode." This was the beginning of an explosive growth of Internet services over wireless phones in Japan. (The name "DoCoMo" is an English acronym that stood for "Do Communications over the Mobile network." The name was also a play on words in that dokomo means "anywhere" in Japanese. The i in i-mode supposedly stood for "interactive, Internet, and independence.")[40]

The i-mode service was tremendously successful, with almost 21 million users (out of Japan's 127 million people) as of March 2001[41] and another 300,000 new users signing up each week.[42] Every day, millions of Japanese used their i-mode phones to surf Web sites, exchange e-mails or photographs, download their horoscopes, or play with popular Japanese cartoon characters. The rollout of wireless application services in North America and Europe paled in comparison. For example, Sprint PCS, the leading carrier for these services in the United States, had a mere 1 million users at the end of 2000.

When DoCoMo was created, however, most NTT staff did not want to leave the parent company for what was seen then as a less exciting venture. Uncharacteristically, the new start-up hired workers from outside NTT, and these people brought in a spirit of entrepreneurship. The initial head of the i-mode project, Keiichi Enoki, was a young engineer inspired by his teenage daughter's enthusiastic exchanges of gossip over e-mail using her PC. He also saw his son playing endless hours of games on his PC and thought it would be possible to enable people to play electronic games on the move.[43] Enoki hired two people who became key players in the DoCoMo venture: Mari Matsunaga and Takeshi Natsuno, both lured in 1997 from an Internet start-up (a classified-ad magazine group) and both concerned more with the business model than with the technology.

NTT DoCoMo became a market leader in Japan by focusing on three areas: the technology platform, a new business model, and unique content. As of this writing, the company was also laying the foundations for moving its platform and services into other countries. This was the major challenge for the 2000s. But it remained unclear whether DoCoMo would be able to push its platform—a unique blend of modified standard technologies and content—or its business model and content in other countries with different market conditions and user preferences. In other words, although DoCoMo was a platform leader in Japan for wireless Web services and content, it remained a platform-leader wannabe in the rest of the world. This section describes the specific elements of NTT DoCoMo's efforts to establish its platform in Japan and extend its leadership position beyond Japan.

The i-mode Technology Platform

The i-mode technology platform consisted of two standards for creating content and for transmitting data wirelessly: (1) an application programming language for small-screen Web devices (c-HTML) and (2) a data transmission standard (first PDC, then PHS, and in the future W-CDMA). Both sets of technologies were derivations of open industry standards.

C-HTML PROGRAMMING LANGUAGE   Although DoCoMo expressed an early interest in the alternative WAP technology, it instead designed its own proprietary system based on HTML (the basic Web programming language since the early 1990s)—"compact HTML," also known as c-HTML. Content providers for the i-mode system had to use c-HTML to create their Web page screens and link to the network. Because of its similarities to HTML, c-HTML made it easy for Web developers to write applications without having to learn an unfamiliar programming language. With DoCoMo's control over the handset user-interface, c-HTML also guaranteed a consistent and high level of end-user experience.

DATA TRANSMISSION STANDARD   For its data transmission standard, DoCoMo relied initially on the Personal Digital Cellular/Personal Handyphone System (PDC/PHS), an early packet-switching technology used in Japan that sent data at the rate of 9.6 kilobytes per second (kbps). i-mode was not particularly fast; 9.6 kbps was the same data rate as most of the rest of the world's networks. That fact alone, however, demonstrated a key element of i-mode's success: High data rates were not necessary to woo a large number of customers. This ran counter to what had been the conventional wisdom in the wireless industry.

Ahead of other wireless carriers, DoCoMo planned to upgrade in 2001 to a new "third-generation" (3G) data transmission standard—jW-CDMA for Japanese W-CDMA (W-CDMA stood for Wideband Code Division Multiple Access). It offered much faster data rates—up to 2 megabytes per second, which was forty times faster than existing analogue modem technology—and better spectrum efficiency. Even if its customers did not press for higher bandwidth services, DoCoMo as an operator had to upgrade because it had barely any capacity left on the PDC system.

We should note, however, that DoCoMo's proposed jW-CDMA technology differed from the standard accepted by the International Telecommunications Union (ITU). The jW-CDMA had certain peculiarities as well as proprietary protocols. Vendors also had to sign nondisclosure agreements to build products using the new standard. DoCoMo had lined up Matsushita (Panasonic) to be its first handset supplier, although delays in making the jW-CDMA chip sets created some problems in launching the upgraded service in October 2001.

Even before DoCoMo introduced 3G transmission technology, the i-mode platform surpassed alternatives in both transmission efficiency and content. The PDC/PHS technology was packet based, unlike the circuit-switched solutions that most WAP carriers traditionally offered. Packet-based transmission allowed DoCoMo to offer a service in which users were essentially online twenty-four hours a day but paid only for each packet of data they sent or received. By contrast, GSM (Global System for Mobile Communications) networks, the current-generation standard in Europe (with over 100 million users worldwide, including the United States), required a dedicated-line connection or circuit each time a user wanted access to a service. This is why WAP phones took half a minute just to connect to a Web page. This consumption of time and dedicated lines also helped explain why WAP phones were more expensive than DoCoMo's offerings.[44]

WAP phones received a lot of publicity when they appeared in large numbers during 1999 in Europe, but results fell short of expectations. Not only was service slow, but the screens were often difficult to read, and little compelling content made its way onto the networks. Not surprisingly, there was widespread consumer indifference—called "WAPathy" by some industry executives.[45] In the first six months of usage, for example, T-Mobil, a unit of Deutsche Telekom AG, reported that customers with WAP phones were accessing the wireless Internet less than once a week. There was clearly room in the industry for a better combination of technologies. Microsoft was a loud critic of WAP and announced it would launch an i-mode browser in 2001. DoCoMo itself chose to participate actively in the WAP Forum, an industry group that tried to set standards for the WAP technology, in an effort to improve the standard and bring it closer to c-HTML. This seemed to be under way as of this writing. In fact, at least some industry analysts believed that within two years there would be little difference between WAP and i-mode as wireless operators and applications developers adopted extended versions of HTML.[46]

DoCoMo also had great influence over the design of hardware (the handsets) that customers had to use with its service. With a group of 900 R&D engineers and $825 million in R&D funds, DoCoMo designed the world's smallest and most sophisticated handsets. Katrina Bond, a senior analyst covering the mobile sector for Britain's Analysis Ltd., commented: "NTT DoCoMo is one of the few operators that can dictate [technological specifications] to handsets manufacturers."[47]

Standards Battles in Wireless Transmission Technologies

During the late 1990s and early 2000s, the wireless world experienced a "battle of the standards." The battle was intense because the standard that emerged would be global; operators wanted their customers to be able to use their phones around the world. There were also potentially vast economies of scale in equipment purchases, content management, and operations. Operators that bet wrong might find that handsets and equipment for their standards were scarce and costly, and new content they were preparing might not work properly on different platforms. Equipment and content vendors, too, had to choose one standard or set up to handle multiple standards. Which standard would win, however, was by no means clear in 2001.

In the early and mid-1990s, the ITU, an international body dedicated to global standard-setting activities, tried to promote one global standard for 3G wireless services. That vision collapsed under pressure from regional standards bodies. By 1998, the ITU had proposals for thirteen different interface standards based on CDMA. All that happened while Ericsson and QUALCOMM were embroiled in a highly publicized patent dispute. QUALCOMM and backers of the Interim Standard 95 (IS-95) favored one "harmonized" CDMA standard based on their chosen technology, cdma2000, because it provided backward compatibility to older systems. Ericsson and the GSM camp wanted their own technology, W-CDMA, which was incompatible with IS-95 systems.[48]

A compromise emerged, scaling the thirteen proposals into a single CDMA standard that encompassed three optional modes: W-CDMA, cdma2000, and Time Division Multiple Access (TDMA), a variation of W-CDMA. The specifications for interoperability were finished as of early 2001, but problems remained. Operators and OEMs that offered services or made transmission equipment would ultimately decide the standard. Two versions of the technology, W-CDMA (backed initially by Ericsson and Nokia) and cdma2000 (backed primarily by QUAL-COMM), remained the major competitors.

W-CDMA, with its global roaming capabilities and promises of huge economies of scale, was gaining most of the industry's attention. CDMA operators also had the easiest migration path to high-speed data services of any technology operator because they could perform upgrades primarily in the software. All of Europe's operators—including Vodafone, the world's largest cell-phone operator—planned to deploy the technology as it became available.[49] NTT DoCoMo first allied with Ericsson and

Nokia in 1997 and promised that its version of W-CDMA would be backward compatible with GSM. DoCoMo and J-Phone, another Japanese operator, also received 3G licenses and planned to deploy W-CDMA systems around 2002. But technical issues, such as chip set and handset availability, were likely to delay the wide deployment of W-CDMA until 2003.

The other standard—cdma2000—trailed W-CDMA in global acceptance and roaming capabilities, but had benefits in availability and cost. This technology offered extra capacity and packet-data services on backward-compatible handsets. The cdma2000 technology could also add voice capacity and high data speeds within existing spectrum constraints. Operators in Korea already deployed the cdma2000 technology in their systems, and some North American operators planned to migrate to it in the near future. However, the W-CDMA community received a boost when South Korea's mobile operators began heavily advocating W-CDMA. They were reluctant to become the only Asian operators using the cdma2000 standard. In this area of the world in particular, DoCoMo's support of W-CDMA was impacting the adoption decisions of other companies.

DoCoMo also embarked on an aggressive strategy to expand globally by investing in operators with the expectation that they would build W-CDMA networks. The Japanese company took stakes in operators in Europe, Asia, and North America, such as with its 2001 investment in AT&T Wireless. AT&T Wireless had already committed to the TDMA standard, but it announced plans to deploy GSM services with a migration path to W-CDMA for its 3G services. AT&T's affiliate partners, including Canada's Rogers Cantel and TeleCorp PCS, agreed to do the same.

The standards battle still waged, and there were risks for both DoCoMo and AT&T because there was no easy transition to W-CDMA. CDMA technology was inherently complex, and W-CDMA, originally designed for military purposes, contained elements that differed from current CDMA systems.[50] Manufacturers of W-CDMA transmission equipment were also ahead of handset manufacturers, which could prove to be a problem—customers needed new handsets to use the new service. Another factor delaying the rollout was continuing debate over technical standards and interoperability with other systems.

Because of the problems in the W-CDMA camp, the cdma2000 standard continued to have its backers, particularly in the United States and Latin America. BellSouth International, for example, decided to overlay cdma2000 technology with its existing TDMA networks in Latin America. U.S. operator Nextel, which used a GSM-derivative technology, and other U.S. operators that used TDMA, were also considering cdma2000.

On the equipment side, QUALCOMM hoped to supply CDMA-based 3G chip sets for both standards, and was pushing operators to adopt integrated handsets that could handle both the cdma2000 and W-CDMA technologies. The ITU was working on core network standards that would enable global roaming across various flavors of 3G networks and aimed to have the standards work done by the end of 2002. Some compromise on the standards was likely to ensure extensive interoperability, which would make it easier for DoCoMo to extend its services outside Japan. Meanwhile, operators around the world were upgrading their second-generation systems to something in between second- and third-generation technologies. As long as there was no great demand for new types of wireless content that required higher bandwidths, there was no great need for 3G technologies—another obstacle that DoCoMo faced as it tried to become an international player in wireless content and services.

The i-mode Business Model

DoCoMo was not isolated from the standards battle—to the contrary, it was a major force in determining which content rendering and transmission standards won out. But what distinguished DoCoMo most was not so much its technology platform as its business model and content offerings. To understand i-mode's success, at least in Japan, it is necessary to look at i-mode as a business model as well as a technology.

The i-mode business model began with the company's strategy for content. First, DoCoMo maintained complete control over which devices (Web-phone handsets) i-mode subscribers could use, even to the point of mandating the number of pixels on a handset screen. This meant that developers designed applications only for one "form factor," rather than for the larger number of screen forms possible with WAP devices. WAP developers, remember, had to support the lowest common denominator among screen form factors because they were never sure which device a customer might be using.[51] Developers for i-mode content, on the other hand, followed one standard, and this standard offered a relatively rich user experience. Like other platform leaders and wannabes, DoCoMo encouraged third parties to create complements for its platform—in this case, innovative wireless content accessible over Web sites. DoCoMo formed application partnerships with some 800 companies and had "official" Web sites that customers could access with a touch of a button from the handset. DoCoMo also made it simple for third parties to set up unofficial sites on the belief that more interesting content would draw more users to i-mode.[52] In total, the i-mode network contained nearly 40,000 Web sites.[53]

In addition to a common platform for creating and viewing content, DoCoMo offered an attractive pricing model for its partners. i-mode customers could subscribe to the service for a monthly cost of about $2.50 and a per-packet charge of less than one-quarter of 1 cent. DoCoMo added these charges to the total service bill. After collecting fees from sites that charged for their service and taking a 9 percent commission, DoCoMo gave the remainder of the fees to the Web sites, eliminating the headache of billing and collection for the sites. Its 21 million wireless Internet users in Japan generated an average of $20 in revenue (plus voice fees) per month.[54] DoCoMo's revenues came not only from subscriptions and carrying charges for data packets but also, and increasingly, from e-commerce—collecting commissions on transactions over the network. In March 2000, for example, about 70 percent of i-mode subscribers purchased services over the network, totaling about $3.8 million in transactions for the month. The percentage of users was approximately double the number a year earlier.[55]

The i-mode Content and Delivery Process

i-mode attracted both users and content providers because of its compelling content and unique delivery process. When DoCoMo launched i-mode in February 1999, the company emphasized the ability to check news headlines and conduct stock trades on the move. As the service evolved, however, entertainment-based content emerged as the most popular service. Table 6–3 contains a sample of content available on i-mode phones in 2001.

The delivery process was also a key selling point: i-mode services were available twenty-four hours a day without the user having to log on

Table 6-3 English Language Content Available on i-mode Phones

MENU LIST	INFORMATION PROVIDER	CONTENTS	INFORMATION CHARGE
NEWS/INFO			
CNN	CNN	CNN news and information delivery twenty-four hours a day and information via per month mobile communications	300 yen
Nikkei News	Nihon Keizai Shimbun, Inc.	Stories from the *Nihon Keizai Shimbun* translated into English	FREE
Dow Jones	Dow Jones	News about global financial markets	300 yen per month
Bloomberg	Bloomberg LP	Top news stories, market data, stock quotes, and a personal watch list (20 min. delayed prices) in English and Japanese	FREE
BRIDGE	Bridge Japan	Foreign exchange rate, index price, financial news, stock price, company-related news, charts, portfolio	300 yen per month
Weathernews	Weathernews, Inc.	Weather news around the world	FREE
The Chosun Ilbo	The Chosun Ilbo	*The Chosun Ilbo* (daily) (the largest circulation in South Korea)	FREE
People's Daily	People's Daily	Comprehensive news about China and the world	FREE
Asahi Shimbun	The Asahi Shimbun	General news and popular newspaper column "TENSEIJINGO (Vox Populi, Vox Dei)"	100 yen per month
ENTERTAINMENT			
Disney-i	Disney	Games involving Disney characters, news about Disney and Disneyland	100 yen per month
MiracleGP	Hudson	Motor racing game	300 yen per month
UNIVERSAL-J	USJ Co., Ltd.	Information about Universal Studios Japan	FREE
FORTUNE-i	Telsys Network Co., Ltd.	Horoscope and tarot cards	170 yen per month
RINGING TONE			
Pokemelo JOY	XING	"Harmony ring tones" from Pokemelo JOY	300 yen per month

Table 6-3 **Continued**

MENU LIST	INFORMATION PROVIDER	CONTENTS	INFORMATION CHARGE
DATABASE			
i-Townpage	NTT Directory Services Co.	English version of the Japanese Yellow Pages. It allows users to search for businesses from a database of over 70,000 listings	FREE
Tokyo-Q	Nokia Japan	Guide to what's going on in the city, with a list of favorite places	FREE
TokyoFoodPage	Nokia Japan	Guide to eating and drinking in Tokyo, with hundreds of restaurant listings plus weekly food and restaurant news	FREE
Kyoto info	Matsushita Electric Industrial Co., Ltd.	Information on restaurants, stores, hotels	FREE
TokyoWine News	Nokia Japan	Wine information and wine criticism	FREE
Cooking Japan	Osaka Gas Group	Basic Japanese cooking recipes and cooking hints	FREE
OTHERS			
Citibank	Citibank NA Tokyo	Information on rates, accounts, transfers, branch/ATM maps	FREE
TMTDW	Tokyo-Mitsubishi TD Waterhouse Securities	Financial market news in English Equity trading service, the first service available by i-mode	FREE
ERICSSON CAFÉ	Ericsson	World Tour games, ring tones to download, Swedish cooking recipes	FREE
FedEx	Federal Express	Track the status of your package on i-mode anywhere any time	FREE

Source: Data compiled from <http://www.nttdocomo.co.jp/english/p_s/imode/index.html> (accessed 20 November 2001).

to the Internet. This approach contrasted with WAP services, where users had to dial in to the network each time they wanted to use the server. DoCoMo services were always available, and the user paid only for services used. This model for offering mobile wireless services was attractive to users, especially if service providers all used the same or compatible technologies.

In Japan, the variety of content appealed to users. Most Japanese customers checked their horoscopes every day, especially during long commutes on public transportation. i-mode was especially popular among young people between twenty-four and thirty-five, especially women in their late twenties—a large consumer segment with high disposable incomes. Teenagers enjoyed playing electronic games and exchanging digital pictures. Despite the variety of content, always-on e-mail remained the most popular i-mode service. Sending messages over i-mode phones was less expensive for Japanese than a phone call over a fixed line. In addition, Internet penetration in Japan remained lower than in the United States or Europe, which made i-mode a cheap way to get onto the Internet, albeit in a limited form.

DoCoMo did not offer a general Internet-access service so i-mode users could not roam freely over the Internet. Users could only view Web sites specially designed to be compatible with the i-mode service. Similar to the proprietary portion of AOL, DoCoMo managers selected the content available on i-mode phones. Natsuno, one of the DoCoMo founders who took charge of content business development, insisted that quality of content was a major factor in DoCoMo's success. He emphasized four criteria: (1) Content should be fresh. (2) Content should be "deep" (i.e., more than a simple short message service [SMS]), which might require "drilling down" to other levels. (3) Content should encourage repeat visits (e.g., games). And (4) the user should be able to see the benefit.[56] Enoki, a DoCoMo VP, used a metaphor to describe what i-mode offered:

> Think about department stores. You don't go there very often. But when you go, you spend a lot of money. Just the opposite is the convenience store. You don't buy lots of things. The variety is limited. But you go there every day. I thought that same concept could be applied to information. Mobile content is inferior to other media in terms of speed and screen size. But in terms of ease of use and convenience, it's far superior.[57]

As this quote indicates, DoCoMo executives were aware that specific content could play up to i-mode's unique strengths. Their approach kept fancy graphics to a minimum, but the platform still allowed for services, such as home banking, that consumers and content providers were willing

to pay for. Enoki commented on the banking service: "What you're interested in is numbers: your balance. On i-mode, you can't sell, for example,
neckties because you require good pictures. But on the other hand, i-mode
offers access to the Internet anytime and anywhere, and we emphasize that
benefit."[58] Even with the upgrade to 3G network capabilities, DoCoMo was
not likely to abandon the convenience store strategy. Enoki continued:

> I have no intention to make it a department store even with 3G. If
> you want to do that, you have to offer a large screen, maybe as large
> as a palmtop computer. There is a concept to connect a Palm Pilot
> to a wireless network and offer a new product, but it doesn't sell
> very well. For i-mode to sell well, it's indispensable that people
> carry it around anytime and anywhere and use it conveniently. I
> don't want to do anything to damage these benefits.[59]

Attracting Third-Party Complementors

Although DoCoMo managers selected content, they depended on third-
party vendors to provide that content—without which i-mode would be
no more than a cell-phone and e-mail service. The strategy was, again,
simple and clear: DoCoMo tried to offer a "total package" of content and
services that management thought would be valuable to consumers. The
emphasis was not on high data rates and large amounts of bandwidth.
Good content attracts users, which in turn attract more content: This is
the positive feedback loop essential to platform leadership. Natsuno's
comments in a recent speech show that he fully understood this
dynamic: "Content is everything. If you have good content, you will get
subscribers, and if you have subscribers, you will get even more content.
You also have to have the best business model for content providers. If
you do that, it eventually will be profitable for us."[60] To attract compelling content, Natsuno lined up partners in and outside of Japan. By
the time i-mode started in February 1999, he already had signed up
sixty-seven application providers. The idea was to provide content and
services along the lines of AOL in the United States, but over wireless
phones. By March 2001, the network of 800 partners and 40,000 official
and unofficial Web sites was generating $400 million revenue annually
just for content providers.[61]

DoCoMo's choice of c-HTML rather than WAP also appeared to be a
clever move. It made its network of Web sites proprietary rather than

available to anyone with a Web browser and an Internet connection. In addition, content providers found the language easy to use. Keiji Tachikawa, the president of NTT DoCoMo, explained their reasoning in an October 2000 speech:

> We considered i-mode a new style of media, so we think content is very important. That's why we decided to use an HTML browser: For them to provide content, it was important for us to use the de facto standard of the Internet. . . . We took a strategy that [lets] us reutilize existing content as much as possible. That is why we decided to use cHTML instead of WAP. This was very much welcomed by the content providers. This decision allowed us to achieve a win-win relationship [with] the providers of information.[62]

The Japanese company was not neglecting technological innovation, however. In addition to 3G transmission technology, which provided much greater bandwidths (useful for graphics, speedy connections, and network capacity increases), DoCoMo announced in February 2001 that its new phones would support the Java programming language as well as a new service, called i-appli. i-appli allowed customers to download and run small Java applets (small applications written in the Java programming language). There were thirty-eight applets from a variety of content providers available immediately, ranging from information content to entertainment and games.[63]

DoCoMo's Globalization Strategy

With little room to grow in Japan, DoCoMo was intent on extending its operations and influence to other countries. In Japan, it was relatively easy to impose its choice of technical standards (c-HTML and W-CDMA) and line up content providers. DoCoMo would like its platform to become the global platform to enable its customers and its partners' customers to access the same services anywhere in the world and to gain even more economies of scale in its operations. DoCoMo President Tachikawa noted that "We consider our [version of the] 3G standard to be very good, one that can be adopted worldwide. So we're going to use our influence to spread it around the world."[64]

For this global strategy to succeed, however, a majority of service providers around the world had to adopt a compatible configuration of technologies for data and voice transmission and for access to Web content. Toward this end, DoCoMo had already begun to form partnerships and to make investments in overseas service providers, usually in exchange for their agreements to adopt a compatible set of technologies and become a partner in content creation. DoCoMo also took some minority stakes (between 15 and 20 percent) in local operators outside Japan that needed cash and technology, such as Hutchison Telecom, Hong Kong's largest mobile phone operator; Taiwan's KG Telecom; KPN Mobile, the wireless unit of the Dutch national phone company; and Hutchison 3G UK holdings, which owned a British license for 3G cellular services and planned to develop next-generation cellular services in Europe. DoCoMo expected to increase its investment in these firms gradually to as much as 50 percent and to pursue mobile content and application ventures.[65] In September 2000, DoCoMo also bought 16 percent of AT&T Wireless for $9.8 billion. This brought to $17 billion the amount that DoCoMo spent since early 2000 for minority stakes in cellular operators in Asia, Europe, and the United States.[66] In addition, DoCoMo was organizing partnerships with companies based in the United Kingdom to bring its i-mode and W-CDMA services to Europe.[67]

DoCoMo's partnership with AOL was a learning experience in globalization. In September 2000, DoCoMo took a 42.3 percent stake in AOL Japan, a subsidiary that AOL founded in 1996 as a joint venture with the Japanese publisher Nihon Keizai Shimbun and the trading company giant Mitsui & Co.[68] In exchange for its shares, DoCoMo invested $100 million cash and other noncash contributions to the unit. The broad pact included plans to develop Internet businesses jointly and to invest in markets outside Japan. The relationship was mutually beneficial. DoCoMo learned how AOL selected and managed its content offerings. AOL learned how DoCoMo tailored Internet content to Web phones and managed functions such as billing customers for wireless access to the Web. The DoCoMo brand was so strong in Japan that, four months after the deal, AOL renamed its Japan unit DoCoMo AOL.[69]

DoCoMo was also forming alliances with U.S. companies. For example, in 1999, DoCoMo began partnering with Microsoft to develop mobile access services for corporate users starting in Japan and later moving to the United States. DoCoMo also joined with Sun Microsystems to develop the handsets incorporating Sun's Java software. In February 2001,

Palm and NTT DoCoMo announced plans to launch a jointly developed PDA featuring wireless communication capabilities along the instantly available i-mode approach.[70]

The venture with AT&T Wireless drew considerable attention because it was such a large investment and meant that the i-mode service would come to America. AT&T and DoCoMo planned to set up a new division and introduce a joint service sometime in 2002. The two companies expected to start operations in one city (such as Seattle) and expand to the other parts of the United States within a year or two. Services were likely to be a subset of what DoCoMo offered in Japan, such as e-mail, stock quotes, and local information on restaurants and movies. DoCoMo management expected U.S. i-mode fees to be similar to those in Japan—about $70 per month on average for voice service, and an extra $20 per month for access to i-mode content. AT&T was also considering the alternative of a flat monthly fee, which had proved popular with AOL's customers. The key issue for AT&T was to learn from DoCoMo how to select content partners; AT&T managers were aware that content that was attractive when accessed through the Internet would not necessarily translate well onto wireless Web phones.

Future Prospects for DoCoMo's Platform Strategy: Success or Failure?

NTT DoCoMo had established itself as a platform leader in Japan for wireless Web services and content, but the company was not without challenges. Again, we can view these challenges from the Four Levers Framework. First, there was the problem of profitability throughout the value chain (a Lever 3 problem—external relationships). Although DoCoMo and its customers benefited from the low pricing structure, content providers in Japan were making little if any profit.[71] This situation raised questions about the sustainability of DoCoMo's business model and strategy for attracting (and retaining) content. Third-party providers need adequate incentives to innovate and continue participating in the network of suppliers. How would DoCoMo handle this challenge? It was possible that increased usage of the system would lead to higher revenues and more profits for content providers. Or, DoCoMo could share more revenues or raise prices. As DoCoMo moved overseas, it needed to make sure that the business model worked for complementors as well as for itself.

Second, could DoCoMo duplicate its success with i-mode outside Japan (Lever 1—scope of the firm)? The United States in particular was a much different and more competitive market, for several reasons. First, when i-mode initially appeared, the penetration of the Internet in Japan was low (about 13 percent, compared to 35 percent in the United States). For most Japanese, i-mode was their introduction to the Internet and, in particular, e-mail. U.S. customers familiar with the Internet needed stronger motivations to use the service. Second, the price of telephone communications in Japan was much higher than in the United States— another reason for Japanese to use i-mode services that did not exist in the United States. Third, NTT had a near-monopoly over wireless phone services in Japan and used this base as a marketing tool. The United States and Europe had much more competition in wireless services and rising competition in wireless content. Not only did Palm have wireless offerings with its Palm.net service (discussed earlier in this chapter), but AOL planned to move much of its content to wireless devices. And, of course, U.S. cell-phone operators such as Nextel, Sprint PCS, Verizon, and VoiceStream were all lining up content partners that would allow them to compete with AT&T and DoCoMo (see table 6–4).

Third, would the c-HTML programming language be a boon or a barrier for DoCoMo (Lever 2—product technology)? WAP was the most popular format in the United States and Europe for rendering Web content over wireless devices. The lack of compatibility between c-HTML and WAP provided DoCoMo with an advantage in that it created a proprietary network. On the other hand, the lack of compatibility could delay moving Web content to the i-mode networks outside Japan—a serious issue since U.S. and European competitors were moving quickly in the same space. If the two standards converged, such as into a proposed "xHTML" language being developed by the World Wide Web Consortium, then DoCoMo would gain easier access to content but lose its proprietary edge.

Harvesting User Innovation:
Linux and Open Source Software

Platform leaders can benefit from tapping into the creativity of third parties for complements as well as for help in evolving the platform

Table 6-4 **Content Partners for U.S. Wireless Carriers**		

U.S. WIRELESS CARRIER	NUMBER OF CONTENT PARTNERS	SAMPLE LISTING OF CONTENT PARTNERS
AT&T Wireless	80	ABCNews.com, Allrecipes.com, AOL Mobile, Barnes&Noble.com, Delta Airlines, eBay, eCompare, E*TRADE, excite, FTD.com, ESPN.com, MapQuest, Weather Channel, Traffic Station, Travelocity.com, *Wall Street Journal*
Nextel	33	CNETNews.com, *New York Times* Digital, SmartRay, LifeMinders, MobileID Office, mySimon, ShowNow, Vicinity Brandfinder, TicketMaster, MSN Mobile
Sprint PCS	100	Ameritrade, CBS Marketwatch.com, Charles Schwab, CNN.com, Go2 Online, Indiqu, InfoSpace, MapQuest.com, MSN Mobile, Northwest Airlines, Storerunner.com
Verizon	35	Amazon.com, Barpoint, CitySearch, DLJ direct, Fidelity, Fox Sports, GetThere, Go2 Online, MapBlast, Vicinity BrandFinder, Zagat
VoiceStream	11	Webraska, Network Commerce, Realnames, PocketThis, Exit Source, Qsent

Source: Data compiled from "Content Kingpins," in S. Marek, "Carriers' Content Maneuvers," *Wireless Week,* 29 January 2001, 30.

itself. Handspring, for example, helped Palm evolve its hardware archi-tectures, and many other firms produced complementary add-ons and software applications. And DoCoMo succeeded in Japan at least in part because it tapped into the innovative power of outside firms to generate a rich set of complements and services. Linux involves an extreme case of relying on contributions from outsiders, including individuals who use the platform and have good ideas for new features and complements. Of course, the idea that users can be a valuable source of innovation is not new. In academic circles, scholars such as Nathan Rosenberg at Stanford and Eric von Hippel at MIT have discussed the important role users can play in developing innovations. But the idea is potentially new and pow-erful for platform leaders.

Now, on to the story of Linux, which is described in more detail in a recent book by Glyn Moody called *Rebel Code.* Linux is a freely available, open source operating system modeled after UNIX and developed by

Linus Torvalds of Finland (for whom it is named), with the assistance of thousands of individual volunteers. Commercial companies such as Red Hat and VA Linux also distributed Linux with a variety of complementary products and services. They hoped to see this operating system overtake Microsoft Windows and even UNIX as the dominant software platform for PCs and more powerful computers known as workstations and servers. Backers of Linux as a new software platform need to understand the dynamics of platform leadership to evolve the platform and generate complements that make Linux more compelling to use. But we also believe that platform leaders and wannabes in general should find lessons here for how to mobilize and coordinate independent volunteers to create complements and services as well as help them evolve key features and standards within the platform itself.

Linux might be an unusual case. For perhaps the first time in history, several thousands of individuals from around the world (and not part of a single company) successfully created—together—a sophisticated and complex product. In 2001, estimates of Linux users numbered some 10 million or so worldwide. Its use as an operating system for servers running Web sites may best display its strengths. Linux was generally thought to be more reliable than Microsoft Windows NT/2000 and, of course, was much less costly to use than Windows or commercial versions of UNIX, such as from Sun Microsystems.

The successful evolution of Linux into a rock-solid operating system was itself improbable due to the large number of seemingly uncoordinated independent software developers. Furthermore, Linux and other open source developers did not seem to respond to common economic incentives such as the profit motive. A lot of people spent countless hours for no pay and charged no fees for their work. They enriched their creation incrementally through constant feedback, trial and error, and sharing of what they learned and built. Platform leaders and wannabes would do well to have this level of user activity and innovation tied to their platforms. Why did Linux generate this level of quality as well as interest? These are the questions we probe in this section.[72]

Some Background: Richard Stallman and GNU UNIX

The origins of Linux are closely tied to the creation of the operating system that proved to be its inspiration—UNIX, designed by AT&T in the

1970s.[73] UNIX had a unique design in that its modular, file-based structure allowed the system to evolve piecemeal. In other words, many software developers could work independently on various parts of the program. Another important event was the development of a free clone of UNIX, called the GNU UNIX, by Richard Stallman, an independent programmer based at MIT.[74]

Stallman wanted to design an operating system that worked like UNIX, would be free, and would be usable on different kinds of computers. UNIX had the portability characteristic—AT&T engineers had written it in a programming language (C) that ran on different kinds of computers. The problem was that AT&T owned UNIX; the software had to be licensed and, after 1979, AT&T did not reveal the source code. Consequently, Stallman became determined to create a "UNIX-like" operating system that would be free and open to all.[75]

Since UNIX was a modular system, Stallman was able to replicate its functionality piece by piece. He began the project in 1984 with minor parts, gradually designing more complex components. His software acquired an excellent reputation for quality, which he attributed not only to a good basic design but also to the feedback he received from users as he released parts of his program.[76] The compatibility of his system with UNIX ensured that Stallman had a large base of users for his free software. Stallman, however, was slow to write a new operating system kernel (the set of components that contained the most important basic functions, such as for managing system access, file storage, memory usage, device drivers, and processor scheduling). This delay provided an opportunity for Linus Torvalds, which we describe below. Most important, though, was that Stallman inspired a group of programmers to gather around him, and this gave him the idea to found the Free Software Foundation (FSF) in 1985. Stallman compensated some of these programmers from his teaching salary and the commissions he earned from a commercial version of a compiler that he wrote (the GNC C Compiler [GCC]). But the basic software products that the group produced were free. FSF grew to about forty people, some paid staff and some volunteers, by the end of the 1980s.

Stallman insisted that the code he and his colleagues at FSF created should remain free and open for all future users who might want to use the products or improve them. This policy required a new and innovative strategy for treating intellectual property. Stallman designed, with the help of a lawyer, a new kind of license that he called the GNU General Public License or GPL. He wanted to protect a particular kind of right for users of his products: the right to use, copy, and modify the software. This new "copyleft" (contrary to copyright) allowed the users of any part of the GNU project software to use it, copy it, and modify it. It also allowed users to sell the original or the modified version, but they had to be "copylefted" as well. Any modification to a copylefted program had to be copylefted. Furthermore, if software released under the GNU GPL were combined with proprietary software, the resulting combination had to be released under the GPL. This means that the GNU GPL transformed any piece of software that was used in combination with GCC into free and freely available software. Stallman's philosophy is captured in the following comment:

> The overall purpose is to give the users freedom by giving them free software they can use and to extend the boundaries of what you can do with entirely free software as far as possible. Because the idea of GNU is to make it possible for people to do things with their computers without accepting the domination of somebody else. Without letting some owner of software say, "I won't let you understand how this works; I'm going to keep you helplessly dependent on me and if you share it with your friends, I'll call you a pirate and put you in jail."[77]

Stallman later received a MacArthur Foundation grant for his software work, which provided him with some income. In general, though, he lived the life of a virtual monk: no car, no house, no wife or children. He slept in his MIT office. Nonetheless, his accomplishments and the FSF had enduring consequences for the emergence of a broader movement to produce free software, including Linux.

From Minix to Linux

The other major figure in the open source software movement, Linus Torvalds, got his start while in college in Finland. The story goes that he was using a program called Minix, an educational operating system developed by Andrew Tanenbaum, a professor at the Free Amsterdam University. Tanenbaum, frustrated when AT&T decided to make new releases of UNIX proprietary, decided to write an operating system similar to UNIX that would not be based on AT&T's code. He started in 1984 and finished in 1986. At this time, Tanenbaum also created a "Usenet group," a chat group that communicated over the Internet. This forum was helpful in sending him feedback and comments. Tanenbaum called his UNIX-like operating system Minix. He also wrote a book, *Operating Systems: Design and Implementation*, which came with a copy of Minix as an educational tool. He continued to generate new releases of Minix that incorporated comments from users, but Tanenbaum did not think of Minix as a commercial product and did not evolve the system as fast as some users—Torvalds included—wanted.

Another important event came in 1990. Intel launched the 80386 chip, which was a major improvement over previous PC microprocessors. Torvalds bought his first PC in January 1991 and installed the version of Minix that had been adapted to the Intel 80386 chip. He played with it, downloaded Stallman's GNU C Compiler, and started writing programs to experiment with his PC running Minix. Torvalds wrote several programs that allowed him to do things such as read Usenet group notices on the university system from his bedroom through a modem connection.[78] He went on to write other programs and eventually thought about the possibility of making "a Minix that is better than Minix."[79]

In August 1991, Torvalds posted in the Minix Usenet group an e-mail announcing that he was working on a free operating system for 386 and 486 PCs (or IBM AT clones as they were called at the time). His posting drew immediate interest. He put together a list of the ten to fifteen people who had responded to his e-mail, posted his first version (version 0.01), and solicited their comments and feedback. The project fell neatly between the Minix program (that Tanenbaum was not so keen on evolving) and the promising but unfinished GNU project. Torvalds defined his project as a "program for hackers by a hacker." It is interesting to consider the evolution of Linux: It started as a complement to Minix, then could function without the help of Minix, and ended up as a substitute for Minix and a superior product.

The More Users, the More Innovators and Testers

In 1991 and 1992, more and more software developers became involved with Linux. They were attracted to the possibility of a stable operating system that would let the users add new features themselves and learn more about operating systems and how they worked in the process. Many programmers sent their contributions to the source code. Linux filled the vacant place of the GNU kernel that still was not built and fulfilled Stallman's dream of a complete UNIX clone, now called the GNU/Linux operating system.

Torvalds used the Usenet posting to receive information from many Usenet members. In a year he became the leader of a group of programmers who were building a UNIX kernel. This example from 1992 is typical of the types of requests Torvalds posted in the Linux Usenet group: "Please try it all out, give it a real shakedown, and send comments/bugs-reports to the appropriate place. The changes are sometimes bigger than we prefer, so the more testers that try it out, the faster we can try to fix any possible problems."[80] The heavy reliance on the work and creativity of users, and the emergence of group norms for eliciting feedback and introducing suggested changes in a quickly released new version, became the distinctive style of Linux development.

This idea of releasing code and encouraging users to submit feedback and modifications or improvements was also a part of the UNIX culture, but it became more pronounced and fundamental to free software. Developers of Linux harnessed this idea, allowing quick releases of new versions that contained improvements submitted by many users.[81] The Internet also played a major role in enabling this rapid creation and release of new versions of the product, as well as frequent exchanges of comments, suggestions for code patches, and sharing of code. Torvalds claimed that the best design decision he ever made on Linux was to make it available by File Transfer Protocol (an Internet communications protocol that allowed Internet users to download files). The Internet freed users and testers from geographic constraints and allowed Torvalds to receive immediate feedback from all over the world.

Coordination Mechanisms and a Modular Architecture

Tanenbaum had warned Torvalds in 1992 that "coordinating 1,000 prima donnas living all over the world will be as easy as herding cats."[82] Indeed, there was nothing in the GPL that prevented developers from taking Linux in a direction that Torvalds did not want. Responding to hundreds and then thousands of users who wanted to add different features to

Linux and build special programs—all of which we consider as complements to the original platform—also became a logistical problem.

At first, users suggested only a few, relatively small changes to the operating system. Torvalds usually communicated with these users by e-mail, and got to know many of them. In this way, he managed to retain personal control over the platform as it evolved. He also released new versions at an astounding pace, albeit with mostly small modifications. As of May 1992, for example, Linux was already in its ninety-sixth edition—version 0.96. The "release early, release often" philosophy allowed Torvalds to "treat his users as codevelopers in the most effective way possible."[83] In contrast, producers of proprietary operating systems such as Microsoft (at least prior to the final settlement of the most recent antitrust case) do not allow users to see actual source code and tend to release major new versions of the product every two or three years, sometimes with minor updates or patches to fix bugs or omissions every few months. Also important to the ability of Linux to evolve was a modular architecture.[84] The modular architecture, modeled after UNIX, facilitated distributed development through separate, well-defined and partitioned tasks or subtasks. Thousands of users could build complementary features and have Torvalds or his colleagues incorporate them into the platform.

The kernel—the core set of basic features that Torvalds had mostly designed and written on his own—was not itself modular. In fact, Tanenbaum even complained that the Linux core was too "monolithic" in that the components were large and did not follow his principles of "micro-kernel" design.[85] But what Torvalds had done was create a small, stable core that could easily accept additional functionality as separate modules.[86]

As Tanenbaum had predicted, some disagreements emerged among Linux users on how to move forward. But Torvalds was able to exert leadership based on his legitimacy as a programmer. In addition, "lieutenants" appeared in the form of volunteers who specialized in particular areas and were willing to answer user questions in their areas and help guide the design. As a result, the distributed innovation process did not lead to chaos. With this partitioning of authority among a select group of users and the originator of the system, Linux continued to evolve as a programming platform and take on additional functionality. In this evolution, the development of a reputation among one's peers was essential to the assignment of responsibilities. Stephen Tweedie, a Scotsman who became a senior Linux developer, explained:

> It's very simply a case of who is actually working on something, and who has got a track record of making good choices. And if you are working on something and you have got the credibility in the eyes of other people who are doing that, then other patches [pieces of software code that add or fix functionality in the main program] tend to come to you. These are people who are generally recognized as being not owners but simply experts in particular areas. The community takes advantage of that and works through those people to get work done in those areas. . . . It is very much a meritocracy.[87]

Tweedie's comment represents a view of the allocation of responsibility as the outcome of natural selection by the local community.[88] Other observers of the open source movement have echoed this theme of reputation in an attempt to answer the puzzling question of what motivated software developers to do so much work to evolve the Linux platform, create new features, even whole applications such as the Apache Web server, and then "give them away" to the world.

Motivations of Open Source Developers

We do not believe that all the contributors to Linux, Apache, and other open source projects such as Sendmail (an early program that defined the standards for sending e-mail over the Internet), Perl (one of the first programming languages that made it possible to create interactive Web sites), or Mozilla (Netscape's open source version of the Navigator browser), were acting on purely altruistic motives. We tend to agree with Rishab Aiyer Gosh, who described an economy of "cooking pots" to qualify the nature of the exchanges taking place.[89] In this metaphor, the project being developed is the cooking pot to which many people individually bring one parsnip here, one leek there; they are all contributing to the good soup that is stewing. And they know that as long as they are contributing in this manner, there will always be soup in the pot. It is more a barter economy than a set of transactions each with a specific price.

Furthermore, individual contribution and collective experience are intricately linked in the process of software development. Eric Raymond, the author of the famed essay on open source, "The Cathedral and the Bazaar," wrote the following:

> While coding remains an essentially solitary activity, the really great hacks come from harnessing the attention and brain power of entire communities. The developer that uses his or her brain power in a closed project is going to fall behind the developer who knows how to create an open, evolutionary context in which feedback exploring the design space, code contributions, bug-spotting, and other improvements come back from hundreds (perhaps thousands) of people.[90]

Raymond suggested that "Linus's method was a way to create an efficient market for ego boosting—to connect the selfishness of individual hackers as firmly as possible to difficult ends that can only be achieved by sustained cooperation."[91]

Besides "ego boosting," individual rewards to the developers included a sense of belonging to a community and the satisfaction that comes with participating in a project that has value for society. These rewards may be less tangible than getting a paycheck, but they are no less real. Stallman provided an extreme example of this behavior. But one can imagine (and economists have) other, more self-interested motives.[92] A person can derive benefits from building a good reputation such as by getting a well-paid job to keep producing the same kind of high-quality software in a profit-oriented venture. This happened to Torvalds, who took a job with Transmeta, a new for-profit microprocessor design company. Torvalds also admitted in a 1996 interview that he was driven in the early days not only by his joy of programming but also by a desire to "show off."[93]

Last but not least, contributors to open source software seemed to truly enjoy programming. They have fun, and they usually learn new things at the same time. In addition, programmers who contributed a lot to the movement, such as Torvalds and Stallman as well as Raymond (with Sendmail), usually had other personal motivations, such as the desire to rebel and do things differently. This culture of rebellion was also a part of the innovation process.

Open Source and For-Profit Companies

Several entrepreneurs were interested in making a profit from Linux. Their companies included the well-known Red Hat, VA Linux, Caldera, and TurboLinux, which sold special versions of Linux that packaged the free software with a bundle of utilities (such as special installation programs) and applications (such as Star Office, a competitor of Microsoft Office) as well as service and support. As of 2001, however, none of these companies had managed to turn a profit. Some had large public stock offerings in the late 1990s, but share prices came quickly down to earth even before the crash of the Nasdaq stock market in 2000–2001.

Overall, there were difficulties in business models that tried to combine free software with for-charge products and services. Perhaps the major problem was that most Linux users were sophisticated enough not to need the services or bundles of complements that the commercial Linux companies offered. Nonetheless, there were companies that explored different ways to take advantage of the open source movement to enhance their platforms or generate complements.

NETSCAPE'S MOZILLA   In March 1998, Netscape (purchased by AOL in the fall of 1998) became a major participant in the open source software movement.[94] As a last-ditch effort to mobilize outside programmers to help in its losing browser war with Microsoft, Netscape decided to give the source code away for its browser and make this an open source project, combining efforts of Netscape programmers with open source developers. Netscape called the open source project "Mozilla." Developers signed a license that resembled the GNU GPL, although Netscape retained some special rights to package the Mozilla code into commercial versions of Navigator that included proprietary code from other sources.

The results were disappointing, however, for a variety of reasons. First, the Navigator code that Netscape released to the public was a 3-million-line pile of "spaghetti," not a neatly modularized system.[95] Second, Navigator and its suite version, Communicator, contained a lot of proprietary code that Netscape had licensed from other companies. These other companies, including Sun Microsystems, which had components such as a Java interpreter embedded within Navigator, were not willing to give away the source code. This meant that the Mozilla team had to write these components from scratch or find substitutes. They did the job successfully, but it delayed the release of a finished product. Third, Netscape found it difficult to manage the Mozilla project without allocating a large number of its own engineers—about a hundred—to the work of redesigning key features and subsystems or adding new functions. Mozilla attracted some thirty enthusiasts who volunteered to write or rewrite parts of the system. But Netscape, perhaps because it was a for-profit company and perhaps because the task was so daunting technically, was never able to motivate hundreds and thousands of individuals to contribute to the effort, as in the case of Linux. As a result, introducing the next major release of Navigator that truly benefited from the Mozilla project took about two years and not the several months that Netscape managers had initially expected.[96]

On the positive side, the Mozilla project gave Netscape a much better browser. Netscape was also likely to continue to receive at least some innovative contributions from the Mozilla developer and user communities in the future. The Mozilla project also demonstrated that it is possible to evolve a commercial platform product with the assistance of open source developers. This was true even though the process was slow for Netscape and required considerable in-house resources to manage and complement the outside contributions. Moreover, combining open source methods with internal work improved Netscape's development abilities. Company engineers were forced to write in a more modular fashion. They had to document their work better so that outside developers could understand what they were doing. And more eyeballs looking at the code found more bugs and raised expectations for higher quality and reliability.[97] Still, in 2001, the jury was still out with regard to how widely used new versions of Netscape Navigator or open source versions of Mozilla would become in future years.

IBM'S APACHE   In contrast, IBM found another way to take advantage of the open source movement to enhance one of its major platform products—in this case, a hardware server. In June 1998, IBM announced that it would ship its Websphere Application Server with Apache, the open source software that was the world's leading Web server product in terms of market share. Apache was originally built by Rob McCool at the University of Illinois around 1994 while he was working part-time at the

National Center for Supercomputing Applications (NCSA). This was the same organization where Marc Andreessen and a handful of other University of Illinois students developed the first popular graphical Web browser—Mosaic. Mosaic was another piece of free software, at least initially, and provided the design concepts for Netscape Navigator, which the same group of programmers built for commercial purposes. McCool himself later joined Netscape. After he left NCSA, a group of programmers added new code or "patches" to his work, and released the first version of Apache in 1995. It quickly became the most popular Web server software, which is used to host Web sites and run small Web applications.[98]

Although IBM had a Web server product of its own, it had a minuscule market share. The company decided to drop its in-house product and to adopt and enhance Apache, adding any new code to the open source pool. The purpose, of course, was to sell more servers by treating Apache as a complement to its hardware platform. The ploy worked, at least after IBM committed to offering technical support for Apache as well. IBM later decided to adapt Linux to work on its servers—another move that made the IBM server hardware more popular.[99] For IBM, a major commercial producer of hardware and software, to embrace Apache truly stood out as a landmark move. It signaled that Apache was an important complement to Linux, the "killer app" that made Linux a serious alternative platform to Windows NT/2000 and UNIX. IBM's move, as well as a later decision to give away millions of dollars worth of open source development tools, also gave tremendous credibility to the open source movement as a mechanism to generate complements for a platform product.

The news was not all good, however, for companies that were selling Web servers (such as Netscape) or Linux bundles and support services (such as Red Hat and VA Linux). As IBM and then other major hardware vendors, such as HP and Compaq, introduced server hardware bundled with Linux, users found less need to buy what the for-profit Linux companies offered. Another route for these companies was to follow the example of Red Hat, which made a deal with IBM and sold some Linux bundles with IBM server and database software.[100] Although Red Hat had yet to generate a profit as of late 2001, the strategy was to combine the ability of the open source movement to enhance a platform or generate complements with the ability of for-profit firms to offer unique combinations of free software with proprietary products and services. It was a potentially win-win scenario for platform leaders as well as for complementors and users.

Conclusion: Leader Wannabes Need to Stimulate External Innovation

Microsoft, Cisco, Palm, NTT DoCoMo, and open source vendors of Linux and other software products all grappled with common problems: (1) how open to make the interfaces to their platforms without giving away too much information or advantage to competitors (Lever 2) and (2) how to guarantee the availability of enough complements to make their platforms successful in the marketplace (Levers 1, 3, and 4). It is clear from these cases that firms had a wide range of options. Not everyone followed the Intel model.

For example, companies need not rely on proprietary interfaces to their platforms, although they do need to find some way to establish and maintain an advantage over the competition. Cisco faced this problem in the early 2000s: Since its interfaces were open, competitors were able to jump in with cheaper and sometimes better products that did the same things. NTT DoCoMo, despite some proprietary elements in its platform, was likely to face the same problem as content providers formed alliances with other wireless operators. Platform leaders and wannabes also varied how much emphasis they placed on particular approaches; most decisions were not black and white. For example, companies might not want to have a large in-house complements business, but they might establish a small in-house effort while a market was still evolving or a pilot-type operation to help seed new complementary markets.

Palm originally set hardware and software architectural standards for the PDA industry and licensed its operating system to potentially important complementors such as Handspring. In addition, Palm was still filling in the details on its vision for what the PDA product could become— a device that was essential for the mass market because it proved useful for so many daily tasks and basic communications functions, especially e-mail, and in a wireless mode. But Palm did not demonstrate that it was the only company capable of providing a vision for the future and leading the way in terms of technical standards that facilitate the work of complementors. Handspring and Microsoft were also important innovators. We did not think Palm would prevail in a head-to-head battle with Microsoft to design PC-like PDAs or win a head-to-head battle with Symbian to provide operating system software for Web phones. Palm's best shot for platform leadership is probably to continue doing what it does well—designing the operating system for handheld devices. Palm also needs to forge more alliances and partnerships to keep a steady stream of complements and services coming into its own Palm Economy, rather than into the broader PDA market.

The challenges that NTT DoCoMo faced as it prepared for global expansion raised the question of what was truly distinctive and difficult to imitate about the company's offering: Was it the technology platform, the delivery process, the business model, or the content? The platform was unique but other service operators were also adopting W-CDMA. c-HTML was proprietary to DoCoMo, but was likely to evolve into a common standard. The delivery process and business model—always-on twenty-four-hour service and low charges only for services used—were novel but easy to imitate technically, though it might not make business sense for all carriers. We are left with content. It was, no doubt, the biggest challenge for DoCoMo and its overseas partners to continue finding compelling content that differed from what the competition offered or from what was freely available over the Internet. We expect that the advantage in content that was a distinguishing feature of i-mode in Japan would be difficult and perhaps impossible to repeat in overseas markets. On the other hand, i-mode was a compelling total package. With aggressive marketing, DoCoMo and its partners are still likely to become powerful competitors in the United States and other markets, even if they never achieve the near-monopoly status that DoCoMo enjoys in Japan.

Finally, we saw in the case of Linux factors that contributed to the successful development and diffusion of a new programming platform:

- the open availability of the underlying technology (the source code), which encouraged tinkering and innovation;
- a modular architecture, which facilitated distributed innovation with loose controls;

- the existence of the Internet, which enabled rapid exchanges of components and communication among users;
- leadership behind the project, which had one person and then a small group of experts in clear charge;
- and a novel treatment of intellectual property rights, which encouraged people to innovate and required that they contribute their innovations back to the open source pool.

These conditions, together with the widespread availability of inexpensive PCs and the large number of skilled programmers worldwide, created the conditions that made Linux and other open source projects successful in many respects. The open source movement provided an example that both Palm and DoCoMo should find useful for stimulating third parties to offer complements and services for their respective platforms.

It seems that one approach to pushing a platform or attracting complements may be better or worse than the alternatives depending on factors such as the state of the market or technology in question, or what capabilities a firm has, which are essential to implement a given strategy. We will review the range of strategic options as well as key issues related to implementation of a platform leadership strategy in chapter 7.

Chapter Seven

Conclusion

The Essence of Platform Leadership

Becoming a platform leader is like winning the Holy Grail: Many seek it, but few achieve it. By definition, platform leaders who succeed can exert a strong influence over the direction of innovation in their industries and thus over the network of firms and customers—the "ecosystem"—that produces and uses complements. But not all industries are suitable for platform leadership strategies. The dynamics that make it possible occur only under certain conditions. A fundamental condition is that the firm's product has limited value when used alone but gains in value when used along with complements. For Intel, the starting point was recognizing that, without innovation on complements and evolution of the PC platform, its main product line—the microprocessor—would have very limited appeal. Intel managers went so far as to consider their situation to be "desperate." Other platform leaders and wannabes that we examined—Microsoft, Cisco, Palm, NTT DoCoMo—might not have used such strong language to describe their situations, but they shared a similar predicament.

The realization that demand for one's core product depends on an array of complements—and, therefore, that one's destiny depends on the decisions and actions of others—is the starting point for thinking like a platform leader. It can also be a painful realization for managers as well as boards of directors, investors, employees, and customers. It can be disturbing to hear that your company or product line has great potential only if you acknowledge how little you can do on your own. Once they have recognized this, however, managers in platform leaders and wannabes can then get down to work. They can create a strategy to deal with issues such as how to encourage complementary innovation and how to evolve the platform interfaces and architecture. The situation of platform leaders and wannabes can become less desperate as they exert more control over their fates: Platform leaders and wannabes can transform constraints stemming from their dependencies into competitive advantages. Platform leadership, combined with complementary innovation, can result in win-win scenarios for the platform leader, complementors, and customers, if everyone works together.

The Four Levers of Platform Leadership

In this book, we discussed the Four Levers that managers can use to implement a platform leadership strategy or make their existing strategy more effective.

Lever 1: Scope of the Firm

Platform leaders need to recognize that they depend on an ecosystem or network of innovation to produce complements that make the platform more valuable. This should be a *thriving* ecosystem for the platform to be as successful as possible. Therefore, determining the scope of the firm— in other words, what complements to make inside and what to leave to external firms—is probably the most important decision that platform leaders have to make. This is usually not a one time decision; platform leaders such as Intel and Microsoft, for example, were constantly debating the issue as new technologies and applications appeared. Nor is it an either–or decision; companies usually can do at least part of the innovations in-house *and* add new functionality to their core products. Another part of this decision-making process, as discussed in chapter 4, involves how platform leaders can stimulate external innovation, and how they can choose appropriate levels of investment and involvement in venture capital activities or acquisitions aimed at evolving the platform or helping the complements business.

Companies that want to become platform leaders need to assess— like Intel's managers did—whether they really need innovation to happen on complements and how desperate they are. They also need to determine what actions would most increase demand for their product as well as the platform overall: Do they need an ever-increasing variety of complements, or just a few stable complementary applications? Palm, for example, stimulated the external development of over 8,500 applications. NTT DoCoMo encouraged the creation of 40,000 official and unofficial Web sites for its services in Japan. Cisco acquired each year dozens of complementary firms and potential substitute technologies that it could tie into its platform concept. Microsoft, in contrast, developed the most popular applications for Windows in-house and severely damaged the businesses of many prior complementors, including Netscape, Novell, WordPerfect, and Lotus.

The capabilities of the firm matter greatly in this decision. It makes no sense for a platform leader or wannabe to develop its own complements if it does not have the technical and organizational skills or the financial capacity to compete in the relevant markets. Intel, for example, though it has thousands of software engineers who program microprocessors and research complementary technologies, is not a commercial software company and would thus struggle to compete with the likes of Microsoft in operating systems or software applications. Nor is Intel a consumer electronics company, which suggests that it will have difficulty competing in consumer mass markets with its entry in MPEG music players or digital cameras.

Microsoft clearly had the technical skills to move from building PC programming languages and operating systems to software applications. Still, Microsoft generally stayed with "horizontal" applications, such as Office or broadly used database management programs that fit well with its platform technology. Microsoft avoided developing software for specific markets, such as computer-aided design systems for the aircraft industry or information management systems tailored to hospitals or other industries, where specialized firms with deep industry knowledge were likely to have the advantage. Microsoft did well in video game markets for the PC, but it may not have all the capabilities (such as marketing skills) to compete in consumer hardware products such as video game boxes, a business it entered in fall 2001 with the Xbox.

Cisco provided perhaps the most complex example of platform leadership that we looked at in this book. It seemed willing to invest in any technology that could work with Internet routers or packet switches. It did not build many end-user applications itself, but rather expanded through acquisition into different infrastructure products that enabled various types of networking applications. Cisco did not simply rely on the market to provide these different technologies and applications. It primed and directed the market, as well as diversified its product lines into areas that we considered complements to the basic Internet router. As noted in chapter 5, some of these technologies were also potential substitutes for the router, though Cisco and its customers often used them as complements, tied together by software in hybrid networks.

Platform leaders and wannabes both need to have a vision of what product or platform they want to develop in the future—based on assessment of their existing capabilities and where they see the industry or technology evolving. They need to focus on developing a platform where they will have an advantage over competitors and where the core technologies will be difficult to imitate. Then, they need to determine whether outside firms possess the capabilities to contribute to the success of the platform by developing complements. If these capabilities exist in outside firms, then the platform leader or wannabe needs to consider whether these external developers have enough incentives to work on complements to a platform they do not own or control. In one extreme case, that of the Linux operating system, external developers had enough incentives to devote enormous amounts of time to evolving the platform and creating complements. Their motivation, at least in part, seems to have come from their open access to the inner workings (the source code) of the platform. As we saw in this book, platform leaders exert a lot of energy and resources trying to entice external firms to develop complements. We will summarize later in this section the variety of methods firms can use to encourage external innovation.

Another critical issue is whether an actual or potential complements market—a group of firms able to build complements—already exists. If there is no market, then a platform leader or wannabe might well decide to build these complements itself. Palm, for example, had to include some applications with its Palm Pilot or the product would have failed immediately. Linux vendors such as Red Hat may need to invest more in developing or packaging software applications for the mass market that run on the Linux operating system; otherwise these complements may never become widely available. Similarly, NTT DoCoMo's i-mode service was likely to fail in the United States unless it could line up distinctive and compelling content attractive to U.S. users.

Basing your advantage on the absence of an infrastructure-type market such as one that produces complements and doing everything yourself may not be wise in the long run. As industries evolve, specialists will emerge. If the product turns out to be successful with customers, specialist firms are likely to jump into the market. Often, they become better at specific tasks (like hardware design or applications design) than firms that try to do everything.[1] Automobile companies, for example, used to make nearly all their components before auto parts and materials suppliers existed. Some companies (like Ford) even ran their own rubber plantations and steel mills to guarantee supplies of these materials. Once the automobile became a successful mass-market product, however, specialist firms emerged in every area of the value chain, and automobile companies began the process of "de-integrating" or using the market to obtain the components and materials they needed. It is no different with complements for platform producers in other industries.

Among the companies we looked at, Palm probably had the most difficult choices to make in the area of what to do in-house. In 2001, it was both a hardware platform company—the main PDA maker—and a software platform company—the Palm OS maker. It had the capabilities to do both types of innovation well, but for how long? The software platform was obviously Palm's unique strength, and it had less competition there than in hardware design. But Palm OS still had competition, and fierce competition at that—Microsoft's Pocket PC. Palm had built some software applications for the Palm Pilot. Should it try to develop more applications of broad appeal to PDA users, as Microsoft had done with its applications business, and potentially double its revenues?

Again, issues to consider are capabilities, resources, and the state of the market. Could Palm afford to focus on software only, perhaps by spinning off the hardware design group? If it did this, should it focus just on Palm OS or try to build some key complements that took advantage of its basic software? Or would Palm compete too directly with existing complementors and possibly force useful partners out of the market or into the Microsoft camp? Was the market already crowded with complementors developing applications for PDAs? Palm managers needed to study these issues carefully as they moved forward with their platform and tried to maintain their position as the market expanded.

This leads to the question: What does a platform leader or wannabe do if the platform needs a variety of complements to succeed and they do not have the in-house capabilities to develop those complements? Management might well decide not to build these complements in-house. If so, the platform leader can still exert great influence over the design and production of these complements by acting on the incentives and capabilities of external complementors. There are many ways to encourage and channel the development of complements.

For example, platform leaders or wannabes can share technical information about their own products and platform interfaces, as well as dispatch engineers to help complementors build compatible products. Or platform leaders can use a "rabbit" strategy as we saw Intel do in chapter 3. This approach targets a promising developer of complements and helps the company in a very visible way so that other firms feel encouraged to follow. The rabbit strategy draws the attention of investors and complementors to a potentially lucrative new market and signals to the world that the platform leader intends to stay out of this complementary market while encouraging competition in that market. Another way to achieve the same objective is to make venture investments in start-up firms that plan to build complements. The platform leader or wannabe can also develop enabling technologies, such as API and SDKs (as did IAL) and share them either free of charge or for low royalties to stimulate the development of complements. Finally, platform leaders or wannabes can share market information and provide marketing funds to help complementors in their efforts.

Even if a firm decides to rely on external developers for complements, however, it still should try to keep in-house the capability to venture into those complementary areas in the future. We saw Intel accomplish this with its chip set group. Cultivating such in-house capabilities gives the platform leader or wannabe three possible benefits: (1) the expertise necessary to define the interface between its product and complements; (2) the ability to enter the complementary market directly, should outside firms decline to enter or fail in the attempt; and (3) some bargaining power with complementors.

Venture investments as well as mergers and acquisitions also affect the scope of the firm and its ability to influence complements production. Intel, Microsoft, Cisco, and Palm all took equity positions in complementors. Intel, Microsoft, and Cisco have also made many acquisitions. The first approach—equity investments—helps complementors by providing funding and creating a formal mechanism for the platform leader or wannabe to steer the complementor in a particular direction. An investment from the likes of Intel, Microsoft, Cisco, or Palm also provides an impressive seal of approval that can help new firms get additional funding and customers.

The second approach—acquiring a complementor—yields a subtler question of conflicting interests. The main problem is that the merger blurs the line between core product and complement. Once the complementor is acquired, the platform leader or wannabe becomes the source of the complement and thus a competitor in the marketplace of former partners making the same complements. This situation might lead to reduced incentives for other firms to position themselves in the complementary market, resulting in less competition—and possibly less complementary innovation. The outcome can be bad not only for complementors but for the platform leader and its end users.

In short, there is no simple answer regarding whether to make complements in-house or encourage the market to provide them. We know that platform products need complements to offer value to customers and that platform leaders need to guarantee the market presence of key complements. Consequently, it seems wise for a platform leader or wannabe to have at least some in-house complements capability. This capability can be useful to develop products directly or, at a minimum, to "seed" the market and provide direction and competition for third parties.

Lever 2: Product Technology

ARCHITECTURE Architectural decisions have enduring power. Roman roads still provide an important grid for major routes in France,

Italy, and other countries of the Mediterranean. A platform architecture—the high-level design of the system and the interface designs that determine how components or subsystems work together—can have a similarly profound and lasting impact on the structure of an industry and the nature of innovation. Architecture can determine who does what type of innovation as well as how much investment in complements occurs outside the platform leader. Whether a firm chooses a modular architecture (made of separable components with open interfaces) is particularly important because modularity facilitates the development of complements. Modular designs can reduce the costs of innovation for outside firms and encourage the emergence of specialized companies that may invest heavily and creatively in complements. This phenomenon operates in the case of the highly modular PC, for example, with both hardware complementors and software complementors. Nonmodular or "integral" architectures can make it more expensive and technically difficult to create complements because of the many system and interface issues that arise.

We saw Intel, Palm, NTT DoCoMo, and Linux developers all adopt modular types of architectures for their platforms. Even the operating systems sold by Microsoft and Cisco, despite their somewhat haphazard evolutions (except for Windows NT/2000), had modular characteristics that allowed many firms to create complements both in parallel and independently. A modular architecture makes it possible to break down the tasks necessary to build components of the platform and a family of complements. It facilitates the dispatching of tasks to distinct groups. It is the ideal approach to system design for platform leaders that want to take advantage of third-party innovation.

INTERFACES   For a modular architecture to encourage third-party innovation, the interfaces should be open—in other words, the platform leader should specify publicly how to link complements to its platform. Such open disclosure, however, has potentially problematic consequences in that it could give competitors too deep an understanding of how a competing product works. Intel, for example, jealously guarded the internal architecture of its microprocessors, even though it shared the specification of interfaces such as the PCI bus and the USB that linked a computer to its peripherals. Similarly, Microsoft did not give away Windows source code, which would expose the internal structure of the software platform, but it revealed detailed specifications on the Windows programming interfaces.

Intel and Microsoft continually evolved their technologies to retain their positions as leaders of the PC platform. Intel microprocessors once encountered threats from different architectures, such as the ultrafast, reduced instruction set designs used in high-powered workstations, and the superior graphical capabilities of Motorola chips used in Apple Macintosh computers. These products were no longer a major threat to Intel because it redesigned its microprocessors to compete more effectively in terms of speed, processing power, graphics, and other dimensions. Microsoft also continually upgraded Windows and built Windows NT/2000, a high-end operating system with a modern and professional architecture, to compete more effectively with UNIX and Linux in the corporate server market. The challenges for Palm, NTT DoCoMo, and even the Linux community are to keep evolving the platforms they defined and keep the competition at bay. It was not clear at the end of 2001 whether they had the ability to succeed.

Cisco also had challenges, but of a somewhat different nature. Its platform was essentially an operating system based on open standards—standards that Cisco alone did not define. Therefore, the company had to make its software and hardware products compatible with any new communications technology that emerged, leaving it vulnerable to competition from alternative technologies and specialized niche players. In 2001, it was unclear if Cisco would be able to keep pace with all the innovations happening externally and maintain its historically high growth rates. There was no shortage of acquisition candidates, but Cisco no longer had the same powerful currency (its stock) that it once had.

Intel is a consummate example of a platform leader that both evolved the architecture of the system and disclosed its interfaces. As we saw in chapters 3 and 4, Intel designed many of the PC interfaces and rallied firms around these technical standards. Intel routinely invested in architectural PC innovations, standard-setting activities with low royalty return, even subsidizing the costs of some complementors. A significant effect of these investments was to reinforce the architecture Intel supported. In the process, however, Intel also facilitated modular, complementary innovation throughout the industry. By designing in part the PC interfaces and by successfully rallying other firms around them, Intel achieved important outcomes. It was able to influence the future supply of complements, whose supply in turn affected the demand for Intel's products. It was able to promote industrywide consensus on technical specifications and avoid potentially detrimental standards wars. Through a long process of interfirm collaboration, interfaces such as PCI, AGP, and USB were created. Once defined and adopted by the marketplace (i.e., by vendors and end users), these standards become difficult for any single actor to remove. The standards become historical legacies that direct the attention of a multitude of players to a specific set of technical issues deemed as "relevant."

Defining the architecture of a system product can also be a powerful way to raise barriers to entry for potential competitors that might consider offering a competing architecture with different interfaces. A potential competitor to Intel, for example, would not only have to invent a microprocessor with a better price-performance ratio, it would also have to rally complementors and OEMs to adapt their designs to this component. This change could incur huge switching costs for the complementors. Having a coalition of other firms with their interests aligned with yours through common interfaces is a powerful deterrent for potential entrants. Platform-specific complements can then create, as in the Microsoft antitrust trial, an "applications barrier to entry" for firms that would like to compete with alternative platforms.[2]

Fears of market dominance may plague antitrust watchers. We learned during the Microsoft trial, however, that it is not illegal for a company to achieve a large market share or even a monopoly, usually defined as possessing 70 percent or more of a specific market. What is illegal is to *abuse* a monopoly position, such as by using dominance in one market to try to dominate another market or by overcharging customers or manipulating suppliers. Remember, too, that firms around a platform leader can compete with it while benefiting from the platform leader's dominance if it uses this position to coordinate innovation throughout the industry. Competitors of Intel, for example, adopted Intel-sponsored PC interfaces without having to invest their own R&D resources.

INTELLECTUAL PROPERTY　A carefully chosen strategy for IP can help achieve platform leadership. IP rights are tools that firms can use either to preserve or destroy third parties' incentives to innovate. When a platform leader or wannabe exchanges interface technical specifications with third parties, it stimulates the development of complements. Absent this interface information, third parties find it difficult—if not impossible—to design complements. Hence, a platform leader or wannabe's decision to make the specification of its interfaces available to the public (open) lowers third parties' costs to innovate. In contrast, a decision to withhold the specification (closed) raises these costs, sometimes dramatically.

Most of the platform leaders discussed in this book, except those competing in open technologies such as Linux software, have been reluctant to reveal too much architectural information about the inner workings of their product. However, they have willingly disclosed information regarding interfaces that remain external to their product. Cisco relied primarily on open standards, DoCoMo was pushing for the adoption of W-CDMA (also an open standard), and Intel adopted a free and open IP policy on the PCI, USB, and AGP interfaces. Palm chose to license its Palm OS to complementors but also to Handspring, which was both a complementor and a competitor. We believe that disclosing information about interfaces is a powerful way to encourage external innovation. But as we said before, disclosing too much may also facilitate imitation.

In the development of Linux, it was particularly striking to see how the disclosure of full product information had a turbo effect on external innovation. Literally thousands of developers, without pay, devoted their time to develop modules of the Linux operating system or complementary utilities and applications. Granted, there could be no such thing as "too much disclosure" in the open source movement. Since the authors of products such as Linux and Apache were not out to make a profit, they had nothing to lose, at least in theory. But the story of the open source movement provides different insights into the role of IP for encouraging innovation than we would get from studying only Intel. As opposed to conventional wisdom on how to stimulate innovation (e.g., patents, secrecy), the commitment to disclosure (as stipulated in the copyleft mechanism) seemed to be a fundamental mechanism to protect incentives to innovate for potential contributors—by preserving their freedom to innovate. The copyleft mechanism perpetuates a full-disclosure effect. In the open source movement, it proved to be an extremely effective tool to unleash the innovative efforts of thousands of developers because this measure spoke directly to their motivations.

This observation points to the fundamental trade-off between secrecy and disclosure (when one aims to stimulate innovation), two strategies for dealing with IP that have different consequences for innovation. Secrecy protects the incentives of inventors. It guarantees they will reap financial rewards because it reduces the possibility of copying. So, secrecy is good to block substitute innovation and to encourage profit-seeking entrepreneurs to innovate on a stand-alone product. Patents are good for temporarily blocking substitute innovation as well. But disclosure is best suited for encouraging complementary innovation because it allows the involvement of many inventors, even if they do not profit financially from their work. Economists used to believe that, without clear financial incentives, no one would innovate. But the open source movement shows that the issue is more complex. Linux developers, for example, had plenty of incentives to innovate—otherwise, why would they? They built useful products, made Linux more functional, gained recognition from their peers (and sometimes employers), and they had fun. In the case of Linux, the lack of secrecy around the IP increased their incentives and ability to innovate. The tricky part for commercial firms trying to exploit the open source movement, such as Netscape and IBM, or even Linux vendors such as Red Hat, is to combine disclosure with some protection of IP for products not built under the open source rules.

In short, decisions about product technology—architecture, interfaces, and IP—are critical to platform leadership. Successful firms need to build modular architectures and openly disclose external interfaces necessary to create complements, while still protecting their competitive advantage. Resources spent on design issues such as platform architecture and interfaces, or on activities to promote industry consensus around interface standards, are not wasted. They give the platform leader or wannabe an opportunity to shape the industry and the ecosystem in which it operates.

Lever 3: External Relationships

To be a platform leader as we define it implies that a firm is highly dependent on external companies for complements that make the platform more valuable to end users. Platform leaders, therefore, have to devise strategies to collaborate with and influence a broad set of firms. Intel in particular implemented elaborate programs to work with both established complementors and new potential complementors, helping the latter gain industry credibility and raise capital, as well as assisting them with technical issues.

CONSENSUS AND CONTROL   To be effective over the long term, platform leaders and wannabes need to pursue at least two objectives simultaneously: First, they must try to obtain consensus among key complementors with regard to the technical specifications and standards that make their core products work with other products. Second, they must try to maintain control over critical design decisions at other firms that affect how well the core product and complements continue to work together through new product generations. Attempting to control what other firms do is usually not a good way to get them to be partners. Consequently, pursuing consensus and control at the same time can be quite a challenge.

Our study strongly suggests that consensus among industry players is probably impossible to achieve without at least one firm driving the process that leads to consensus. One firm must also exert some degree of control (such as over interfaces between components, or layers between the hardware platform and the software operating system); that is, define the parameters of choice rather than forcing a choice itself. Platform leaders or wannabes do not need to care which exact complements can be made, as long as they are compatible with and add value to the platform. The flip side, of course, also seems true: Control is probably impossible to achieve without some degree of consensus. In other words, platform industries seem to require at least one firm to act as the technical leader to maintain compatible standards, but this kind of leadership is possible only when firms agree to follow a platform leader.

In the Intel case, the company had to cultivate the technical capability to design interface standards that defined how the microprocessor "talks" to other components. Intel also cultivated the organizational capability to gain the support of other firms to design their own products around these interfaces. But, as we observed, it was difficult for Intel to influence the complete set of PC interfaces because some were not part of the microprocessor. If a critical mass of key players does not agree on interface specifications for the whole product, then the industry will not develop complementary and compatible products, or the industry will innovate in these kinds of products only very slowly—perhaps too slowly to match the pace of demand that the platform leader wants.[3]

COLLABORATION AND COMPETITION   Observing Intel closely suggested that specific management processes can help a platform leader achieve consensus and maintain control at the same time. One "secret" to Intel's success was in the way the company managed relationships with complementors: Intel engaged in a deliberate balancing act of collaboration and competition with other firms. To a large extent, this reflected a relationship of mutual dependency. Both Intel's future and the future of many complementors depended on how well these firms cooperated.

This balancing act requires firms to trust the platform leader as a partner. But maintaining trust is difficult because the relationships can be ambiguous. It is not always clear if another firm is a supplier, competitor, or complementor, or if a supplier or complementor today will become a competitor tomorrow. Some firms also play multiple roles. For example, IBM bought lots of Intel microprocessors, but it also made its own, such as the PowerPC, which competed with Intel products.

Then there is a real threat to complementors that "dance with the elephant." Some firms that today are suppliers or complementors of a platform leader might face direct competition from their much more powerful partner in the future. For example, Intel or Microsoft might decide to absorb features of complements into the microprocessor or Windows, or to offer very similar capabilities. Cisco was continually expanding the portfolio of networking products that it offered. Palm was continually adding functionality to its operating system. Platform leaders do not move into the markets of their partners very often, but they do it frequently enough to make outside firms wary of them and anxious to keep innovating in ways that benefit the platform. A platform leader may be less likely to intrude on the turf of a complementor if that firm can innovate in ways that the platform leader cannot.

In the Intel case, it was important for the platform leader to play multiple roles, (1) driving architectural, systemic innovation; (2) stimulating innovation on complements; and (3) coordinating. The first role is of a firm deeply concerned with the common good, in other words, with expanding the "pie" for everyone. For example, Intel was particularly concerned with decisions related to building consensus around technical interface standards. These interfaces offered standardized hardware or software "plugs" that firms developing complements could use to connect their products to Intel's microprocessors. In computing and telecommunications industries, or in game software, having platform interfaces that are open—publicly available and free of charge—makes it relatively easy for firms to enter the complements business. Platform leaders should always try to create these win-win situations: They promote competition and innovation in complements, and these innovations benefit the complementors, platform leader, and customers.

A second role for platform leaders is that of industry enabler. Enabling the industry to innovate in ever-better ways around a platform sometimes requires the platform leader to sacrifice its own private interest, at least for the short term, in favor of the common good. This was Intel's attitude, for example, when it invested in interface standards and relinquished royalty rights for technologies that facilitated evolution of the PC as a system. Intel signaled its publicly minded behavior when it gave away enabling technologies to encourage innovation and competition in complementary markets and coordinated the efforts of hundreds of engineers in developers' forums and the PlugFest compliance workshops.

A third role that platform leaders must play is similar to the classical position of firms that pursue their own best interest, such as to maximize their own profits or market share. This means that the platform leader sometimes makes decisions that might hurt some external firms, even if they were complementors in the past (and still might be in the future). Platform leaders need to be willing to play this traditional role because, in many cases, their incentives do not align with complementors. Objectives might diverge for several reasons. For example, complementors might bear larger risks and have shorter time horizons. If that happens, we believe that a platform leader or wannabe should try to share the risk with potential complementors. But platform leaders might also lead on complementors, when they either fail to have the patience to wait for a complement to arrive (such as Intel with Rambus) or when they enter complementary markets and compete with complementors. Of course, external firms would not be so loyal to platform leaders and support their standards if the complementors felt constantly threatened that the platform leader might move into their territories. For this reason, platform leaders have to be extremely careful with decisions that extend the functional scope of their products or extend their lines of business. Examples include Intel's successful incorporation of graphics and mathematical processing features into its basic microprocessors, as well as its gradual move into selling complete computer systems.

We can also cite Microsoft's incursions into various software applications and Internet content—competing head-on with companies such as Netscape, AOL, Lotus, Corel, Intuit, and Oracle, which were partners of the Windows division. (If non-Microsoft applications did not work properly on the Windows platform, then the Windows developers would have failed to maintain their product as the industry's software platform.) Often we find platform leaders taking specific actions to signal firms that they want to be a long-term partner and have no plans to move into their markets. Again, however, reputation and trust are essential. Successful platform leaders have to build reputations as organizations that do not impulsively or carelessly step out of their product boundaries into the territories of their complementors.

We saw various types of reputations and relationships among the platform leaders we discussed. For example, Intel had a reputation for being careful not to destroy the business models of its complementors (usually), whereas Microsoft did not. Cisco was likely to acquire firms that were key complementors or that posed a threat. Palm and Handspring also had a complex relationship that was likely to become more so in the future. Handspring was both a complementor to Palm (since its Visor product worked on Palm OS) and a competitor in the PDA device market, with a rapidly rising share and architectural leadership ambitions, at least in the hardware space. Handspring also had the ability to switch operating system vendors should Palm fall behind in software technology or try to overcharge Handspring for Palm OS.

Platform leaders have to find ways to manage these kinds of external tensions. Intel found that the best way to proceed is to adopt a gradual, low-key approach when pushing a particular agenda because this allows input from collaborating firms—and permits both sides to "test the waters." For example, when Intel failed to take a careful approach with its first foray in videoconferencing and tried to impose a new standard while there were strong incumbents, the effort failed. Intel came close to destroying the ability of complementors to make a profit. But Intel also learned to push an agenda more subtly and successfully with PCI, and the company repeated this success with the AGP and USB standards. Platform leaders also need to assure their partners that critical technical information will remain open and that there will be adequate protection of proprietary IP. Platform leaders or wannabes need to gain the trust of third parties. Building trust can take years, and, once established, is easily damaged. Platform leaders have to act fairly when their motives are questioned. They need to establish credibility in technical areas where they want to influence future designs or standards and allow potential complementors to feel comfortable that the platform leader is acting on behalf of the whole industry or ecosystem, and not just for itself.

The Intel employees we interviewed consistently held the view that third parties did not naturally have a lot of incentives to follow Intel's lead. Intel had to make it worth their while, but establishing the proper incentive for complementary innovation was usually not possible through written contracts or direct subsidies. Intel excelled at establishing long-term relationships with third parties that partitioned innovation efforts between the platform leader and complementors. In drafting interface specifications, for example, Intel did not insist on complete ownership of all related IP. It also encouraged technical input from select firms and only later—once the specifications were almost stable—opened up the process of standards setting to a broader set of firms. With this low-key, gradual approach, Intel seemed to have found a way to overcome the recurring difficulties of obtaining consensus that plagued other more "democratic" technical consortia. By relinquishing royalties on technical standards and by spinning off the effective management of standardization groups, Intel also allowed many firms to have a say in the specification of interfaces that would affect them, while strategically enrolling their support. Later, as we saw in chapter 4, Intel learned to distinguish between IP related to the specification of an interface versus the ability to implement that interface. Intel would retain some rights over implementation IP in order to preserve the possibility that it might enter the complementary market itself, if management decided this was necessary sometime in the future. The platform leader may find it helpful to signal a clear commitment to the financial success of its complementors. For example, Intel's gradual process of standardization around AGP and USB allowed it to define goals jointly with complementors and reduced the reluctance of these third parties to allocate resources to develop products that would complement Intel's future product generations. Long-term relationships favored these kinds of commitments.

In short, platform leaders have to pursue several roles at once: collaborating with external complementors while championing the public interest, but also competing with external complementors when this proved necessary to stimulate a new complements market. Platform leaders and complementors may be "friends" or "foes," and the ambiguity of relationships may generate tensions. Platform leaders and wannabes have several alternatives for managing these external tensions: establish trust-based long-term relationships; take a low-key, gradual approach in standards setting; and act as a neutral broker between external firms. In managing these external relationships, platform leaders need to maintain a reputation for not stepping over boundaries, and this sometimes includes restricting the scope of their own product lines. Finally, platform leaders and wannabes should retain a genuine sense of responsibility with respect to the business viability of their complementors. It could not possibly help the ecosystem if the platform leader extracts too much profit for itself and watches complementors struggle or fail.

Lever 4: Internal Organization

A platform leader may rely on specific internal organizational approaches to manage external relationships with complementors more effectively. Again, the problem is usually how to compete and collaborate simultaneously. These goals are difficult to balance because some groups within a platform leader might compete with complementors, while other groups might try to get those same complementors to cooperate and adopt the platform's technical standards.

We believe that these internal tensions must, and can, be managed. Intel's solution was to have some groups within the company focus more on competition with other firms (e.g., the product groups), while other groups focused more on cooperation and building consensus with partners (e.g., an R&D lab, IAL). Intel recognized the necessity of pursuing those conflicting goals—referred to by everyone within Intel as Job 1 (sell more microprocessors), Job 2 (compete directly in complementary markets), and Job 3 (build new businesses potentially unrelated to the core microprocessor business). Job 1 also included encouraging external, demand-enhancing innovation on complements. Intel's top management openly acknowledged that there were conflicts among these goals. Entering complementary markets directly brought Intel into competition with partners, but management sometimes decided that these moves were necessary. Investing heavily in new business development also sometimes distracted groups from focusing on the core businesses, but sometimes this seemed necessary to help the firm diversify.

STRUCTURE   Platform leaders and wannabes need to think hard about how to organize internally given the internal and external tensions likely to arise. They should consider maintaining a clear separation between units charged with achieving different goals, such as stimulating innovation by complementors versus investing directly in complementary markets. This organizational separation seems to facilitate trust with external partners.

Intel, for example, separated internal groups with different goals so that outside firms could more easily trust and exchange confidential information with Intel people. Microsoft separated its operating systems and applications groups, which helped its relationships with competitors who were also complementors such as IBM/Lotus, Netscape, Intuit, and Oracle. Cisco also kept its product units relatively independent, which enabled them to work with outside firms that competed with other Cisco groups.

PROCESS AND CULTURE   But organizational design is usually not enough. Internal processes are necessary to set goals, build consensus, and make the structure work. Intel, for example, had an elaborate process for holding meetings at various levels to set strategies and goals, and assess and resolve internal conflicts. Intel also relied on internal processes such as formal planning and off-site meetings and on several senior executives to fill an arbiter role to resolve conflicts that might arise among the various units within the company. Top management of platform leaders should also foster an organizational culture that encourages debate and tolerates ambiguity, such as permitting different groups to pursue some-times conflicting goals.

"SYSTEM" MINDSET AND NEUTRALITY   Finally, we noted that plat-form leaders had a better chance of success if they were able to cultivate the organizational capabilities to view the platform as a system and have a vision for how to evolve that system. As we saw, this often means involving external partners in its development and acting as a neutral broker between them. IAL embodied these capabilities. NTT also had large R&D resources that it devoted to studying technologies of general utility to the wireless industry. Microsoft, Cisco, and Palm also demon-strated their recognition that their platforms contributed to particular systems, whether it be the PC, Internet-based networks, or PDAs and handheld computers. But it was not clear that these firms had the same ability or willingness to act as neutral industry brokers as did Intel with IAL. Windows.NET is a good example: Was this new platform architec-ture an attempt to improve the working of the Internet for the benefit of complementors and users, or an effort to provide Microsoft with greater proprietary control and influence over Internet standards and technolo-gies? The jury is still out.

Some Limits to Platform Leadership

We could not conclude this book without saying something about the limitations of platform leadership as a competitive strategy. Three closely related issues particularly concerned us. First, even successful platform leaders can fall prey to problems that arise from too much of a platform-centric mentality. There are other ways to compete. Second, platform leaders can become so tied to certain technologies that they find it diffi-cult to evolve their platforms. Evolution is often important to long-term survival. And third, there may be some confusion as to whether market leadership is a necessary precondition for platform leadership. We believe that it is useful to clarify the distinction among these issues.

The Problem of Platform-Centric Mentalities
Technologies evolve, industry structures evolve, and user needs evolve. Even the most advanced platforms and vibrant ecosystems can fail when

new technologies or user patterns emerge. The danger for platform leaders is to become entrenched in one vision of an industry. Often, firms, especially if they are successful, become less aware of possible radical changes in their environment or product lines. The ecosystem that platform leaders create and nurture is likely to limit their view of the world and potential options for the future.

All the companies and technologies discussed in this book are affected by this limitation. Intel, for example, despite some efforts to be broader, remained closely tied to the x86 microprocessor family. It was unlikely to move to radically new types of processing models, such as using optical technologies. Microsoft continued to have a very "Windows-centric" view of the Internet. It may never take full advantage of the benefits of open standards or the open source movement. Cisco depended heavily on its ability to weave multiple technologies together through its IOS software. But IOS was a patchwork of code and standards that would someday outlive its usefulness. Palm was quickly becoming a hostage to the internal architecture and the external interfaces that defined Palm OS. Even NTT DoCoMo had to live with the consequences of its decisions as to what standards to adopt for wireless data transmission and content rendering. And Linux was essentially a UNIX clone, with all the benefits and constraints that this implied for future models of computing.

The Need to Evolve the Platform

We could also see some platform leaders struggling with the issue of what is their real "platform" in industries where the technology was rapidly evolving or consisted of multiple types of potentially compatible or interoperable alternatives. For some Intel groups, the platform was becoming the Internet and the different kinds of servers and devices that ran Internet software, rather than the Windows-based PC and the x86 microprocessor family. Microsoft was struggling with how to reconcile the Internet as a computing platform versus Windows. Cisco found itself moving beyond the Internet router as a platform to various types of networking equipment that communicated through Internet protocols. In any case, figuring out how to be a platform leader in one setting may not help a firm figure out what the next industry paradigm or ecosystem is likely to be. A dominant position in one technology is more likely to constrain a firm's ability or its incentives to invest in a new ecosystem that can threaten current sales and profits.

Product architectures also tend to be long-lived. This is often as much an organizational problem as it is a technical one. Firms usually contain different departments or groups that create different components. A product often reflects the internal organization of the producer.[4] In the computer or telecom industries, or all de-integrated industries, it is not only several departments within a given firm, but several firms in the industry that make the components of a system. This situation has made the adoption of a "big picture" or systemwide view (i.e., a systemic understanding of the product) difficult. Platform leaders that reveal enough architectural information to promote a deep understanding of the systems they are building can address this problem as well as encourage innovation both within and outside the firm.

We saw that Intel established the IAL to be a repository and disseminator of system knowledge. The activities of many firms to optimize their products reinforced its competencies. It functioned as an industry consensus-builder. But when an industry is fragmented and consists of many specialist firms developing components that fit in an architecture that is the legacy of times past, there is certainly no guarantee of short-term profit from creating and sustaining an organizational repository of system knowledge. It requires long-term vision from component makers to invest in and create such organizations. In that same fragmented industry, an architectural change may not be possible without industry reorganization. Any firm aiming to institute an architectural change at the system level would not only have to overcome the division of labor that is structured and reinforced by existing partitioning of economic activities (reflected by the existing map of firms' boundaries), but would also have to gain industry consensus around the new architectural interfaces that would bound the scopes of products developed by an array of independent firms.

Long-term success at platform leadership, therefore, requires the ability to evolve the platform while rallying other firms around these changes. Evolving the platform has the effect of reinforcing the system architecture. By contrast, one could suggest that weak technical leadership could easily lead to obsolescence of the system architecture and the overall platform, and can eventually create a risk for the entire set of firms that depend on that platform for their livelihoods.

Confusion between Technical versus Market Leadership

This brings us to another question: Should a platform-leader wannabe try to drive technical standards first, in the hopes that technical leadership translates into market leadership? Or should wannabes try to grab market share first, and then invest in technical leadership? We know from history that platform leaders in competitive markets usually emerge through the mechanisms of the marketplace, rather than through some magical process that recognizes technology leaders. This was true with radio, television, VCRs, PCs, and many other products. As a result, trying to become the de facto market leader should put a firm in a good position to evolve into being the technical leader for its platform.

Of course, there are some technologies that might require industry-level agreements among firms and government agencies for platform standards and complementary markets to emerge. In these cases, it makes lots of sense for firms to develop lobbying and negotiation capabilities, and to promote their solution as the industry solution. This seems to be the case with high-definition television, for example. Without confidence that particular technical specifications will become the industry standards, consumer electronics companies will be reluctant to make products with particular capabilities, broadcasters will be reluctant to buy new equipment and broadcast in particular formats, and consumers will be reluctant to buy new TV sets. Here the quest for market share coexists with the desire to impose one's solution as a standard, either de facto or de jure in collaboration with external firms. The same phenomenon may eventually be true for the wireless Web. Although different systems currently coexist, there are many inconveniences today for users who cannot use their phones or wireless PDAs in all locations. In these kinds of cases, the variable seems to be the technology: How interoperable or compatible are different systems, and how well can the market mediate differences and bring producers and users toward a common standard?

Although a high market share and a high degree of innovative capabilities are important and necessary conditions to achieve platform leadership, they alone do not suffice. A company has to be able to engage complementors and place itself in the center of the network of innovation around its platform. Of course, market share and innovative capabilities facilitate platform leadership in the sense that, when a firm makes an attractive product and sells it well, this increases the incentive for potential complementors to adapt their innovations to the platform leader's product. Palm, for example, sold over one million units of its Palm Pilot before it became vocal about its platform ambitions and started explicitly encouraging external developers to develop applications—an approach that attracted complementors. On the other hand, when Apple's CEO John Sculley touted that the Newton would be the platform for handheld computing before its success in the market place, this led to a resounding flop that froze further development on PDAs for several years.

We also believe that a firm cannot become a platform leader without first having a large market share for its product. Although this strategy is possible, the platform-leader wannabe would have to pursue a technical leadership strategy very aggressively and truly land itself at the technical frontier of the industry. QUALCOMM, for example, tried to do this in wireless transmission technology by establishing a large number of patents and licensing them broadly. The technical leader should also do whatever it can to become a market leader in the future. Why? Since the main goal of platform leaders is to maintain their position as an essential piece of a thriving and innovative ecosystem, it has to offer external developers the most attractive proposition. Developers will most likely choose to invest in products that complement the platform-leader wannabe's product only if they believe this platform is the best alternative in its category and will eventually attract the most customers.

Again, there is no simple answer here. Both market leadership and technical leadership are important and useful to achieve platform leadership. We can say, however, that de facto market leadership—such as through mass-market designs and prices aimed at encouraging volume sales—usually puts a firm in a strong position to exert technical and standards leadership. But neither get to the essence of what platform leadership is really about.

Final Thoughts

So what is the essence of platform leadership? It is recognizing that certain kinds of products have little value by themselves but can be extremely valuable as the center of a network of complements. Platform leadership forces managers to consider the effect of their decisions not only on one firm, but on an entire industry. Platform leaders and wannabes must maintain incentives for third parties to produce complementary innovations and help them do so, or the strategy will fail. We are talking about a strategy of interdependence—creating a vibrant ecosystem—that entails a fragile existence for firms that are part of the network.

In conclusion, we can say that the essence of platform leadership begins with a vision that extends well beyond the business operations of one firm or the technical specifications of one product or one component. It is a vision that says the whole of the ecosystem can be greater than the sum of its parts, if firms work together and follow a leader. The vision and decisions of platform leaders can affect not only the immediate competitive environment but also the evolution of technologies and entire industries. Their decisions may or may not facilitate investment in research and new product development in the broader industry. In other words, platform leaders, with the decisions they make and do not make, can greatly influence the degree and kind of innovations that complements create. This is what platform leadership is all about! Platform leadership and complementary innovation are not things that happen spontaneously in an industry. Managers make them happen—if they know what to do and how to do it.

Notes

Preface

1. C. W. Baldwin and K. B. Clark, *Design Rules: The Power of Modularity* (Cambridge, MA: MIT Press, 2000).

2. R. N. Langlois, "External Economies and Economic Progress: The Case of the Microcomputer Industry," *Business History Review* 66, no. 1 (1992): 1–51; R. N. Langlois and P. L. Robertson, "Networks and Innovation in a Modular System: Lessons from the Microcomputer and Stereo Component Industries," *Research Policy* 21 (1992): 297–313.

3. F. Fisher, J. McGowan, and J. E. Greenwood, *Folded, Spindled and Mutilated: Economic Analysis and U.S. vs. IBM* (Cambridge, MA: MIT Press, 1983).

4. C. Shapiro and H. R. Varian, *Information Rules: A Strategic Guide to the Network Economy* (Boston: Harvard Business School Press, 1999).

5. J. Farrell and G. Saloner, "Installed Base and Compatibility: Innovation, Product Preannouncements, and Predation," *American Economic Review* 76, no. 5 (1986): 940–955; J. Farrell and G. Saloner, "Dynamic Competition with Switching Costs," *RAND Journal of Economics* 21, no. 2 (1988): 275–292. Farrell and Saloner have written many articles on network externalities since. J. Farrell, H. K. Monroe, and G. Saloner, "The Vertical Organization of Industry: Systems Competition versus Component Competition," *Journal of Economics and Management Strategy* 7, no. 2 (1998): 143–182; M. L. Katz and C. Shapiro, "Technology Adoption in the Presence of Network Externalities," *Journal of Political Economy* 94, no. 4 (1986): 823–841; M. L. Katz and C. Shapiro, "Product Introduction with Network Externalities," *Journal of Industrial Economics* 40, no. 1 (1992): 55–83.

6. T. F. Bresnahan and S. M. Greenstein, "Technological Competition and the Structure of the Computer Industry," *Journal of Industrial Economics* 47, no. 1 (1999): 1–40.

7. R. Sanchez and J. T. Mahoney, "Modularity, Flexibility and Knowledge Management in Product and Organization Design," *Strategic Management Journal* 17 (winter 1996): 63–76.

8. M. A. Schilling, "Towards a General Modular Systems Theory and Its Application to Interfirm Product Modularity," *Academy of Management Review* 25, no. 2 (2000): 312–334.

9. B. Gomes-Casseres, *The Alliance Revolution: The New Shape of Business Rivalry* (Cambridge, MA: Harvard University Press, 1996); B. Gomes-Casseres, "Group Versus Group: How Alliance Networks Compete," *Harvard Business Review*, July–August 1994, 62–84.

10. R. Garud and A. Kumaraswamy, "Changing Competitive Dynamics in Network Industries: An Exploration of Sun Microsystem's Open Systems Strategy," *Strategic Management Journal* 14 (1993): 351–369.

11. A. McGahan, D. B. Yoffie, and L. Vadasz, "Creating Value and Setting Standards: The Lessons of Consumer Electronics for Personal Digital Assistants," in *Competing in the Age of Digital Convergence*, ed. D. B. Yoffie (Boston: Harvard Business School Press, 1994).

Chapter One

1. M. A. Cusumano, Y. Mylonadis, and R. Rosenbloom, "Strategic Maneuvering and Mass-Market Dynamics: The Triumph of VHS Over Beta," *Business History Review* 66 (spring 1992): 51–94; M. A. Cusumano and R. Rosenbloom, "Technological Pioneering and Competitive Advantage: The Birth of the VCR Industry," *California Management Review* 29, no. 4 (summer 1987): 51–76.

2. Microprocessors, veritable "computers on a chip," are the ubiquitous core hardware component of the PC. In 2001, Intel provided over 80 percent of them.

3. Definition adapted from J. L. McClelland and D. E. Rumelhart, *Parallel Distributed Processing* (Cambridge, MA: MIT Press, 1995) as quoted in C. W. Baldwin and K. B. Clark, *Design Rules: The Power of Modularity*, 63.

4. C. W. Baldwin and K. B. Clark, *Design Rules*; R. Sanchez and J. T. Mahoney, "Modularity, Flexibility and Knowledge Management in Product and Organization Design"; M. A. Schilling, "Towards a General Modular Systems Theory and Its Application to Interfirm Product Modularity"; and K. T. Ulrich and S. D. Eppinger, *Product Design and Development* (New York: McGraw-Hill, 1995).

5. M. A. Cusumano and David B. Yoffie, *Competing on Internet Time: Lessons from Netscape and Its Battle with Microsoft* (New York: Touchstone/Simon & Schuster, 1998), 11.

6. Michael Cusumano has written extensively on this issue of mass-market standards and competitive dynamics. For VCRs, see references in note 1. For PCs, see M. A. Cusumano and D. B. Yoffie, *Competing on Internet Time: Lessons from Netscape and Its Battle with Microsoft* (New York: Touchstone/Simon & Schuster, 1998); and M. A. Cusumano and R. Selby, *Microsoft Secrets: How the World's Most Powerful Software Company Creates Technology, Shapes Markets, and Manages People* (New York: Free Press/Simon & Schuster, 1995).

7. Hereinafter, we shall use the term "complementors" for the longer phrase "developers of complementary products." See A. M. Brandenburger and B. J. Nalebuff, *Co-opetition: A Revolutionary Mindset That Combines Competition and Cooperation. The Game Theory Strategy That's Changing the Game of Business* (New York: Currency Doubleday, 1997).

8. See, for example, the feud between Intel and Intergraph. A lawsuit filed in November 1997 by Intergraph against Intel became the cornerstone of an antitrust complaint filed by the U.S. Federal Trade Commission in June 1998. It alleged Intel abused its monopoly power by keeping technical information from computer makers Intergraph Corp., Compaq Computer Corp., and Digital Equipment Corp. (now part of Compaq). One argument was Intel's refusal to disclose interface information

that would help Intergraph prepare ahead of Intel's launch of its new microprocessor new Intel-compatible complementary products. The legal argument presented by Intergraph was based on the notion of the Intel product (or platform) as an "essential facility" in the computer industry. Consequently, Intel was deemed by Intergraph lawyers as exerting a real damage to Intergraph by refusing to share with Intergraph engineers what was, in Intel's eye, proprietary interface information—which Intel felt free to share with whomever they wanted. Intel stopped sharing its specifications with Intergraph after Intergraph made a move that Intel saw as direct competition. Intergraph lawyers accused Intel of withholding the interface information as retaliation. Intel was not condemned. In fact, the FTC formally approved a settlement with Intel in March 1999, on the eve of the trial, when it agreed not to withhold information from its customers. See N. Turner and M. Marsala, "Intel Isn't a Monopoly—for Now," *Investor's Daily*, 18 March 1999; S. Lohr, "Conceding Guidelines and Winning a Bit of Protection," *The New York Times*, 9 March 1999, C4; L. Kehoe and R. Wolffe, "Intel to Take Turn Under the Courtroom Spotlight: The World's Largest Chipmaker Faces Antiturst Charges," *Financial Times*, 22 February 1999; R. Taylor, "Court Victory for Intel," *Financial Times*, 6 November 1999; T. Foremski, "Intergraph's Case Against Intel Dismissed by Judge," *Financial Times*, 15 March 2000.

Chapter Two

1. Microsoft is discussed in more detail in chapter 5.

2. See J. F. Moore, *The Death of Competition: Leadership and Strategy in the Age of Business Ecosystems* (New York: HarperBusiness, 1996) for a discussion of the computer industry using the metaphor of biological "ecosystems."

3. See work by J. L. Bower, *Managing the Resource Allocation Process* (Homewood, IL: Richard D. Irwin, 1970); R. A. Burgelman, "A Process Model of Internal Corporate Venturing in the Diversified Major Firm," *Administrative Science Quarterly* 28 (1983): 223–244; M. D. Cohen, J. G. March, and J. P. Olsen, "A Garbage Can Model of Organizational Choice," *Administrative Science Quarterly* 17 (1972): 1–25.

4. Bala Cadambi, Department Manager, Peripherals & Interconnect Technology, IAL, interview by author, Hillsboro, OR, 4 August 1998. Emphasis added.

5. A. Yu, *Creating the Digital Future: The Secrets of Consistent Innovation at Intel* (New York: Free Press, 1998), 27. Albert Yu is Senior Vice President and General Manager of Intel's Microprocessor Product Group.

6. See A. S. Grove, *Only the Paranoid Survive: How to Exploit the Crisis Points That Challenge Every Company and Career* (New York: Currency Doubleday, 1996). See also J. Farrell, H. K. Monroe, and G. Saloner, "The Vertical Organization of Industry: Systems Competition versus Component Competition," *Journal of Economics and Management Strategy* 7, no. 2 (1998): 143–182.

7. It is possible that IBM's woes with the Department of Justice after its ten-year-long antitrust trial, leaving it "folded, spindled, and mutilated," made IBM cautious about exerting visibly too much power over its suppliers. It also put an enormous toll on its resources and distracted it from strategic issues. See F. Fisher, J.

McGowan, and J. E. Greenwood, *Folded, Spindled and Mutilated: Economic Analysis and U.S. vs. IBM* (Cambridge, MA: MIT Press, 1983).

8. A. Yu, *Creating the Digital Future: The Secrets of Consistent Innovation at Intel.*

9. Dr. Craig Kinnie, Director, IAL, interview by author, Hillsboro, OR, 11 November 1997.

10. Ibid.

11. Ibid. Emphasis added.

12. See <http://developer.intel.com/ial/labs/index.htm>.

13. Dr. Carmen Egido, Director and General Manager of the Applications, Services and Research Lab, IAL, interview by author, Hillsboro, OR, 11 November 1997.

14. Gerald Holzhammer, Co-Director (at time of interview) of the IAL, interview by author, Hillsboro, OR, 11 November 1997. Emphasis added.

15. David Reed, former Vice President and Chief Scientist at Lotus Corporation, interview by author, 13 August 2001.

16. David B. Johnson, Director, the Media and Interconnect Technology Lab, IAL, interview by author, Hillsboro, OR, 20 August 1998.

17. Carol Barrett, Marketing Manager, IAL, interview by author, Hillsboro, OR, 5 August 1998. Also, "Intel Architecture Labs: Overview," undated Intel internal document.

18. Intel internal document, "Intel Architecture Lab: Overview" (1998).

19. Dr. Andrew S. Grove, Chairman, Intel Corporation, interview by author, Santa Clara, CA, 18 August 1998.

20. Dr. Craig Kinnie, Director, IAL, interview by author, Hillsboro, OR, 11 November 1997.

21. Dr. Andrew S. Grove, Chairman, Intel Corporation, interview by author, Santa Clara, CA, 18 August 1998.

22. Dr. Craig Kinnie, Director, IAL, interview by author, Hillsboro, OR, 11 November 1997.

23. Dr. Andrew S. Grove, Chairman, Intel Corporation, interview by author, Santa Clara, CA, 18 August 1998.

24. Industry Standard Architecture (ISA) is the IBM bus design used in most PCs since IBM released the PC-AT in the early 1980s. It is a limited 8-bit and 16-bit bus, but it is so widely compatible that it has outlasted technologically superior—and much faster—bus standards like PCI. (See C Net Glossary, <http://www.cnet.com>.) The legacy of the IBM architecture became a burden to Intel because it did not allow the chip to "show off" its performance.

25. Will Swope, Vice President, Intel Architecture Business Group, and Director, Platform Planning, interview by author, Santa Clara, CA, 20 August 1998.

26. David J. Schuler, Program Manager, Worldwide Sales and Marketing, Intel Corporation, interview by author, Hillsboro, OR, 6 August 1998.

27. David Carson, Manager, Interconnect Architecture, Media Architecture Lab, IAL, interview by author, Hillsboro, OR, 4 August 1998.

28. However, it is important to note that Intel's sponsoring of PCI did not imply that all players in the computer industry who wanted their products to work with an Intel microprocessor would have to adapt their designs to the new bus specification.

New systems could, and were, built using new processors and old system buses. The microprocessor design did not require PCI because PCI is not an interface to the processor but rather an interface between complements surrounding the processor.

29. Dr. Craig Kinnie, Director, IAL, interview by author, Hillsboro, OR, 11 November 1997.

30. David Carson, Manager, Interconnect Architecture, Media Architecture Lab, IAL, interview by author, Hillsboro, OR, 4 August 1998. Emphasis added.

31. This buffer of programmable logic that could simply be changed or reconfigured if a new microprocessor had to be included in a PC came to be simply called "the chip set" (sometimes spelled "chipset").

32. David Carson, Manager, Interconnect Architecture, Media Architecture Lab, IAL, interview by author, Hillsboro, OR, 4 August 1998. Emphasis added.

33. See C. Y. Baldwin and K. B. Clark, *Design Rules: The Power of Modularity* (Cambridge, MA: MIT Press, 2000), for more on the relationship between industrial innovation and modularity in design.

34. See R. N. Langlois, "External Economies and Economic Progress: The Case of the Microcomputer Industry," *Business History Review* 66, no. 1 (1992): 1–51, for an early history of the computer industry and the role of modularity in innovation.

35. Dr. Andrew S. Grove, Chairman, Intel Corporation, interview by author, Santa Clara, CA, 18 August 1998.

36. Ibid.

37. David Carson, Manager, Interconnect Architecture, Media Architecture Lab, IAL, interview by author, Hillsboro, OR, 4 August 1998.

38. Ibid.

39. Bill Miller, Director, Worldwide Media Relations, Sales and Marketing Group, Intel Corporation, interview by author, Santa Clara, CA, 13 August 1998.

40. Dr. Andrew S. Grove, Chairman, Intel Corporation, interview by author, Santa Clara, CA, 18 August 1998.

41. Bill Miller, Director, Worldwide Media Relations, Sales and Marketing Group, Intel Corporation, interview by author, Santa Clara, CA, 13 August 1998.

42. Claude Leglise, Vice President, and Director, Intel Developer Relations Group, Content Group, interview by author, Santa Clara, CA, 13 November 1997. Emphasis added.

43. Dr. Craig Kinnie, Director, IAL, interview by author, Hillsboro, OR, 11 November 1997.

44. See the discussion on ambiguity of specifications in chapter 3 under "Using Public Forums."

45. Bill Miller, Director, Worldwide Media Relations, Sales and Marketing Group, Intel Corporation, interview by author, Santa Clara, CA, 13 August 1998.

46. David J. Schuler, Program Manager, Worldwide Sales and Marketing, Intel Corporation, interview by author, Hillsboro, OR, 6 August 1998.

47. Dr. Craig Kinnie, Director, IAL, interview by author, Hillsboro, OR, 11 November 1997.

48. Claude Leglise, Vice President, and Director, Intel Developer Relations Group, Content Group, interview by author, Santa Clara, CA, 13 November 1997.

49. USB is discussed in chapter 3. AGP, sometimes called Advanced Graphics Port, a new interface specification developed by Intel, is based on PCI, but was designed especially for the throughput demands of 3-D graphics. Rather than using the PCI bus for graphics data, with AGP, a graphics controller can directly access main memory, allowing fast, high-quality display of 3-D and video images.

Chapter Three

1. See chapter 5 for Microsoft and Cisco.

2. See chapter 6 for Palm, Linux, and NTT DoCoMo.

3. FireWire, also called IEEE 1394 (for a definition of IEEE, see note 20), can daisy-chain together up to sixty-three peripherals in a treelike structure (as opposed to SCSI's linear structure; see note 5). It allows peer-to-peer device communication, such as communication between a scanner and a printer, to take place without using system memory or the CPU. It is designed to support plug-and-play and hot-swapping. Its six-wire cable is not only more convenient than SCSI cables but can supply up to 60 watts of power, allowing low-consumption devices to operate without a separate power cord.

4. David Carson, Manager, Interconnect Architecture, Media Architecture Lab, IAL, interview by author, Hillsboro, OR, 4 August 1998.

5. SCSI is a processor-independent standard interface used to connect computers to peripheral devices (e.g., a mouse, hard disks, floppy disks, CD-ROMs, printers, scanners) and to other computers and local area networks (LANs).

6. Bill Miller, Director, Worldwide Media Relations, Sales and Marketing Group, Intel Corporation, interview by author, Santa Clara, CA, 13 August 1998.

7. Jim Pappas, Director, Platform Initiatives, Desktop Products Group, Intel Corporation, interview by author, Hillsboro, OR, 4 August 1998. Pappas also describes the SCSI connectors in the back of the computer as "old, clunky, large, and positioned very inconveniently on the PC."

8. David B. Johnson, Director, Media Architecture Lab, IAL, interview by author, Hillsboro, OR, 11 November 1997. Emphasis added.

9. Carmen Egido, Ph.D., Director and General Manager of the Applications, Services and Research Lab, IAL, interview by author, Hillsboro, OR, 11 November 1997.

10. Dr. Craig Kinnie, Director, IAL, interview by author, Hillsboro, OR, 11 November 1997.

11. See C. W. Baldwin and K. B. Clark, *Design Rules: The Power of Modularity* (Cambridge, MA: MIT Press, 2000); and other references in chapter 1.

12. Dr. Craig Kinnie, Director, IAL, interview by author, Hillsboro, OR, 11 November 1997. Emphasis added.

13. Ibid.

14. Jim Pappas, Director, Platform Initiatives, Desktop Products Group, Intel Corporation, interview by author, Hillsboro, OR, 4 August 1998.

15. Bala Cadambi, Department Manager, Peripherals & Interconnect Technology, IAL, Intel Corporation, interview by author, Hillsboro, OR, 4 August 1998. Emphasis added.

16. Bill Miller, Director, Worldwide Media Relations, Sales and Marketing Group, Intel Corporation, interview by author, Santa Clara, CA, 13 August 1998.

17. Ibid.

18. Ibid. Emphasis added.

19. Ibid. Emphasis added.

20. IEEE (pronounced "i triple e") is a major institution that promotes and helps establish interoperability standards and also publishes scholarly journals in the fields of electrical engineering, electronics, and networking. See <http://www.ieee.org>.

21. The ITU (sometimes referred to by its former official French name, Comité Consultatif International de Télégraphie et Téléphonie, or CCITT) is an international committee based in Geneva, Switzerland, within which governments and the private sector coordinate global telecommunications networks and services. The ITU also recommends telecom standards—for example, the audio compression/decompression standards and the V. standards for modem speed and compression (V.34 and so on)—and is a leading publisher of telecom technology, regulatory, and standards information. See <http://www.itu.int>. (Source: C Net Glossary, <http://www.cnet.com>.)

22. Jim Pappas, Director, Platform Initiatives, Desktop Products Group, Intel Corporation, interview by author, Hillsboro, OR, 4 August 1998. Emphasis added.

23. Ibid. Emphasis added.

24. The name GeoPort refers to an Apple computer high-speed communication architecture inaugurated in 1997. In theory, a GeoPort can transmit up to 2 megabits of data per second. A GeoPort can accept standard DIN-8 serial connectors as well as a new DIN-9 connector used by GeoPort specific devices. The extra ninth pin provides power, and prevents GeoPort devices from getting plugged in to an ordinary serial port. The prototypical GeoPort device is the GeoPort Telecom Adapter, which provides an interface with analogue telephone lines similar to a standard modem.

25. Jim Pappas, Director, Platform Initiatives, Desktop Products Group, Intel Corporation, interview by author, Hillsboro, OR, 4 August 1998. Emphasis added.

26. Ben Manny, Engineering Manager, Residential Networking, IAL, Intel Corporation, interview by author, Hillsboro, OR, 6 August 1998. Emphasis added.

27. Ibid. Emphasis added.

28. The ideas developed in this paragraph also apply to the economics of developing tools or so-called enabling products such as SDKs. See, "Creating and Distributing Enabling Tools" later in this chapter.

29. Dan Russell, Director, Platform Marketing, Desktop Products Group, Intel Corporation, interview by author, Hillsboro, OR, 4 August 1998.

30. Bala Cadambi, Department Manager, Peripherals & Interconnect Technology, IAL, Intel Corporation, interview by author, Hillsboro, OR, 4 August 1998. Emphasis added.

31. Gerald Holzhammer, Co-Director (at time of interview) of the IAL, interview by author, Hillsboro, OR, 11 November 1997.

32. Dan Russell, Director, Platform Marketing, Desktop Products Group, Intel Corporation, interview by author, Hillsboro, OR, 4 August 1998.

33. Jim Pappas, Director, Platform Initiatives, Desktop Products Group, Intel Corporation, interview by author, Hillsboro, OR, 4 August 1998.

34. Author Annabelle Gawer attended the PlugFest as part of her Ph.D. dissertation field research.

35. Dan Russell, Director, Platform Marketing, Desktop Products Group, Intel Corporation, interview by author, Hillsboro, OR, 4 August 1998.

36. Gerald Holzhammer, Co-Director (at time of interview) of the IAL, interview by author, Hillsboro, OR, 11 November 1997. Emphasis added.

37. Not surprisingly (in this context), Jim Pappas—her guide at the PlugFest—asked author Annabelle Gawer to refrain from interviewing other companies at the site in order to preserve the climate of trust and of "engineers working with engineers."

38. Bill Miller, Director, Worldwide Media Relations, Sales and Marketing Group, Intel Corporation, interview by author, Santa Clara, CA, 13 August 1998.

39. Bala Cadambi, Department Manager, Peripherals & Interconnect Technology, IAL, Intel Corporation, interview by author, Hillsboro, OR, 4 August 1998. Emphasis added.

40. Ibid.

41. Ibid.

42. Ibid.

43. An example of such an optimization tool would be the IPEA (Intel Performance Evaluation and Analysis) kit, a set of tools that Intel gives to external designers to help them optimize their graphics circuit, power management, I/O circuitry, or drivers. Dan Russell, Director, Platform Marketing, Desktop Products Group, Intel Corporation, interview by author, Hillsboro, OR, 4 August 1998.

44. Dan Russell, Director, Platform Marketing, Desktop Products Group, Intel Corporation, interview by author, Hillsboro, OR, 4 August 1998.

45. Ibid.

46. David Ryan, Director, Technology Marketing, IAL, interview by author, Hillsboro, OR, 4 August 1998.

47. Ibid.

48. D. Weinstein, "Intel Inside," INSEAD Case (Fontainebleau, France: INSEAD, 1994); A. Yu, *Creating the Digital Future: The Secrets of Consistent Innovation at Intel* (New York: Free Press, 1998).

49. The "Intel Inside" campaign also infuriated many powerful clients of Intel, including the big OEMs, who saw Intel's branding efforts as a direct threat to their own brands and as a move that would benefit their own smaller rivals from the backing of Intel's brand name. Big OEMs feared a shift in the balance of power against them in favor of "low-cost, no-name companies." This led Compaq's then-CEO to publicly attack Intel's move. See T. Jackson, *Inside Intel: How Andy Grove Built the World's Most Successful Chip Company* (New York: Dutton, 1997).

50. See A. S. Grove, *Only the Paranoid Survive: How to Exploit the Crisis Points That Challenge Every Company and Career* (New York: Currency Doubleday, 1996); T. Jackson, *Inside Intel: How Andy Grove Built the World's Most Successful Chip Company*; A. Yu, *Creating the Digital Future: The Secrets of Consistent Innovation at Intel.*

51. David B. Johnson, Director, Media and Interconnect Technology Lab, IAL, interview by author, Hillsboro, OR, 20 August 1998.

52. Ibid.

53. Sally Fundakowski, Director, Business Developer Relations Group, Intel Corporation, interview by author, Santa Clara, CA, 7 August 1998.

54. Ibid.

55. Richard Steinjann, Intel Corporation, interview by author, Santa Clara, CA, 13 August 1998; Claude Leglise, Tom Marchok, Intel Corporation, interviews by author, Santa Clara, CA, 14 August 1998.

56. Claude Leglise, Vice President, and Director, Intel Developer Relations Group, Content Group, interview by author, Santa Clara, CA, 13 November 1997.

57. Ibid.

58. Ibid.

59. Ibid. Emphasis added.

60. Jonathan Khazam, Intel Corporation, interview by author, Santa Clara, CA, 13 August 1998.

61. Ibid.

62. Ibid.

63. ISV stands for independent software vendors.

64. Jonathan Khazam, Intel Corporation, interview by author, Santa Clara, CA, 13 August 1998.

65. Ibid.

66. Mary Murphy-Hoye, Director, IT Strategy and Technology, Intel Corporation, interview by author, Cambridge, MA, 16 January 2001.

67. Intel Corporation, "Intel Reorganizes All Intel Architecture Activities to Provide Platforms and Solutions for the Internet Economy," (press release, 27 April 2000); Intel Corporation, "Intel Builds e-Business Alliances Across the Country with Solution Provider Forum," (press release, 20 July 2000); Intel Corporation, "Intel Details E-Business Solution Integration Strategies," (press release, 24 August 2000). For the online archives, see <http://www.intel.com/pressroom/archive/releases/>.

68. Mary Murphy-Hoye, Director, IT Strategy and Technology, Intel Corporation, interview by author, Cambridge, MA, 16 January 2001.

69. Sally Fundakowski, Director, Business Developer Relations Group, Intel Corporation, interview by author, Santa Clara, CA, 7 August 1998.

70. David B. Johnson, Director, Media and Interconnect Technology Lab, IAL, interview by author, Hillsboro, OR, 20 August 1998.

71. Bill Miller, Director, Worldwide Media Relations, Sales and Marketing Group, Intel Corporation, interview by author, Santa Clara, CA, 13 August 1998.

72. Ibid.

73. Ibid.

74. Rick Yeomans, Capability Manager, Consumer Manager Video Phone and Technical Marketing Group, IAL, interview by author, Hillsboro, OR, 17 April 2000.

75. David Ryan, Director, Technology Marketing, IAL, interview by author, Hillsboro, OR, 4 August 1998.

76. This analogy was suggested by Professor Michael Piore of MIT.

77. Dr. Craig Kinnie, Director, IAL, interview by author, Hillsboro, OR, 11 November 1997.

Chapter Four

1. Source: Intel Corporation, "Mission, Objectives, Values" for 1997 and 1998, unpublished internal documents.

2. By complementary markets, we mean here markets of products that are complementary in demand to the microprocessors.

3. David B. Johnson, Director, Media and Interconnect Technology Lab, IAL, interview by author, Hillsboro, OR, 4 August 1998. Emphasis added.

4. Bill Miller, Director, Worldwide Media Relations, Sales and Marketing Group, Intel Corporation, interview by author, Santa Clara, CA, 13 August 1998. Emphasis added.

5. Ibid.

6. MPEG (pronounced *m*-peg) stands for Moving Picture Experts Group, a working group of the International Standards Organization (ISO).

7. David B. Johnson, Director, Media and Interconnect Technology Lab, IAL, interview by author, Hillsboro, OR, 20 August 1998. Emphasis added.

8. Ibid. Emphasis added.

9. Ibid.

10. Quoted in H. Bray, "Memory He'd Like to Forget," *Boston Globe*, 19 October 2000, C1.

11. W. Isaacson, "The Microchip Is the Dynamo of a New Economy . . . Driven by the Passion of Intel's Andy Grove," *Time*, cover story, 29 December 1997–5 January 1998; and T. Jackson, *Inside Intel: How Andy Grove Built the World's Most Successful Chip Company* (New York: Dutton, 1997). Jackson states,

> [Intel attempted in 1996] to develop a new standard for "native signal processing." NSP allowed much of the manipulation of audio and video traditionally carried out on specialized chips on the computer's motherboard to be built into the microprocessor itself. In principle, NSP was in both companies' interest. . . . The problem was that the NSP technology Intel had developed didn't slot into DOS or Windows. It stood alone, and by doing so, it appeared to challenge Microsoft's hegemony over software standards. The reaction from Microsoft was swift and vicious. Without saying anything to Intel, Microsoft warned the PC manufacturers that it had no intention of supporting NSP in future releases of Windows, effectively forcing them to sacrifice 100 percent compatibility with Microsoft's standards if they went along with Intel's initiative (374).

Both of these sources report that Intel later halted these investments, and "caved," as Andy Grove famously conceded.

12. For example, see M. La Pedus, "Boards' Plunging Prices a Windfall for OEMs—With Intel chip sets populating most Taiwan-made motherboards, price and next-generation features must differentiate products," *Electronic Buyers' News* 16, September 1996, 39. The article opens as follows: "There is no rest for Taiwan's PC-board makers. As Intel Corp. continues to push its own motherboards, Taiwan's board makers are struggling to keep their heads above water by cutting prices."

13. By "accelerate platform transitions" Miller means facilitating the adoption in the market place of computers powered by the newest Intel chip. In Intel managers' language, the word "platform" usually refers to the overall system (here, the PC).

14. Bill Miller, Director, Worldwide Media Relations, Sales and Marketing Group, Intel Corporation, interview by author, Santa Clara, CA, 13 August 1998. Emphasis added.

15. David Ryan, Director, Platform Marketing, IAL, interview by author, Hillsboro, OR, 6 August 1998.

16. Michael Bruck, Director, Market Development, Developer Relations Group, Intel Corporation, interview by author, Portland, OR, 19 August 1998. Bruck was the technical assistant to then-CEO Andy Grove at the time of these negotiations.

17. Reuters (19 January 1999) reported: "Computer giant Intel said today that it will invest $30.5 million in PictureTel, a maker of business conferencing systems, as part of an agreement to develop videoconferencing products. . . . As part of the distribution and joint product development deal, Intel gives PictureTel distribution rights to sell the Intel ProShare Video System 500, and exclusive worldwide distribution rights to sell and support the Intel TeamStation System. PictureTel will provide support services for both products."

18. See R. Burgelman, *Strategy Is Destiny*, forthcoming, (New York: Free Press, 2002).

19. Michael Bruck, Director, Market Development, Developer Relations Group, Intel Corporation, interview by author, Portland, OR, 19 August 1998. Bruck was the technical assistant to then-CEO Andy Grove at the time of these negotiations.

20. David Ryan, Director, Platform Marketing, IAL, interview by author, Hillsboro, OR, 6 August 1998. Emphasis added.

21. David B. Johnson, Director, Media and Interconnect Technology Lab, IAL, interview by author, Hillsboro, OR, 20 August 1998.

22. See M. A. Cusumano and D. B. Yoffie, *Competing on Internet Time: Lessons from Netscape and Its Battle with Microsoft* (New York: Touchstone/Simon & Schuster, 1998).

23. Ron Smith, Director, Computer Enhancement Group, Intel Corporation, interview by author, Folsom, CA, 18 August 1998.

24. Jim Pappas, Director, Platform Initiatives, Desktop Products Group, Intel Corporation, interview by author, Hillsboro, OR, 4 August 1998.

25. Dr. Craig Kinnie, Director, IAL, interview by author, Hillsboro, OR, 20 August 1998.

26. Will Swope, Vice President, Intel Architecture Business Group, and Director, Platform Planning, interview by author, Santa Clara, CA, 20 August 1998. Emphasis added.

27. Dr. Craig Kinnie, Director, IAL, interview by author, Hillsboro, OR, 17 April 2000. Emphasis added.

28. David Ryan, Director, Platform Marketing, IAL, interview by author, Hillsboro, OR, 17 April 2000.

29. Carol Barrett, Marketing Manager, IAL, interview by author, Hillsboro, OR, 5 August 1998. Emphasis added.

30. Claude Leglise, Vice President, and Director, Intel Developer Relations Group, Content Group, interview by author, Santa Clara, CA, 13 November 1997. Emphasis added.

31. David Ryan, Director, Platform Marketing, IAL, interview by author, Hillsboro, OR, 6 August 1998.

32. When competing with Sony and its Betamax standard in the 1970s, Japan Victor Corporation and its parent company, Matsushita, also found a gradual, low-key approach that incorporated the ideas of other leading firms to be critical in establishing VHS as the dominant standard for video recording. See M. A. Cusumano, Y. Mylonadis, and R. S. Rosenbloom, "Strategic Maneuvering and Mass-Market Dynamics: The Triumph of VHS Over Beta," *Business History Review* 66 (spring 1992): 51–94; and R. S. Rosenbloom and M. A. Cusumano, "Technological Pioneering and Competitive Advantage: The Birth of the VCR Industry," *California Management Review* 29, 4 (summer 1987): 51–76.

33. Jim Pappas, Director, Platform Initiatives, Desktop Products Group, Intel Corporation, interview by author, Hillsboro, OR, 4 August 1998.

34. Bala Cadambi, Department Manager, Peripherals & Interconnect Technology, IAL, Intel Corporation, interview by author, Hillsboro, OR, 4 August 1998. Emphasis added.

35. David J. Schuler, Program Manager, Worldwide Sales and Marketing, Intel Corporation, interview by author, Hillsboro, OR, 6 August 1998.

36. Dr. Craig Kinnie, Director, IAL, interview by author, Hillsboro, OR, 17 April 2000.

37. Dr. Andrew S. Grove, Chairman, Intel Corporation, interview by author, Santa Clara, CA, 18 August 1998.

38. Dr. Craig Kinnie, Director, IAL, interview by author, Hillsboro, OR, 11 November 1997.

39. Groups include the Sales and Marketing Group (SMG), which allocates marketing resources to promote new technical initiatives driven by IAL; the Desktop Products Group (DPG), whose Platform Marketing Group launches and ensures the management of standardization groups promoting Intel-driven interfaces, and whose IHV (independent hardware vendors) Ingredient Marketing group ensures that hardware vendors will adapt their designs to them as well; and the Software Development Group (SDG), a part of the Content Group that maintains relationships with a number of independent software developers (ISVs), subsidizes some of them, and shares information that helps these ISVs develop software that will be compatible with the next version of Intel's microprocessor and help showcase its performance.

40. Dr. Craig Kinnie, Director, IAL, interview by author, Hillsboro, OR, 11 November 1997.

41. Dan Russell, Director, Platform Marketing, Desktop Products Group, Intel Corporation, interview by author, Hillsboro, OR, 4 August 1998. Emphasis added.

42. Ron Smith, Director, Computing Enhancement Group, Intel Corporation, interview by author, Folsom, CA, 18 August 1998.

43. Mike Aymar, Vice President and General Manager, Desktop Products Group, Intel Corporation, interview by author, Santa Clara, CA, 13 November 1997. Emphasis added.

44. Thanks to David Reed, reviewer, for clarification on VHDL.

45. Jim Pappas, Director, Platform Initiatives, Desktop Products Group, Intel Corporation, interview by author, Hillsboro, OR, 4 August 1998. Emphasis added.

46. Carol Barrett, Marketing Manager, IAL, interview by author, Hillsboro, OR, 5 August 1998. Emphasis added.

47. See Peter Botticelli, David Collis, and Gary Pisano, "Intel Corporation: 1968–1997," Harvard Business School Case #9-797-137 (Revision 21 October 1998).

48. A. Reinhardt, "The New Intel," *Business Week*, 13 March 2000, 122.

49. Reinhardt, "The New Intel," 111–112.

50. Reinhardt, 113.

51. Dr. Craig Kinnie, Director, IAL, interview by author, 17 April 2000.

52. Shane Wall, Director, New Business Development, IAL, interview by author, Hillsboro, OR, 17 April 2000.

53. Dr. Craig Kinnie, Director, IAL, interview by author, Hillsboro, OR, 17 April 2000.

54. Ibid.

55. David Ryan, Director, Platform Marketing, IAL, Intel Corporation, interview by author, Hillsboro, OR, 17 April 2000.

56. Rick Yeomans, Marketing Manager, IAL, interview by author, Hillsboro, OR, 17 April 2000.

57. Dr. Craig Kinnie, Director, IAL, roundtable discussion with author, 17 April 2000.

58. Mary Murphy-Hoye, Director, IT Strategy and Technology, Intel Corporation, interview by author, Cambridge, MA, 16 January 2001.

59. Data are from <http://www.Intel.com/capital/portfolio/index.htm>.

60. "Intel Capital: Strategic Goals," <http://www.Intel.com/capital/about/goals.htm>.

61. See the Intel Capital Web site for additional information on these funds.

62. Leslie Vadasz, Senior Vice President and Director, Corporate Business Development Group, Intel Corporation, interview by author, Santa Clara, CA, 14 August 1998.

63. Ibid.

64. Ibid.

65. A. Lashinsky, "Intel Backs Its Faith in USWeb with $10 Million in Cash," *San Jose Mercury News*, 11 November 1997, C3. "USWeb Corp. . . . has landed the high-technology world's version of the Good Housekeeping Seal of Approval."

66. Alex Wong, Technical Assistant to the Director, Corporate Business Development Group, Intel Corporation, interview by author, Santa Clara, CA, 24 November 1998.

67. Leslie Vadasz, Senior Vice President and Director, Corporate Business Development Group, Intel Corporation, interview by author, Santa Clara, CA, 14 August 1998.

68. Ibid.

69. This situation seems to be consistent with insights in the literature on R&D competition (between incumbents and entrants), and in particular the recent work of Joshua S. Gans and Scott Stern. See J. S. Gans and S. Stern, "The Product Market and the Market for 'Ideas': Commercialization Strategies for Technology Entrepreneurs," (working paper) 10 January 2001. (The latest version of this paper is available at: <http://www.mbs.unimelb.edu.au/jgans/research.htm>.) See also J. S. Gans and S. Stern, "Incumbency and R&D Incentices: Licensing the Gale of Creative Destruction," *Journal of Economics and Management Strategy* 9, no. 4 (2001): 485–511. Gans and Stern in these papers have explored how the negotiation over the licensing price of a technology that is interesting to an incumbent and developed by a new entrant is determined *in the shadow* of the possibility that the incumbent's internal research teams could also, eventually, develop that innovation.

70. Mike Aymar, Vice President and General Manager, Desktop Products Group, Intel Corporation, interview by author, Santa Clara, CA, 13 November 1997. Emphasis added.

71. Dr. Andrew S. Grove, Chairman, Intel Corporation, interview by author, Santa Clara, CA, 18 August 1998. Emphasis added.

72. Ibid. Emphasis added.

73. Claude Leglise, Vice President, and Director, Intel Developer Relations Group, Content Group, interview by author, Santa Clara, CA, 13 November 1997. Emphasis added.

74. For the 1999 mission statement, see <http://www.intel.com/intel/annual99/letter.htm>.

75. Claude Leglise, Vice President, and Director, Intel Developer Relations Group, Content Group, interview by author, Santa Clara, CA, 13 November 1997. Emphasis added.

76. Ibid.

77. Mike Aymar, Vice President and General Manager, Desktop Products Group, Intel Corporation, interview by author, Santa Clara, CA, 13 November 1997.

78. Ibid. Emphasis added.

79. Gerald Holzhammer, Director, Desktop Architecture Lab, Intel Corporation, interview by author, Hillsboro, OR, 20 August 1998.

80. Claude Leglise, Vice President, and Director, Intel Developer Relations Group, Content Group, interview by author, Santa Clara, CA, 13 November 1997.

81. Claude Leglise, Vice President, and Director, Intel Developer Relations Group, Content Group, interview by author, Santa Clara, CA, 14 August 1998.

82. See A. S. Grove, *Only the Paranoid Survive: How to Exploit the Crisis Points That Challenge Every Company and Career* (New York: Currency Doubleday, 1996). Also, A. S. Grove, "Exploiting the Crisis Points Challenging Every Company and Career," (fifth in a series of lectures hosted by the MIT Center for Technology, Policy, and Industrial Development, MIT Sloan School of Management, 25 September

1996); and Grove's keynote speech at the Academy of Management Annual Meeting, San Diego, August 1998.

83. Claude Leglise, Vice President, and Director, Intel Developer Relations Group, Content Group, interview by author, Santa Clara, CA, 14 August 1998.

84. Bill Miller, Director, Worldwide Media Relations, Sales and Marketing Group, Intel Corporation, interview by author, Santa Clara, CA, 13 August 1998.

85. Ron Smith, Director, Computer Enhancement Group, Intel Corporation, interview by author, Folsom, CA, 18 August 1998. Emphasis added.

86. Dr. Craig Kinnie, Director, IAL, roundtable discussion with authors, 17 April 2000.

87. David J. Schuler, Program Manager, Worldwide Sales and Marketing, Intel Corporation, interview by author, Hillsboro, OR, 6 August 1998. Emphasis added.

88. Jim Pappas, Director, Platform Initiatives, Desktop Products Group, Intel Corporation, interview by author, Milpitas, CA, 7 August 1998. Emphasis added.

89. Dr. Andrew S. Grove, Chairman, Intel Corporation, interview by author, Santa Clara, CA, 18 August 1998. Emphasis added.

90. Dr. Craig Kinnie, Director, IAL, interview by author, Hillsboro, OR, 20 August 1998.

91. David J. Schuler, Program Manager, Worldwide Sales and Marketing, Intel Corporation, interview by author, Hillsboro, OR, 6 August 1998.

Chapter Five

1. This figure for applications developers is from J. Greene, "Windows of Opportunity," *Business Week*, 3 July 2000, 142.

2. Brad Silverberg, Vice President, Personal Systems (Windows/MS-DOS), 4 August 1993. Cited in M. A. Cusumano and Richard W. Selby, *Microsoft Secrets: How the World's Most Powerful Software Company Creates Technology, Shapes Markets, and Manages People* (New York: Free Press/Simon & Schuster, 1995), 167–168.

3. Microsoft Corporation, Annual Report 2000, 16–17.

4. This data is from David Yoffie, Intel Director, e-mail communication, 9 March 2001.

5. Author Michael Cusumano and Richard Selby first made this observation in Cusumano and Selby, *Microsoft Secrets*, 134–135, 445–447.

6. In its commercial literature, Microsoft refers to Windows as a "platform." In this book however—in accordance with the more general meaning of the word in the computer industry where *platform* means the overall system (i.e., the PC in the mid-1990s, and the set of interconnected PCs in early 2000s)—we use the broader definition of an evolving system made of interdependent pieces that can each be innovated upon. To avoid any confusion, we'll use "software platform" for what Microsoft calls the Windows platform. Microsoft's use of "platform" corresponds to what we call a core product; in other words, the main product to which complements are functionally attached, all of them together making up the platform.

7. S. Lohr, "PC Makers and Microsoft Squabble Over Desktop Icons," *The New York Times*, 13 August 2001, C1, C8.

8. S. Lohr, "New Software, New Scrutiny for Microsoft," *The New York Times*, 30 July 2001, C1.

9. J. Greene, "Microsoft: How It Became Stronger than Ever," *Business Week*, 4 June 2001, 76, 79.

10. J. Greene, "Microsoft Ignores Those XP Tacklers," *Business Week*, 6 August 2001, 34.

11. J. R. Wilke and D. Clark, "Microsoft Pulls Back Support for Java, Dealing New Blow to Rival Technology," *Wall Street Journal*, 18 July 2001 (Web edition <http://public.wsj.com/home.html>).

12. S. Lohr, "PC Makers and Microsoft Squabble Over Desktop Icons," C8.

13. J. R. Wilke and J. Bandler, "Kodak Tangles with Microsoft Over Win XP," *Wall Street Journal*, 2 July 2001 (Web edition <http://public.wsj.com/home.html>).

14. N. Wingfield, "Windows XP's Power to Add Links to Other Web Sites Stirs Dissent," *Wall Street Journal*, 8 June 2001 (Web edition <http://public.wsj.com/home.html>).

15. J. Greene, "Microsoft: How It Became Stronger than Ever," 76.

16. C. Gaither, "Palm Urges Solidarity as Competitors Gain," *The New York Times*, 14 December 2000, C4. The prediction for 2004 is from International Data Corporation. See J. Greene, "Microsoft: How It Became Stronger than Ever," 77.

17. For a good discussion of Microsoft's various initiatives, see J. Markoff, "For Microsoft, a Shift Toward New Vistas," *The New York Times*, 18 December 2000, C25; and J. Greene, "Microsoft: How It Became Stronger than Ever," 75–85.

18. Some applications teams even included former Windows developers. Microsoft developers generally stayed in one group for at least two product cycles (two to three years), but some transferred from applications to systems and vice versa. See M. A. Cusumano and R. Selby, *Microsoft Secrets*, 121–122.

19. C. H. Ferguson and C. R. Morris, *Computer Wars: The Fall of IBM and the Future of Global Technology* (New York: Times Books, 1994), 153. See also A. Schulman, D. Maxey, and M. Pietrek, *Undocumented Windows: A Programmers Guide to Reserved Microsoft Windows API Functions* (Reading, MA: Addison-Wesley, 1992).

20. See Cusumano and Selby, *Microsoft Secrets*, 169. Microsoft managers also frequently support their bundling of products together by arguing that end users want well-integrated products that run seamlessly. Underlying this argument is the belief that this task is best done if only one firm (Microsoft) is in charge of presenting the suite of products to the end user.

21. Written comments on the book manuscript from David Reed, former Chief Technical Officer of Lotus Development Corporation, 29 April 2001, as well as telephone interview by author, 13 August 2001.

22. M. A. Cusumano and David B. Yoffie, *Competing on Internet Time: Lessons from Netscape and Its Battle with Microsoft* (New York: Touchstone/Simon & Schuster, 1998), 11; and various sources for more recent data.

23. See Cusumano and Selby, *Microsoft Secrets*, 169–170.

24. R. Needleman, "Home Improvement," *Red Herring Magazine*, 11 January 2001; and R. Buckman, "Microsoft Renames Products in Effort to 'Webify' Its Image," *Wall Street Journal*, 5 February 2001, B5.

25. J. Greene, "Microsoft: How It Became Stronger than Ever," 77.

26. Quoted in S. Manes and P. Andrews, *Gates: How Microsoft's Mogul Reinvented an Industry—and Made Himself the Richest Man in America* (New York: Doubleday, 1993), 433.

27. D. Ichbiah and S. Knepper, *The Making of Microsoft: How Bill Gates and His Team Created the World's Most Successful Software Company* (Rocklin, CA: Prima Publishing, 1991), 101–103, 108–110.

28. Ichbiah and Knepper, *The Making of Microsoft*, 112–113, 118.

29. Ibid.

30. Manes and Andrews, *Gates: How Microsoft's Mogul Reinvented an Industry*, 138.

31. Several of the briefs in the Department of Justice's remedy proposals make this argument about Microsoft Office as a potential competing platform. See in particular the brief filed by Rebecca Henderson: United States of America versus Microsoft Corporation, Civil Action No. 98–1232 (TPJ), "Declaration of Rebecca Henderson," April 28, 2000, <http://www.usdoj.gov/atr/cases/f4600/4644.pdf>. Other documents are available on the Web at <http://www.usdoj.gov/atr/cases>.

32. D. Clark, "Microsoft Will Keep Making Products for Apple's Macintosh, Gates Pledges," *Wall Street Journal*, 22 March 1995, B6.

33. David Reed written comments, 29 April 2001.

34. See T. P. Jackson, "Findings of Fact," United States of America versus Microsoft Corporation, Civil Action No. 98–1232 (TPJ), 5 November 1999, 5B and 5C. For more information see, <http://www.usdoj.gov/atr/cases/ms_findings.htm> and <http://www.usdoj.gov/atr/cases/f3800/msjudgex.htm> (accessed 16 November 2001).

35. Manes and Andrews, *Gates: How Microsoft's Mogul Reinvented an Industry*, 203.

36. See Jackson, "Findings of Fact," 5D.

37. J. Rymer, M. Guttman, and J. Matthews, "Microsoft OLE 2.0 and the Road to Cairo," *Distributed Computing Monitor* 9, no. 1 (January 1994); and L. Flynn, "Preparing for the Battle in Mix-and-Match Software," *The New York Times*, 22 May 1994, F10.

38. See the Department of Justice documents on the Microsoft antitrust trial at <http://www.usdoj.gov/atr/cases/ms_index.htm> (accessed 16 November 2001), as well as D. Bank, *Breaking Windows: How Bill Gates Fumbled the Future of Microsoft* (New York: Free Press/Simon & Schuster, 2001).

39. See Cusumano and Selby, *Microsoft Secrets*, 34.

40. See various accounts of executive departures in Bank, *Breaking Windows*, and J. Greene, "Microsoft's Big Bet," *Business Week*, 30 October 2000, 162.

41. These cases are discussed in detail in Jackson, "Findings of Fact," Sections 5A, 5C, and 5F.

42. Ibid.

43. Cusumano and Selby, *Microsoft Secrets*, 148.

44. See Cusumano and Yoffie, *Competing on Internet Time*, 89–155.

45. Microsoft Corporation, "Microsoft.Net: Realizing the Next Generation Internet," 22 June 2000, <http://www.microsoft.com/business/vision/netwhitepaper.asp>.

46. K. J. Delaney, "Microsoft Will Rent Software on Per-Use Basis in Web Cafes," *Wall Street Journal*, 31 October 2000.

47. J. Markoff, "Starbucks and Microsoft Plan Coffeehouse Web Access," *The New York Times*, 4 January 2001, C4.

48. Quoted in J. Pontin, "Bill Gates Unplugged," *Red Herring Magazine*, 17 August 2000 (Web edition <http://www.redherring.com/>).

49. J. Greene, "Microsoft's Big Bet," *Business Week*, 30 October 2000, 152–163.

50. Microsoft Corporation, "Microsoft.Net: Realizing the Next Generation Internet," 22 June 2000, <http://www.microsoft.com/business/vision/netwhitepaper .asp>. Also, Microsoft Corporation, "What Microsoft's .NET Vision Means for Businesses," 16 October 2000, <http://www.microsoft.com/ business/vision/netvision .asp>.

51. L. Copeland, "Developers Voice .NET Skepticism," *Computerworld*, 17 July 2000, 1, 16; L. Copeland and D. Deckmyn, "Microsoft Still Sketchy on Details for .Net Tool Set," *Computerworld*, 17 July 2000, 16; and W. Wong and M. Ricciuti, "Microsoft strikes at Sun's Java with new standard," *CNET News.com*, 6 July 2000 <http://news.cnet.com/news/0-1003-200-2154069.html?tag=st>.

52. L. Copeland, "Developers Voice .NET Skepticism"; and L. Copeland and D. Deckmyn, "Microsoft Still Sketchy on Details for .Net Tool Set."

53. W. Wong, "IBM Switches Support to Microsoft-Based Web Standard," *CNET News.com*, 27 April 2000, <http://biz.yahoo.com/n/o/orcl.html>.

54. Microsoft Corporation, "What Microsoft's .NET Vision Means for Businesses."

55. R. Buckman, "Microsoft Makes Change to Focus on Internet," *Wall Street Journal*, 10 August 2000, B6; and Microsoft Corporation, "Paul Maritz to Retire After 14 Years at Microsoft," 13 September 2000 (press release <http://www.microsoft. com/PressPass/press/2000/Sept00/MaritzPR.asp>).

56. H. Bray, "Casting a Broad .NET," *Boston Globe*, 31 July 2000, C1.

57. J. Greene, "Windows of Opportunity," *Business Week*, 3 July 2000, 140–144.

58. M. Boslet, "Clash of the Titans," *The Industry Standard*, 19 March 2001, 64–66.

59. Microsoft and Sun Microsystems settled their suit in January 2001. Microsoft agreed to pay Sun $20 million and to terminate its Java license. See D. P. Hamilton, "Microsoft Settles Long Battle with Sun, Will Pay $20 Million to End Java License," *Wall Street Journal*, 24 January 2001 (Web edition <http://public.wsj.com/ home.html>).

60. "Microsoft, Intel Team to Create Bluetooth standard," *CNET News.com*, 13 June 2000, from Reuters, <http://news.cnet.com/news/0-1006-200-2070732.html? tag=st>.

61. Microsoft Corporation, "Forum 2000 Keynote: Bill Gates Speaks About the .NET Platform," 30 June 2000, <http://www.microsoft.com/business/vision/gates. asp>.

62. Microsoft Corporation, "Forum 2000: Steve Ballmer Speaks About the .NET Platform," 30 June 2000, <http://www.microsoft.com/business/vision/ballmer.asp>.

63. Source: Cisco 2001 financial data, <http://investor.cisco.com/ireye/ir_site

.zhtml?ticker=csco&script=11945&layout=7&item_id='his_financials110501.html'>.

64. T. G. Donlan, "Cisco's Bids: Its Growth by Acquisition Will Pose Problems," *Barron's Online*, 8 May 2000, <http://www.barrons.com/>.

65. D. Bunnell, *Making the Cisco Connection: The Story Behind the Real Internet Superpower* (New York: John Wiley & Sons, 2000), 1–21.

66. Cisco Systems, "Cisco Fact Sheet," January 2001, <http://www.cisco.com/warp/public/750/corpfact.html>.

67. Bunnell, *Making the Cisco Connection*, 33–35.

68. Bunnell, 35–37.

69. Bunnell, 57.

70. C. Gaither, "Amid Slump, Cisco Announces a Revamping," *The New York Times*, 24 August 2001, C6.

71. Cisco Systems, Inc., 2001 Financial Statements <http://media.corporate-ir.net/media_files/nsd/csco/reports/sec_segment2001.xls>.

72. This section summarizes Bunnell, *Making the Cisco Connection*, 64–75, which describes the acquisition process in detail.

73. See S. Oster, *Modern Competitive Analysis* (New York: Oxford University Press, 1999), 216–242; and M. Porter, "From Competitive Advantage to Corporate Strategy," *Harvard Business Review*, May–June 1987, 43–59.

74. Bunnell, *Making the Cisco Connection*, 63.

75. Bunnell, 88.

76. Bunnell, 132–134. Also, e-mail comments from Campbell Stras, Chief Operating Officer, Cybergnostic, Inc., 9 February 2001.

77. Bunnell, *Making the Cisco Connection*, 153–160.

78. Cisco Systems, "Cisco IOS Software—Description & Benefits," <http://www.cisco.com/warp/public/732/overview/benefits.html>.

79. See "How Cisco IOS Is Packaged and Sold" on the Cisco Web site: <http://www.cisco.com/univercd/cc/doc/pcat/ion_gl.htm>.

80. See the somewhat different use of this term in Cusumano and Yoffie, *Competing on Internet Time*, 89–155.

81. Bunnell, *Making the Cisco Connection*, 76, 117–119.

82. S. Thurm, "Microsoft's Behavior Is Helping Cisco Learn How to Avoid Antitrust Trouble," *Wall Street Journal*, 6 June 2000.

83. This anecdote is based on Bunnell, *Making the Cisco Connection*, 87, 114–122.

84. A. Reinhardt, "Does Cisco Have a Microsoft Problem?" *Business Week*, 5 June 2000, 103.

85. Bunnell, *Making the Cisco Connection*, 122–124.

86. Bunnell, 125–128.

87. Bunnell, 128–129.

88. Ibid.

89. Cisco Corporation, "Cisco, Intel and Microsoft Join Forces to Accelerate the Use of Networked Multimedia in Business," (press release, 12 March 1997).

90. Bunnell, *Making the Cisco Connection*, 131–132.

91. Bunnell, 111.

92. L. Greenemeier, "Cisco, Cap Gemini Partner in E-Services Company," *Information Week*, 13 March 2000, 149.

93. Cisco Systems, "Collaboration" and "Alliances," <http://www.cisco.com>.

94. See the discussion of Cisco IOS Technologies at the Cisco Web site: <http://www.cisco.comwarp/public/732/Tech/index.shtml>.

95. Cisco Corporation, "Industry Leaders Propose Standards Effort," (press release, 20 February 1998).

96. Cisco Corporation, "EDS, Cisco Systems and HP Team to Speed Business to the Web," (press release, 3 November 1998).

97. T. Uimonen, "Cisco, Motorola to Build Wireless 'Net," *Network World Fusion News*, 8 February 1999.

98. Cisco Corporation, "Cisco Drives Industry Standards for Broadband Wireless Internet Services," (press release, 26 October 2000).

99. Cisco Systems, "Cisco and Akamai Join Forces to Enhance Internet Content Routing and Delivery Services," (press release, 18 August 1999).

100. Oracle Corporation, "EMC, Cisco, and Oracle Form Alliance," (press release, 3 April 2000).

101. S. Thurm, "Microsoft's Behavior Is Helping Cisco Learn How to Avoid Antitrust Trouble," *Wall Street Journal*, 6 June 2000.

102. E-mail communication from Sonny Wu, Nortel Networks, 9 February 2001, regarding Juniper Networks' market share versus Cisco.

103. J. Shinal, "Telecom Turmoil," *Business Week*, 6 November 2000, 170.

104. T. G. Donlan, "Cisco's Bids: Its Growth by Acquisition Will Pose Problems," *Barron's Online*, 8 May 2000, <http://www.barrons.com/>.

105. Ibid.

106. J. Shinal, "Telecom Turmoil."

Chapter Six

1. Estimates from the Gartner Group, quoted by *Bloomberg News*, 28 November 2000, "Pocket PC Devices Make Headway Against Palm," <http://news.cnet.com>.

2. Pui-Wing Tam, "Palm's Sales Miss Upside Hopes and Stock Falls 14% After Hours," *Wall Street Journal*, 21 December 2000, B9.

3. K. Gerard, "The Palm Phenom," *Business 2.0*, 3 April 2001, 76.

4. Filing quoted in an unpublished report by INSEAD M.B.A. students D. Braga, S. Jackson, G. Mak, and V. Noya, "Nokia vs. Palm," 2000.

5. See A. M. McGahan, L. L. Vadasz, and D. B. Yoffie, "Creating Value and Setting Standards: The Lessons of Consumer Electronics for Personal Digital Assistants" in *Competing in the Age of Digital Convergence*, ed. D. B. Yoffie (Boston: Harvard Business School Press, 1997), 227–264.

6. Gerard, "The Palm Phenom," 77, and the Palm Web site, <http://www.palm.com> (accessed March 2001).

7. S. Baker, J. Shinal, and I. Kunii, "Is Nokia's Star Dimming?" *Business Week*, 22 January 2000, 66.

8. This section relies heavily on D. B. Yoffie and M. Kwak, *Judo Strategy* (Boston: Harvard Business School Press, 2001), 93–117.

9. Yoffie and Kwak, *Judo Strategy*, 95–97.

10. Yoffie and Kwak, 104.

11. Quoted in A. M. McGahan, L. L. Vadasz, and D. B. Yoffie, "Creating Value and Setting Standards" in *Competing in the Age of Digital Convergence*, ed. D. B. Yoffie, 232–233.

12. Yoffie and Kwak, draft manuscript for *Judo Strategy*, chapter 5 page 14.

13. See <http://www.palmos.com>. Emphasis added.

14. Yoffie and Kwak, draft manuscript for *Judo Strategy*, chapter 5 page 29.

15. J. Lardner and K. Girard, "Hawkins Talks," *Business 2.0*, 3 April 2001, 84.

16. E-mail communication with Donna Dubinsky, CEO of Handspring, 24 January 2001.

17. Yoffie and Kwak, *Judo Strategy*, 110.

18. Ibid.

19. Yoffie and Kwak, draft manuscript for *Judo Strategy*, chapter 5 page 30. Emphasis added.

20. Yoffie and Kwak, *Judo Strategy*, 113.

21. Ibid.

22. Ibid.

23. See "Palm Sets the Pace With Enhanced Wireless Palm VIIx Handheld," *Business Wire*, 7 August 2000.

24. See Palm Web site <http://www.palm.com/about/corporate/productover view.html>.

25. Conduits are software plug-ins for the HotSync Manager application. They exchange and synchronize data between a desktop PC and a Palm OS platform handheld computer. Most conduits synchronize data such that data on the handheld mirrors the data on desktop. Conduits also transfer, import/export data, or cause Palm OS applications to be installed.

26. Source: <http://www.palmos.com/dev/program/benefits.html>.

27. "Palm Inc. Launches VC Unit to Aid Complementary Firms," *Boston Globe*, 7 September 2000.

28. Ibid.

29. See <http://www.syncml.org/about-intro.html>.

30. See <http://www.handspring.com>.

31. See <http://www.eyemodule.com>.

32. See <http://www.cue.net>.

33. S. C. Miller, "Palm Offers 2 Models That Are Built to Grow," *The New York Times*, 22 March 2001, E3.

34. This piece of information, as well as other facts in this paragraph, was taken from S. Baker, "Why Psion Is Still in the Game," *Business Week*, 3 April 2000.

35. E-mail correspondence with Bengt Holmstrom, Nokia director and MIT professor, 5 October 2001.

36. Source: D. Deckmyn, "Motorola signs up for Palm OS," *Online News*, 15 December 1999, <http://www.computerworld.com>.

37. See M. A. Cusumano, Y. Mylonadis, and R. Rosenbloom, "Strategic Maneuvering and Mass-Market Dynamics: The Triumph of VHS Over Beta," *Business History Review*, (spring 1992).

38. Quoted in Yoffie and Kwak, *Judo Strategy*, 116.

39. I. M. Kunii, M. Johnston, and W. Echikson, "World Domination—on the Cheap," *Business Week*, 28 August 2000.

40. General material on the history of NTT DoCoMo is available in English at <http://www.nttdocomo.co.jp/english/release/index.html>. General accounts of the company in Japanese include Natsuno Takeshi, *imodo sutorateji* [i-mode strategy] (Tokyo: Nikkei BP, 2000).

41. "Wireless Web Content Called More Important than Technology," *Communications Daily*, 22 March 2001.

42. M. Williams, "AOL Japan Renames Itself after Taking NTT DoCoMo as Partner," *InfoWorld*, 12 February 2001.

43. "Keiichi Enoki; Director—Gateway (Internet Business Department), NTT DoCoMo-Japan." *Business Week*, 36, A3.

44. "Europeans Disappointed with Clunky Wireless Internet Services Are About to Get an Infusion of Smart Tokyo-Style Technology. Will It Make a Difference?" *Newsweek International*, Technology Section, The Japan Connection, 12 March 2001.

45. D. Pringle, "E-Commerce (A Special Report): The Technology—Lost in the Translation—i-mode is a huge hit in Japan; Now the big question: Will it travel well?" *Wall Street Journal*, 11 December 2000.

46. L. Luna, "Browser Wars," *Telephony*, 29 January 2001.

47. Kunii, Johnston, and Echikson, "World Domination—on the Cheap."

48. L. Luna, "Battle of the standards," *Telephony*, 19 February 2001.

49. Ibid.

50. Ibid.

51. "DoCoMo Dashes Forward, Wowing The Wireless," *Wireless Week* (special section), 12 March 2001, 12.

52. D. Pringle, "E-Commerce (A Special Report): The Technology."

53. "Lutris and Pixo Partner to Enable Easy Wireless Internet Development: Partnership Opens Doors for Global Economy to Enjoy Same Wireless Internet Success as Experienced in Japan," *Business Wire*, 18 December 2000.

54. "Wireless Web Content Called More Important than Technology," *Communications Daily*, 22 March 2001.

55. R. Clark, "The NTT DoCoMo Success Story: How Mobile Internet Created the World's Most Valuable Telco," *America's Network*, 1 March 2000.

56. Ibid.

57. T. Kridel, "I-opener," *Wireless Review*, 1 October 2000, 22–28.

58. Ibid., 28.

59. Ibid.

60. "Wireless Web Content Called More Important than Technology," *Communications Daily*, 22 March 2001.

61. Ibid.

62. T. Kridel, "I-opener," 24.

63. "NTT DoCoMo Launches First Cell Phones to Support Java," *InfoWorld*, 5 February 2001, 42a.

64. I. M. Kunii, "Look Who's Going Courting in Japan," *Business Week*, 7 August 2000.

65. Kunii, Johnston, and Echikson, "World Domination—on the Cheap."

66. D. Solomon, R. A. Guth, and P. Landers, "A Big Deal for Tiny Screens: NTT DoCoMo Hopes to Boost U.S. Mobile Internet Use Through Stake in AT&T," *Wall Street Journal*, 1 December 2000.

67. "Japan's iMode comes to Europe," *Electronics Times*, 19 March 2001, 68.

68. R. A. Guth, "AOL Deal Marks Radical Move in Japan: NTT DoCoMo Partnership Joins Powerful Forces in Access to Internet," *Wall Street Journal*, 28 September 2000.

69. M. Williams, "AOL Japan Renames Itself after Taking NTT DoCoMo as Partner," *InfoWorld*, 12 February 2001.

70. "Palm, DoCoMo, to Jointly Launch New PDA in Japan," *Global News Wire*, AFX (UK), 14 February 2001.

71. R. Clark, "The NTT DoCoMo Success Story," 46–50.

72. For much of this history of Linux we rely on G. Moody, *Rebel Code* (Cambridge, MA: Perseus Publishing, 2001), 14–213.

73. See P. Salus, *A Quarter Century of Unix* (Reading, MA: Addison-Wesley, 1994).

74. GNU stands for the self-referential, iterative play-on-words GNU's Not Unix. Play-on-words are an integral part of the hacker's culture. Several other famous programs' names or title have this clever, playful feel.

75. Stallman, as quoted in Moody, *Rebel Code*, 20.

76. Stallman, as quoted in Moody, 24.

77. Stallman, as quoted by Moody, 28.

78. See Moody, 38.

79. See Moody, 40.

80. See Moody, 60.

81. See Moody, 23.

82. See Moody, 78.

83. See E. Raymond, *The Cathedral and the Bazaar* (Cambridge, MA: O'Reilly, 2001) <http://www.tuxedo.org/~esr/writings/cathedral-bazaar/>, 9.

84. For a broader discussion of this issue of modularity, see C. Y. Baldwin and K. B. Clark, *Design Rules: The Power of Modularity* (Cambridge, MA: MIT Press, 2000).

85. Moody, *Rebel Code*, 53.

86. See also A. MacCormack, "Product Development Practices That Work: How Internet Companies Build Software," *MIT Sloan Management Review* (winter 2001): 83.

87. Stephen Tweedie as quoted by Moody, *Rebel Code*, 84.

88. See Moody, 84.

89. "Cooking Pot Markets: An Economic Model for the Trade in Free Goods and Services on the Internet," *First Monday* 3, no. 3 <http://www.firstmonday.dk/issues3_3/Ghosh/index.html>.

90. This quote is from the Web version of Raymond's book, which is now also available in print. See <http://www.tuxedo.org/~esr/writings/cathedral-bazaar/>.

91. Ibid.

92. J. Lerner and J. Tirole, "The Simple Economics of Open Source," Mimeo, Harvard Business School, 25 February 2000.

93. *First Monday* interview with Linus Torvalds: "What Motivates Free Software Developers?" <http://www.firstmonday.dk/issues/issue3_3/torvalds/index.html>.

94. This discussion of Mozilla relied on the updated edition of M. A. Cusumano and D. B. Yoffie, *Competing on Internet Time: Lessons from Netscape and Its Battle with Microsoft* (New York: Touchstone/Simon & Schuster, 2000), 217–20 and 335–336.

95. Cusumano and Yoffie, *Competing on Internet Time*, 185–186.

96. See Moody, *Rebel Code*, 202.

97. See M. A. Cusumano, "A Brighter Future: Mozilla and Open Sourcing Redux," *Computerworld*, 1 November 1999 <http:// www.computerworld.com>.

98. Moody, *Rebel Code*, 127–130.

99. Moody, 205–213.

100. See <http://www.redhat.com> for the section on Enterprise Application Bundles.

Chapter Seven

1. See G. J. Stigler, "The Division of Labor Is Limited by the Extent of the Market," *The Journal of Political Economy* 59, no. 3 (1951): 185–193; and P. Geroski and T. Vlassopoulos, "The Rise and Fall of a Market Leader: Frozen Foods in the U.K.," *Strategic Management Journal* 12 (1991): 467–478.

2. United States of America versus Microsoft Corporation, Civil Action No. 98-1232 (TPJ), "Findings of Fact," United States District Court for the District of Columbia, 5 November 1999, <http://www.usdoj.gov/atr/cases/f3800/msjudgex.htm> Section III B.

3. This result has been noticed in the network externalities literature and dubbed the "penguin effect" for its similarity to penguins facing icy water: No firm wants to "dive" first. The insight is that before a technology (or platform) is sure of victory in the war over standards, complementors—facing the risk of being stranded with products specifically compatible to a "losing" or "stranded" technology—are reluctant to bear the risk of investing assets specific to that potentially "losing" technology. See J. P. Choi, "Herd Behavior, the 'Penguin Effect', and the Suppression of Informational Diffusion: An Analysis of Informational Externalities and Payoff Interdependency," *RAND Journal of Economics* 28 (autumn 1997): 407–425.

4. See R.M. Henderson and K. B. Clark, "Architectural Innovation: The Reconfiguration of Existing Product Technologies and the Failure of Established Firms," *Administrative Science Quarterly* 35 (1990): 9–30. Henderson and Clark describe how firms can get bogged down by their own architecture: The internal division of labor is so ingrained that when a firm develops an assembled product, the product architecture—corresponding to that internal division of labor—can be so entrenched that it is unable to adapt to technical change.

Index

About the Authors

ANNABELLE GAWER is Assistant Professor of Strategy and Management at INSEAD, France, where she teaches in the M.B.A. and the Executive Education programs. A specialist of business strategy and management of high-tech companies in the computer and telecom industries, Professor Gawer has lectured on the topic of strategic management of technological innovation at several universities including Harvard Business School, The Wharton School, the University of Michigan Business School, London Business School, the Technion (in Israel), and the Ecole des Mines de Paris. She also consults with major companies in the United States and in Europe. Professor Gawer holds a Ph.D. from the MIT Sloan School of Management and an MSc in Industrial Engineering and Engineering Management from Stanford University. Prior to her doctoral studies at MIT, she worked as an engineer and project manager for a large European telecommunications equipment manufacturer.

MICHAEL A. CUSUMANO is the Sloan Management Review Distinguished Professor at the MIT Sloan School of Management. He is also the former Editor-in-Chief and current Chairman of the Board of the *MIT Sloan Management Review*. Professor Cusumano specializes in strategy and management for high-tech companies, especially in the software and computer industries. He is a member of the board of directors of Infinium Software; Investhink, Ltd.; and Marex, Inc., as well as an advisor and consultant to dozens of other companies around the world. He has published six books, including the international best-seller *Microsoft Secrets* (with Richard W. Selby) and the *BusinessWeek* top-ten book *Competing on Internet Time: Lessons from Netscape and Its Battle with Microsoft* (with David B. Yoffie).